THE CROSS BRONX

by_MICHAEL AVON OEMING & IVAN BRANDON

Color by_ NICK FILARDI

Letters by_ KRISTYN FERRETTI

Cover Art by_ MICHAEL AVON OEMING

Cover & Book Design by_ KRISTYN FERRETTI

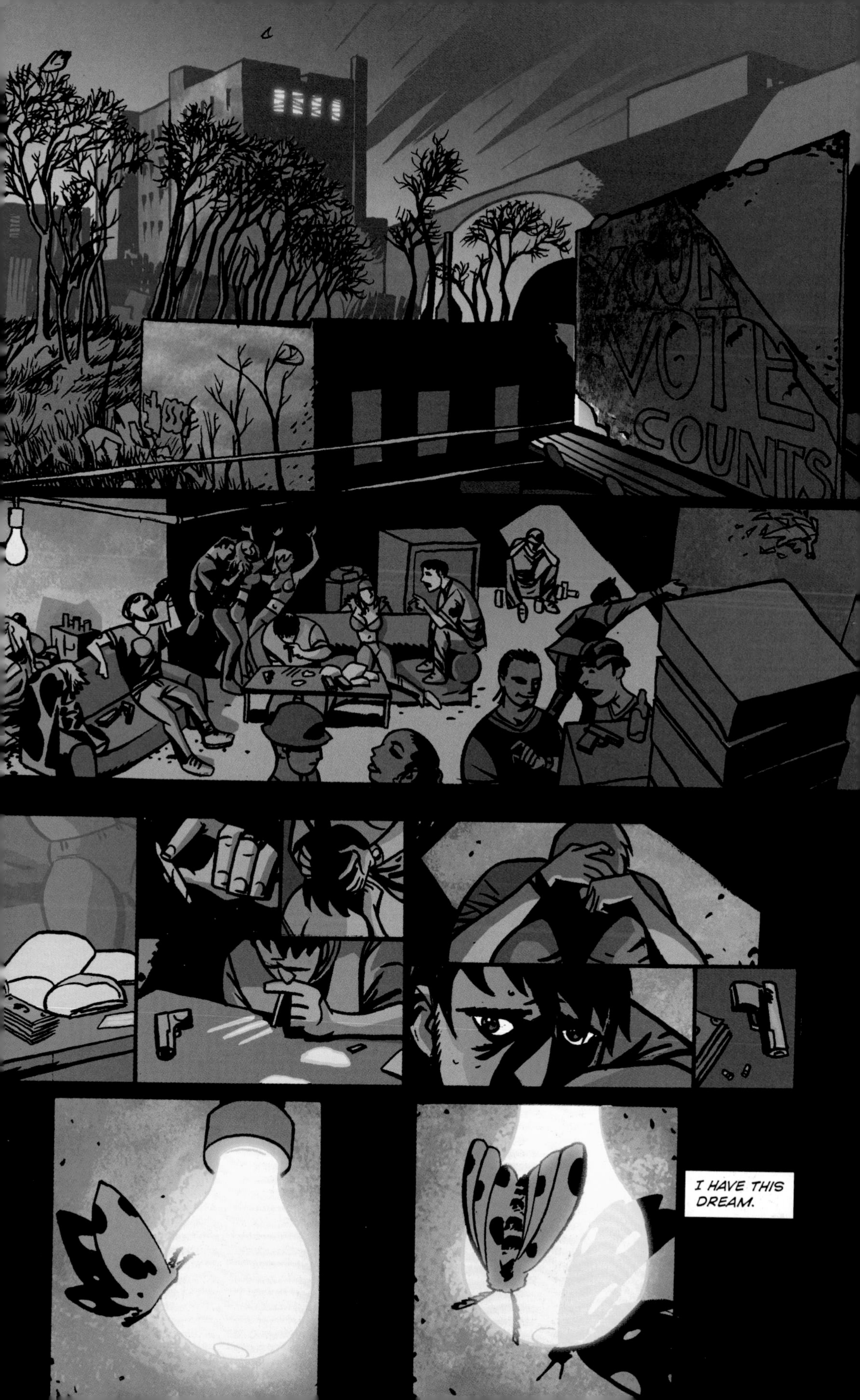
YOUR VOTE COUNTS
I HAVE THIS DREAM.

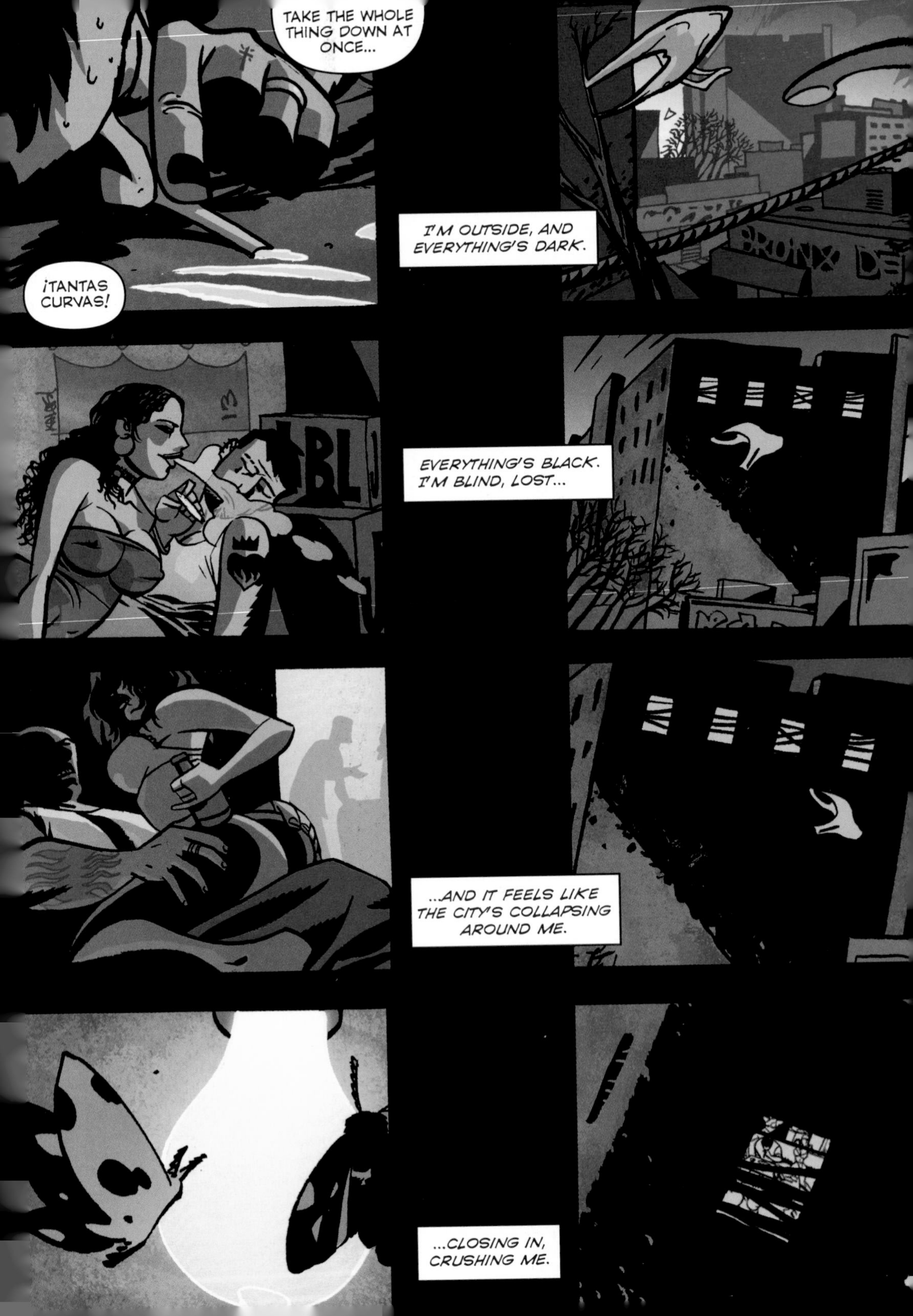
TAKE THE WHOLE THING DOWN AT ONCE...
¡TANTAS CURVAS!
I'M OUTSIDE, AND EVERYTHING'S DARK.
BRONX
EVERYTHING'S BLACK. I'M BLIND, LOST...
...AND IT FEELS LIKE THE CITY'S COLLAPSING AROUND ME.
...CLOSING IN, CRUSHING ME.

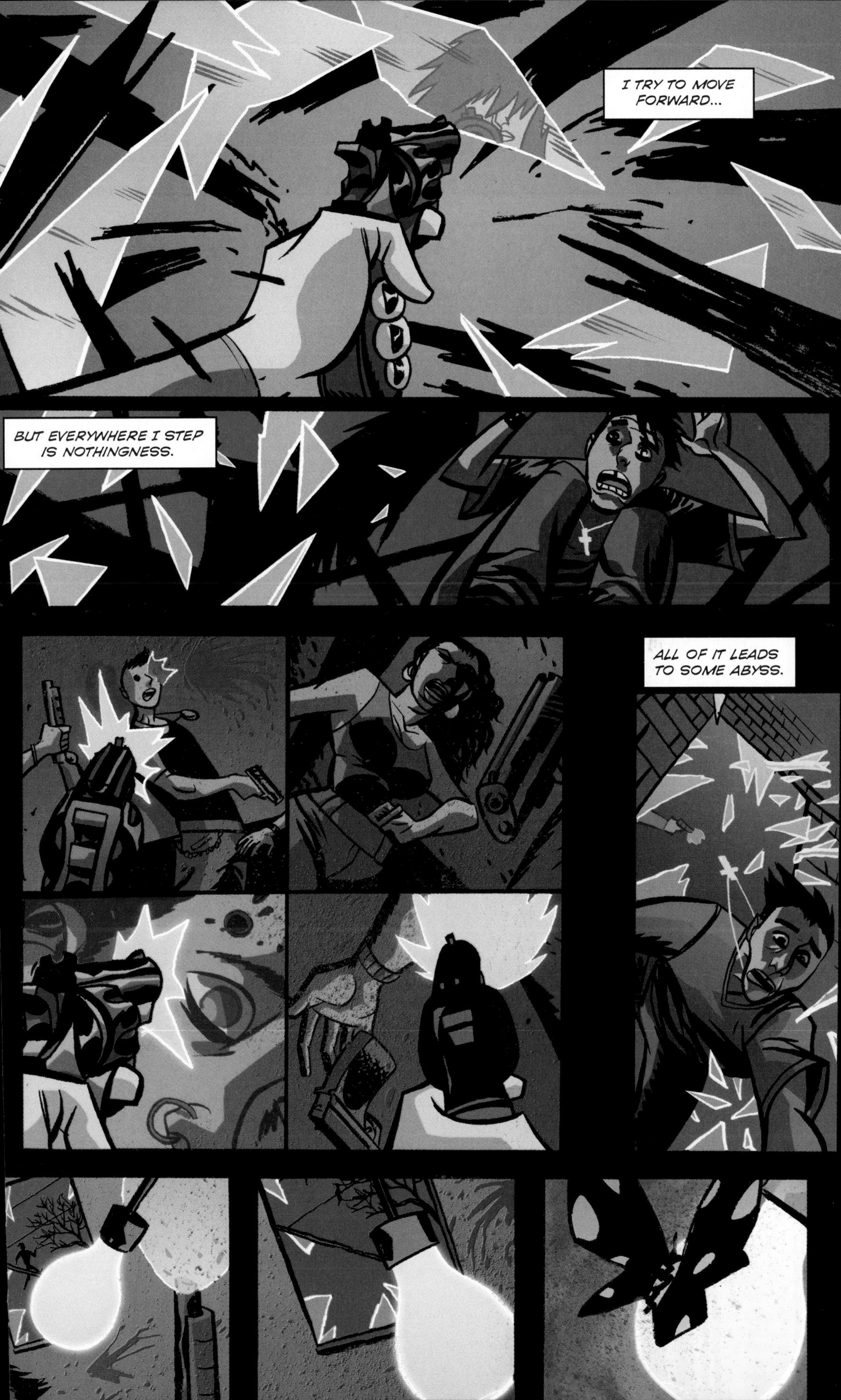
I TRY TO MOVE FORWARD...
BUT EVERYWHERE I STEP IS NOTHINGNESS.
ALL OF IT LEADS TO SOME ABYSS.

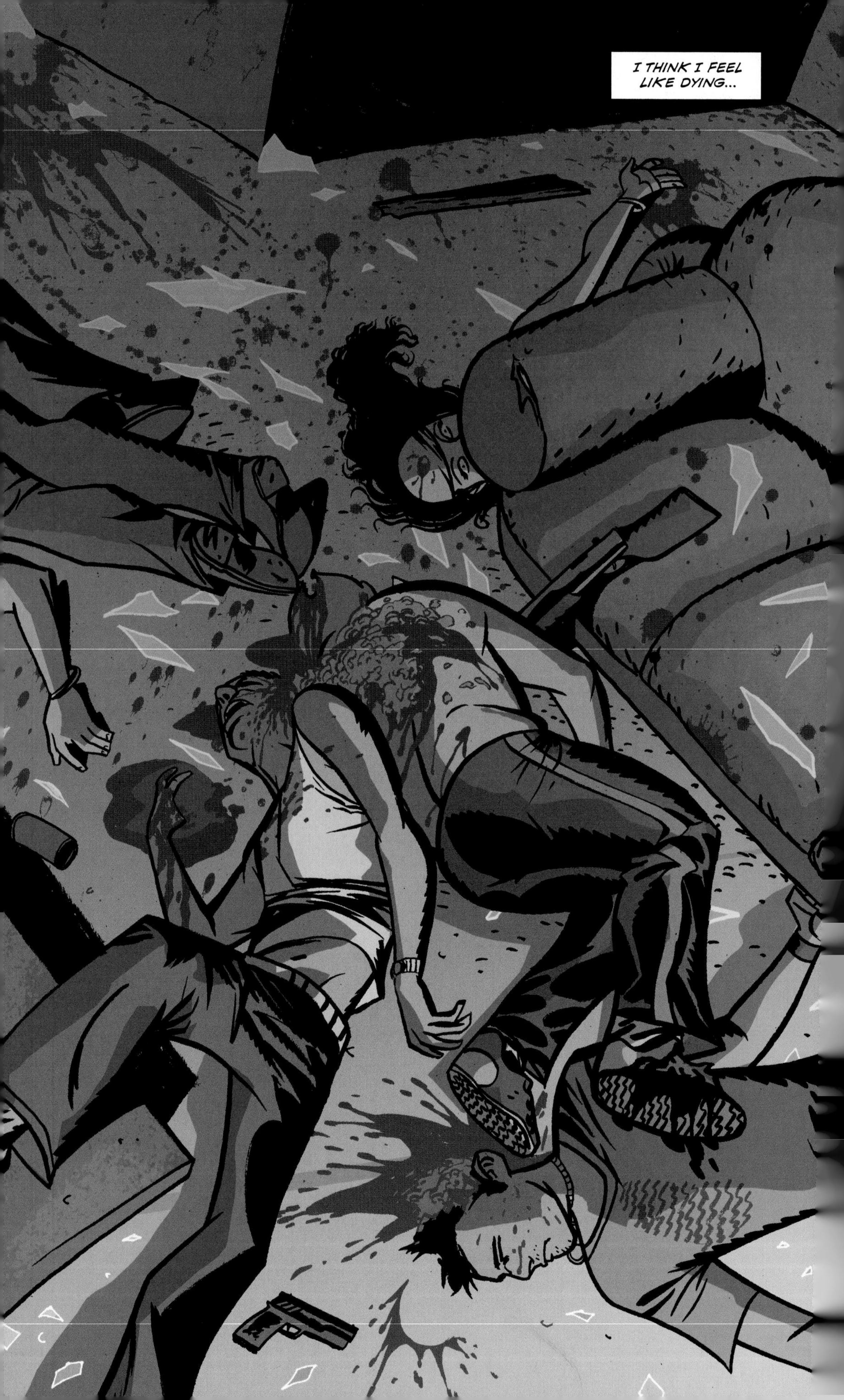
I THINK I FEEL LIKE DYING...

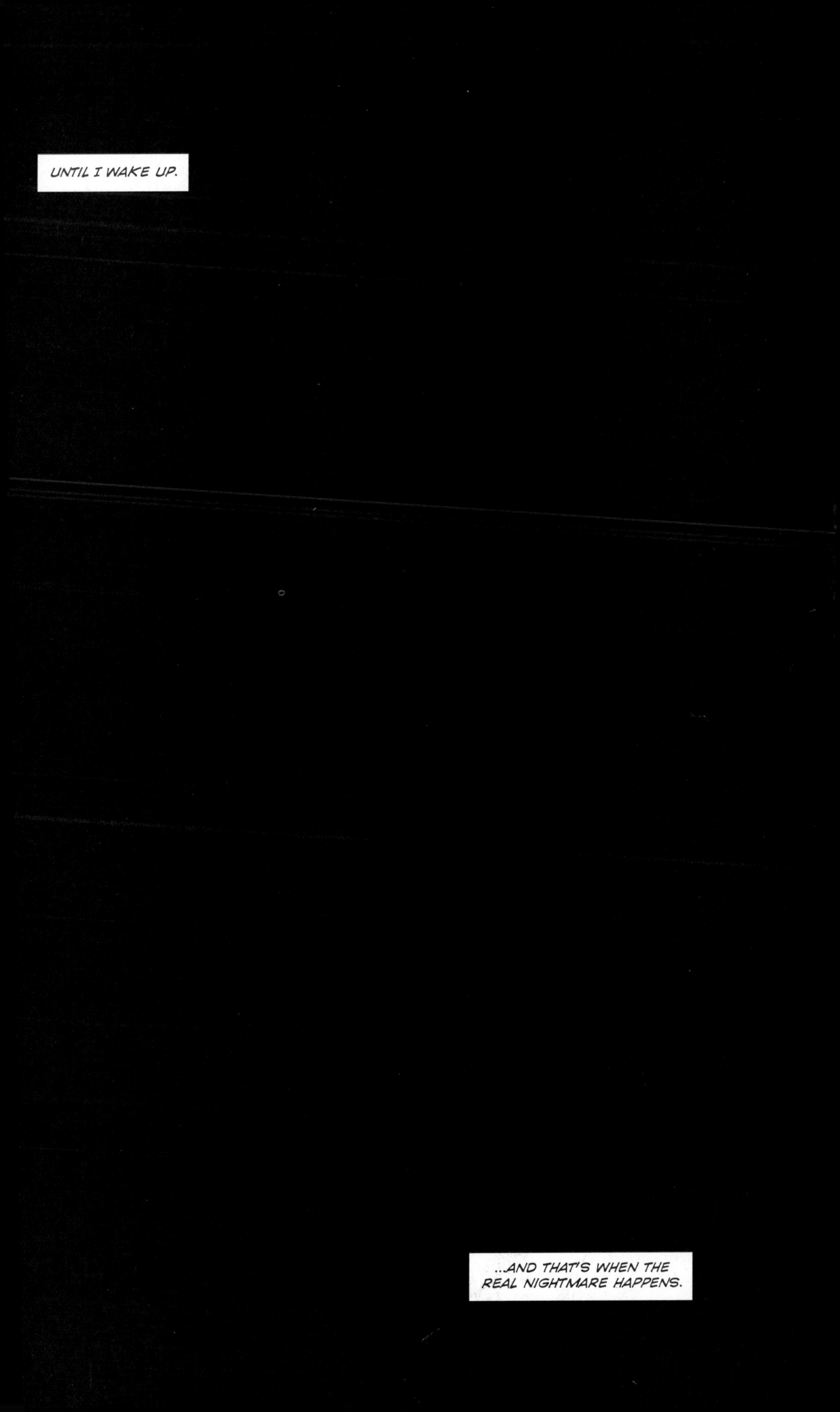
UNTIL I WAKE UP.
...AND THAT'S WHEN THE REAL NIGHTMARE HAPPENS.

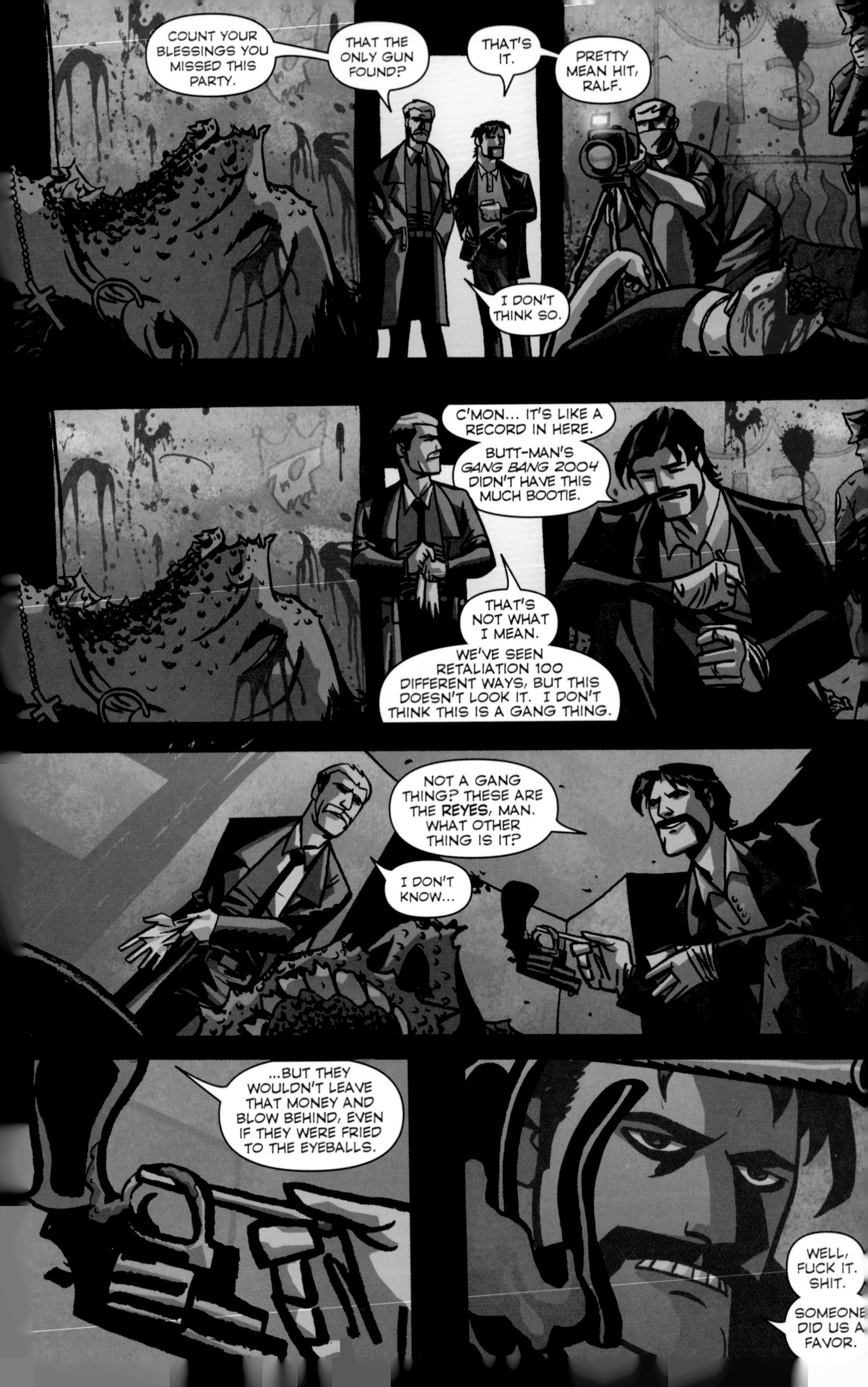

COUNT YOUR BLESSINGS YOU MISSED THIS PARTY.
THAT THE ONLY GUN FOUND?
THAT'S IT.
PRETTY MEAN HIT, RALF.
I DON'T THINK SO.
C'MON... IT'S LIKE A RECORD IN HERE.
BUTT-MAN'S *GANG BANG 2004* DIDN'T HAVE THIS MUCH BOOTIE.
THAT'S NOT WHAT I MEAN.
WE'VE SEEN RETALIATION 100 DIFFERENT WAYS, BUT THIS DOESN'T LOOK IT. I DON'T THINK THIS IS A GANG THING.
NOT A GANG THING? THESE ARE THE **REYES**, MAN. WHAT OTHER THING IS IT?
I DON'T KNOW...
...BUT THEY WOULDN'T LEAVE THAT MONEY AND BLOW BEHIND, EVEN IF THEY WERE FRIED TO THE EYEBALLS.
WELL, FUCK IT. SHIT.
SOMEONE DID US A FAVOR.

IT'S A COP GUN. THE OLD KIND. SERIAL MATCHES THE STANDARD ISSUE OF A BEAT COP KILLED IN THE LINE, 15 YEARS BACK.

DIONISIO ORTIZ, PASSED THE ACADEMY 3 YEARS BEFORE I DID.

PALO AMARGO - Dysentery Bark

RECORD'S SOLID BUT NOTHING THEY'D BUILD A STATUE OVER.

NO RECORD OF THE GUN BEING STOLEN OR SOLD.

THE FATHER FERNANDEZ ASKED ABOUT YOU AGAIN...

PALO AMARGO - Dysentery Bark

LAB SAYS THE RED MESS ON THE HANDLE ISN'T ANYONE'S GUTS.

Palo [...] up to 80 fe[...]nches covered with a smooth, grayish bark.

It has big, bright green, bipinnate leaves, 9" - 12" long, and small, red fruits growing in small clusters. Very small seeds with transparant wings in a brown seedpod.

The leaves and bark were historically used as a remedy for dysentery.
They are very bitter, since it contains, among others, a bitter principle identical with quassin.

Indigenous tribes of Amerindians in the rainforest used it as a hemostat to stop bleeding, for fevers and against dysentery.

In Suriname's traditional medicine, the crushed seeds drawn in alcohol are used against snakebites. An infusion of the bark against malaria, rheumatism, shingles and fever.

Hardiness: USDA zone [...]
Propagation: seeds.
Culture: keep in frost fre[...]
damage at 93° F. seriou[...]

IT'S WAX, MIXED WITH AN HERB CALLED PALO AMARGO.

HE SAYS HE WANTS YOU TO HELP HIM ROB A BANK.

YEP.

RAFAEL!!!

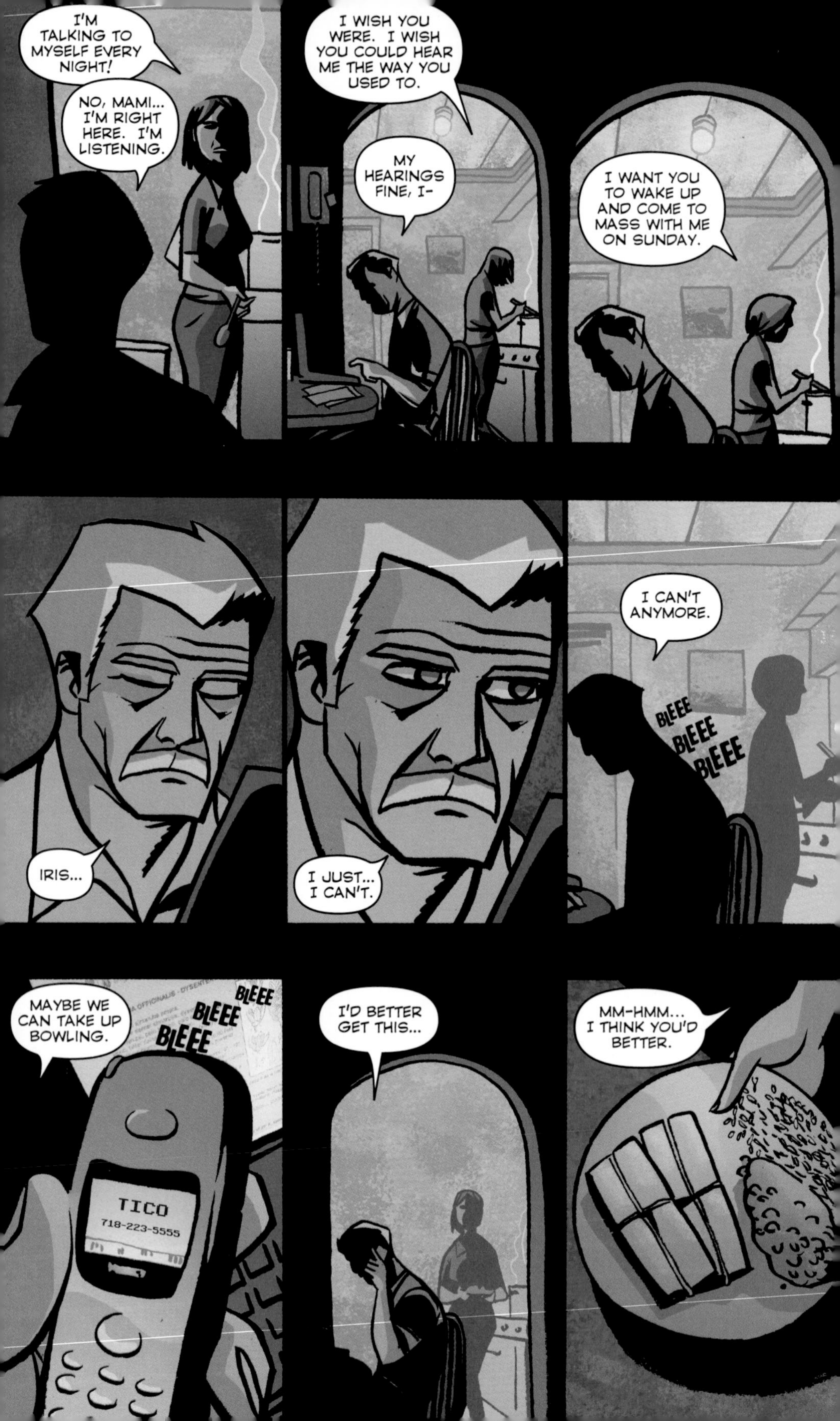
I'M TALKING TO MYSELF EVERY NIGHT!
NO, MAMI... I'M RIGHT HERE. I'M LISTENING.
I WISH YOU WERE. I WISH YOU COULD HEAR ME THE WAY YOU USED TO.
MY HEARINGS FINE, I-
I WANT YOU TO WAKE UP AND COME TO MASS WITH ME ON SUNDAY.
IRIS...
I JUST... I CAN'T.
I CAN'T ANYMORE.
BLEEE
BLEEE
BLEEE
MAYBE WE CAN TAKE UP BOWLING.
BLEEE
BLEEE
BLEEE
TICO
718-223-5555
I'D BETTER GET THIS...
MM-HMM... I THINK YOU'D BETTER.

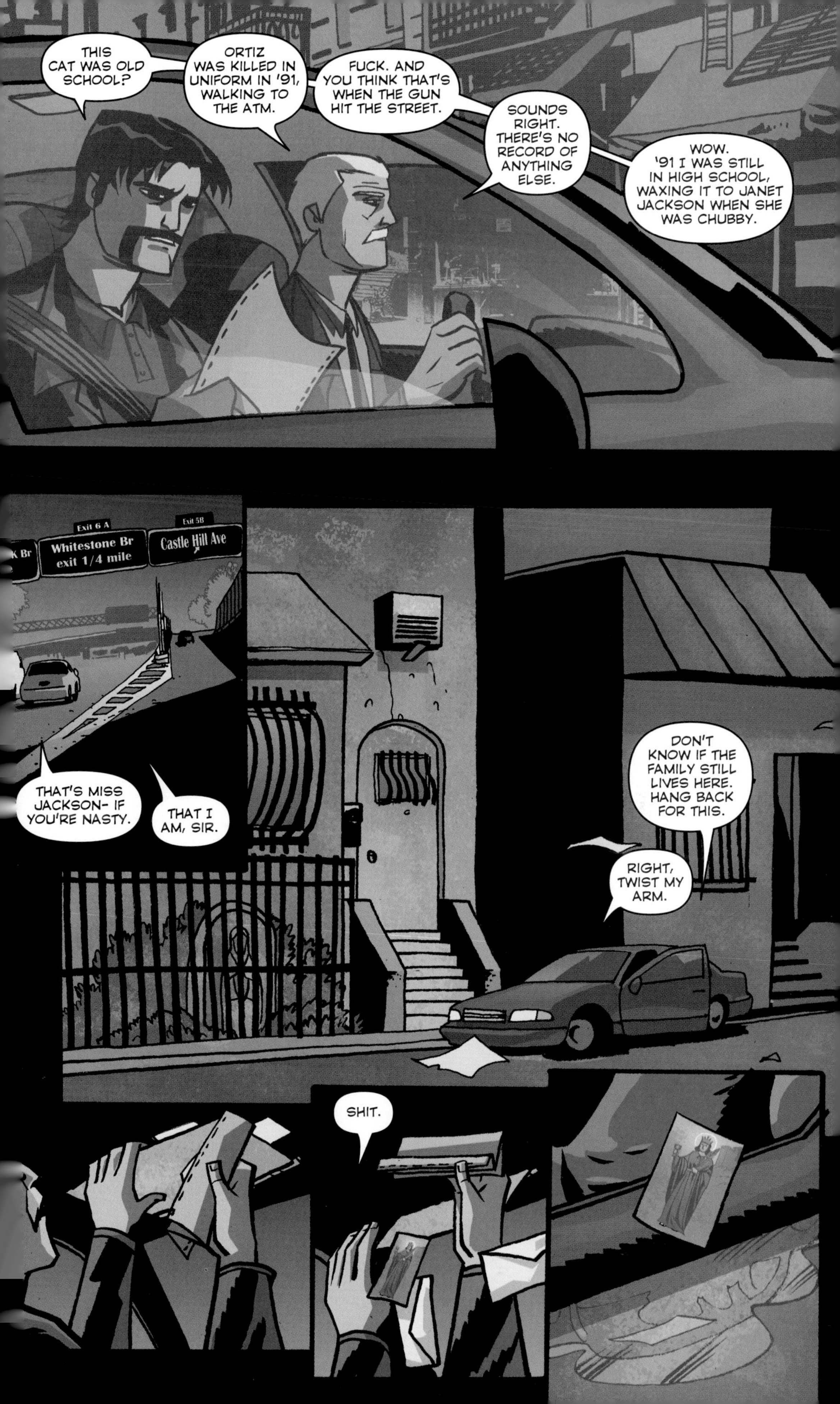
THIS CAT WAS OLD SCHOOL?
ORTIZ WAS KILLED IN UNIFORM IN '91, WALKING TO THE ATM.
FUCK. AND YOU THINK THAT'S WHEN THE GUN HIT THE STREET.
SOUNDS RIGHT. THERE'S NO RECORD OF ANYTHING ELSE.
WOW. '91 I WAS STILL IN HIGH SCHOOL, WAXING IT TO JANET JACKSON WHEN SHE WAS CHUBBY.
Exit 6 A
Whitestone Br exit 1/4 mile
Exit 5B
Castle Hill Ave
THAT'S MISS JACKSON- IF YOU'RE NASTY.
THAT I AM, SIR.
DON'T KNOW IF THE FAMILY STILL LIVES HERE. HANG BACK FOR THIS.
RIGHT, TWIST MY ARM.
SHIT.

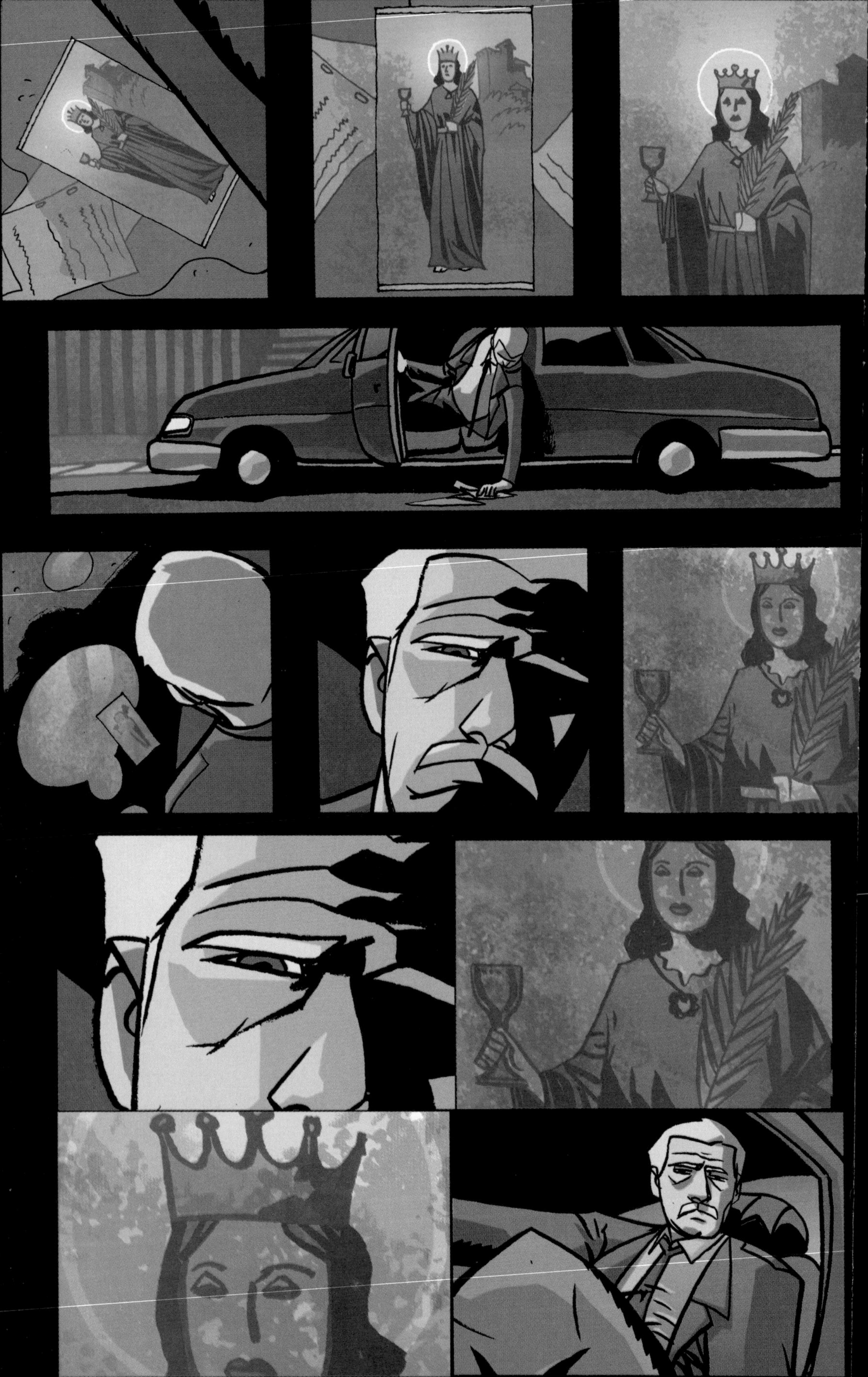

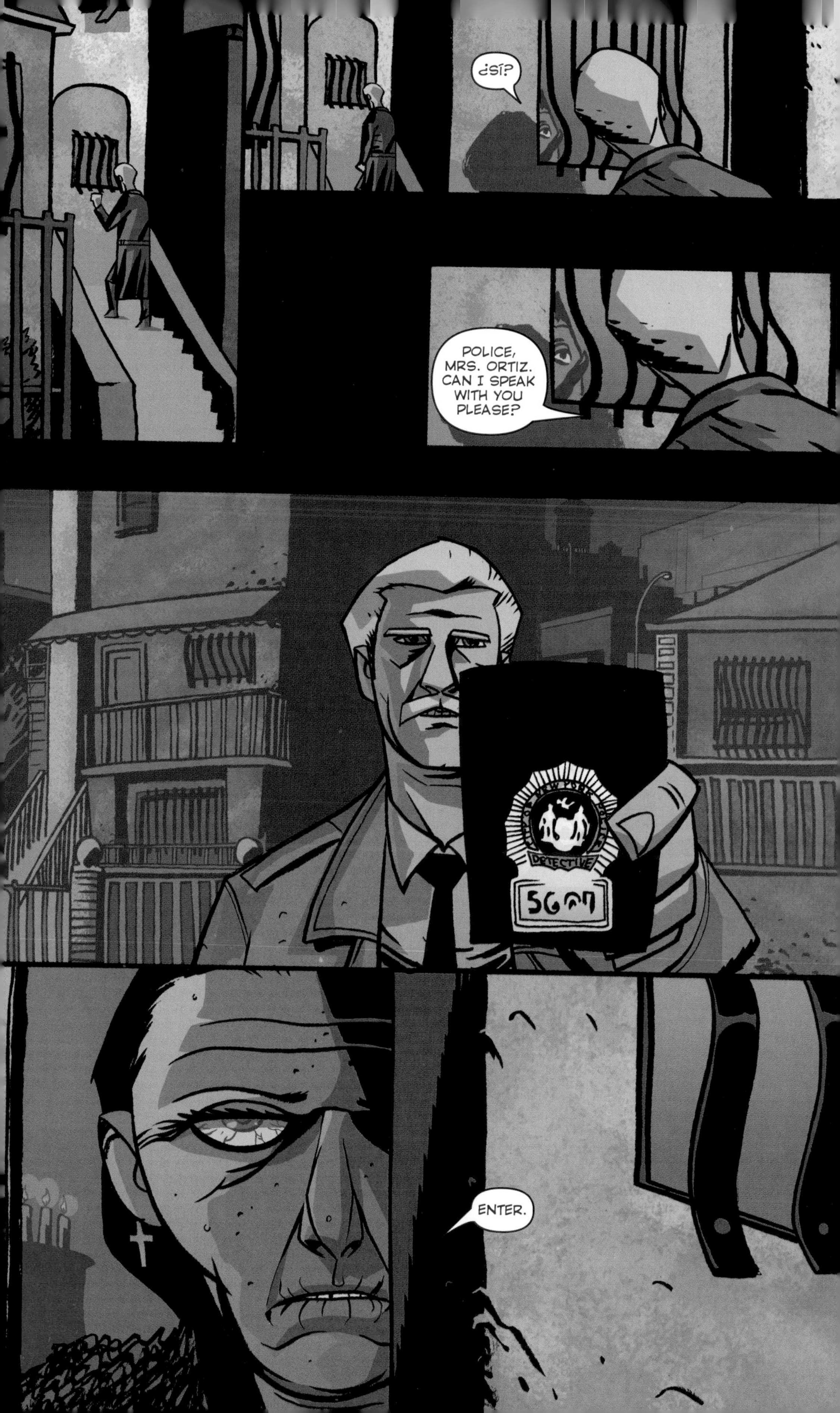
¿SÍ?
POLICE, MRS. ORTIZ. CAN I SPEAK WITH YOU PLEASE?
DETECTIVE
ENTER.

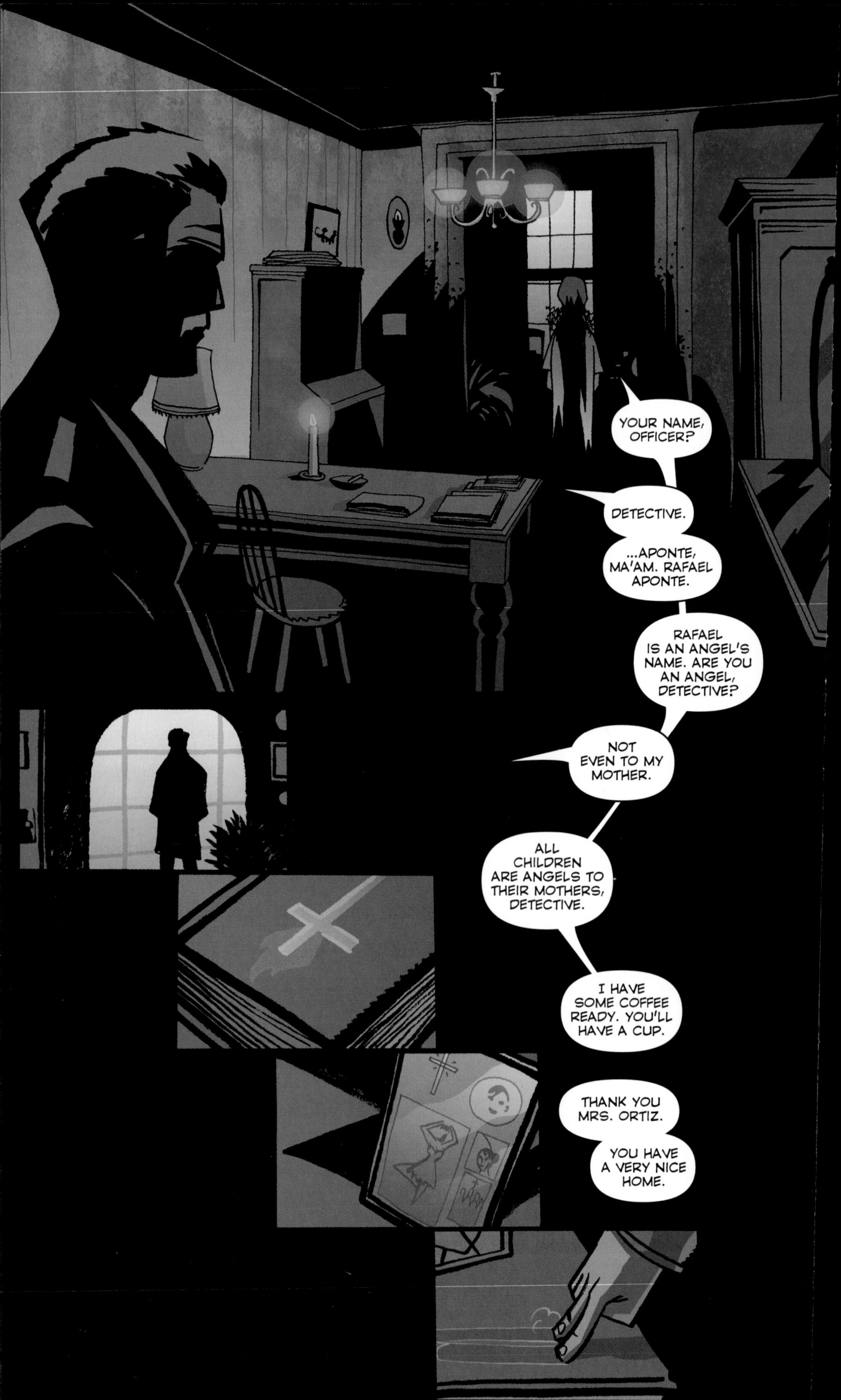
YOUR NAME, OFFICER?
DETECTIVE.
...APONTE, MA'AM. RAFAEL APONTE.
RAFAEL IS AN ANGEL'S NAME. ARE YOU AN ANGEL, DETECTIVE?
NOT EVEN TO MY MOTHER.
ALL CHILDREN ARE ANGELS TO THEIR MOTHERS, DETECTIVE.
I HAVE SOME COFFEE READY. YOU'LL HAVE A CUP.
THANK YOU MRS. ORTIZ.
YOU HAVE A VERY NICE HOME.

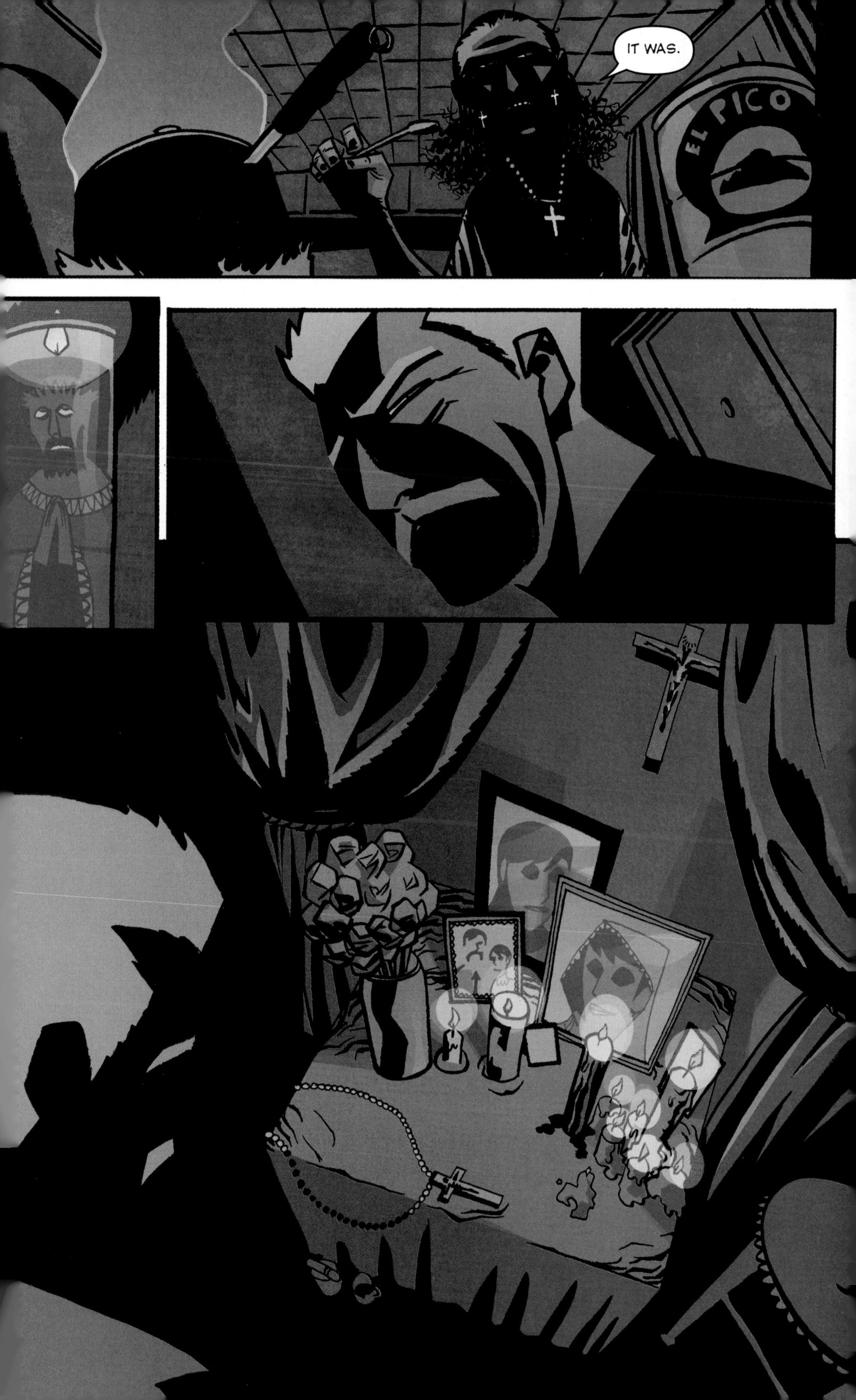
IT WAS.
EL PICO

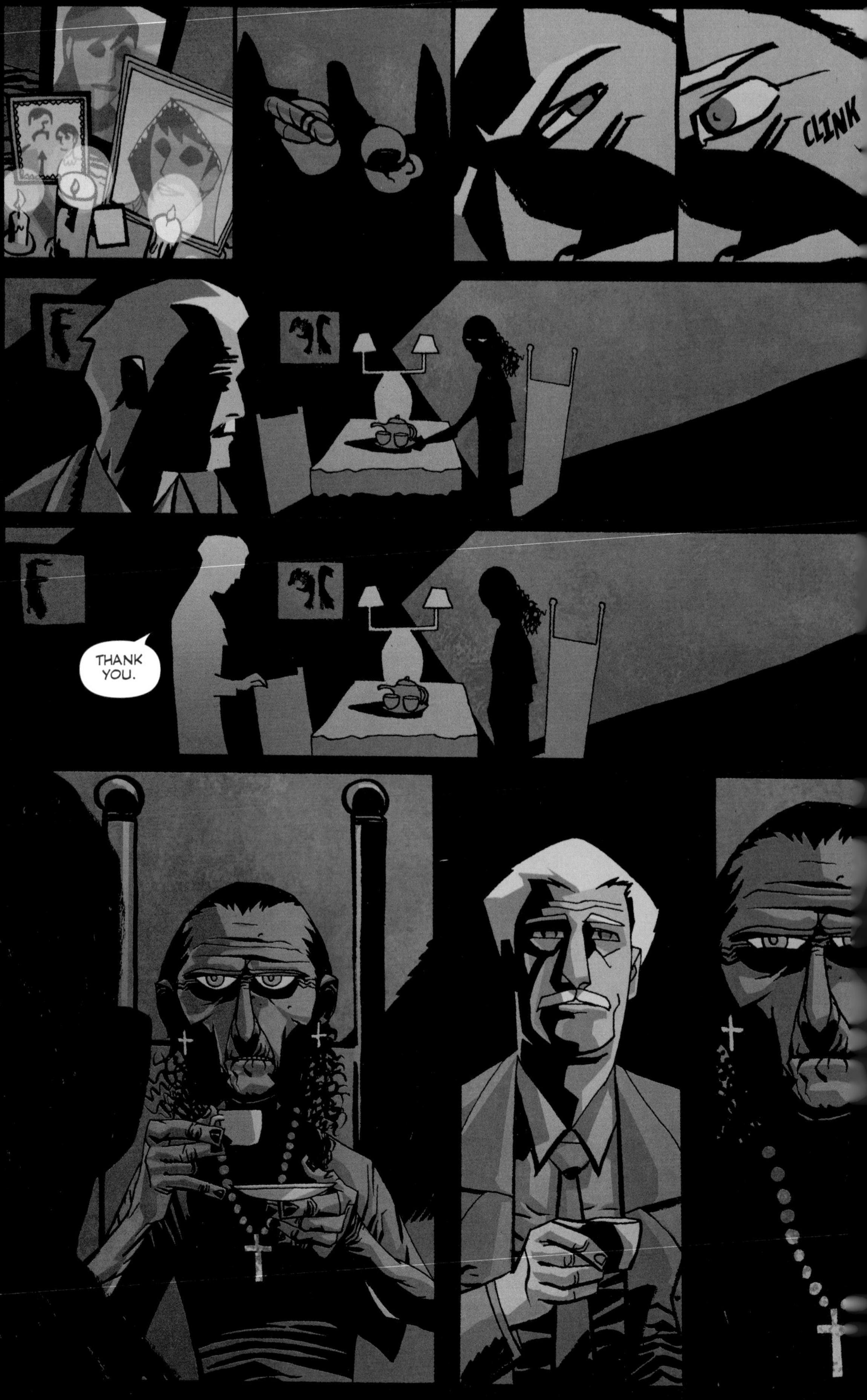
CLINK
THANK YOU.

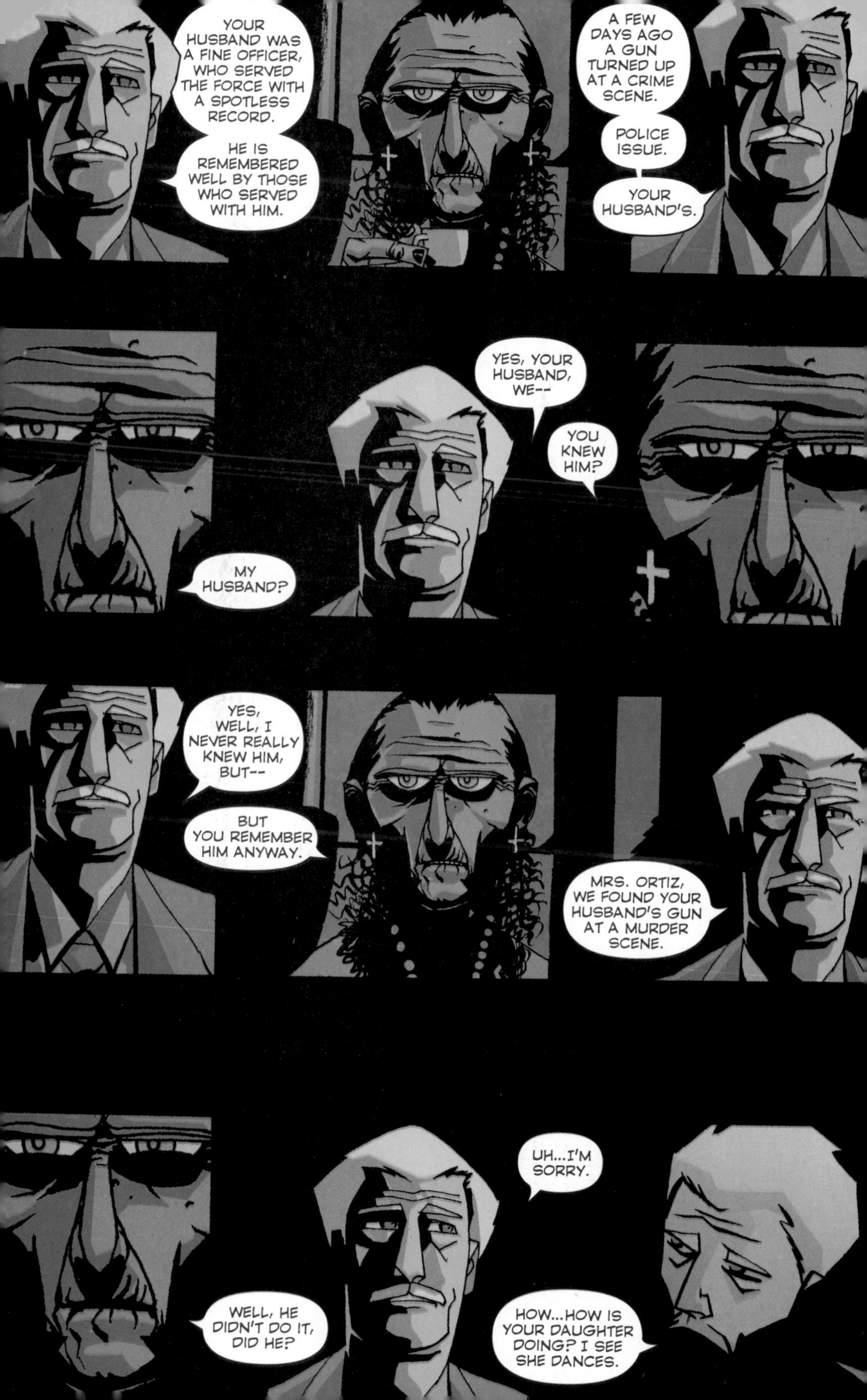
YOUR HUSBAND WAS A FINE OFFICER, WHO SERVED THE FORCE WITH A SPOTLESS RECORD.
HE IS REMEMBERED WELL BY THOSE WHO SERVED WITH HIM.
A FEW DAYS AGO A GUN TURNED UP AT A CRIME SCENE.
POLICE ISSUE.
YOUR HUSBAND'S.
MY HUSBAND?
YES, YOUR HUSBAND, WE--
YOU KNEW HIM?
YES, WELL, I NEVER REALLY KNEW HIM, BUT--
BUT YOU REMEMBER HIM ANYWAY.
MRS. ORTIZ, WE FOUND YOUR HUSBAND'S GUN AT A MURDER SCENE.
WELL, HE DIDN'T DO IT, DID HE?
UH...I'M SORRY.
HOW...HOW IS YOUR DAUGHTER DOING? I SEE SHE DANCES.

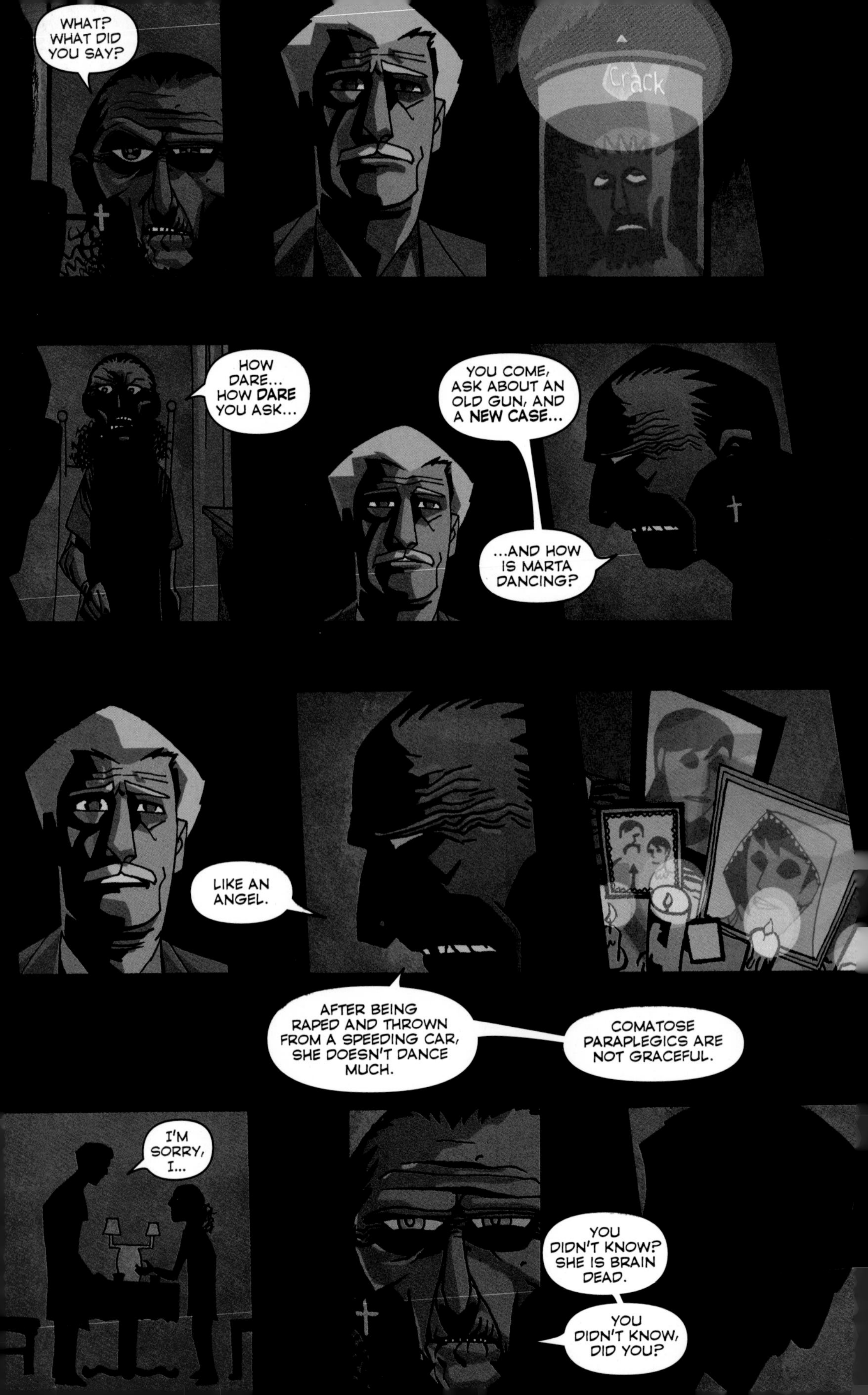
WHAT? WHAT DID YOU SAY?
Crack
HOW DARE... HOW DARE YOU ASK...
YOU COME, ASK ABOUT AN OLD GUN, AND A NEW CASE...
...AND HOW IS MARTA DANCING?
LIKE AN ANGEL.
AFTER BEING RAPED AND THROWN FROM A SPEEDING CAR, SHE DOESN'T DANCE MUCH.
COMATOSE PARAPLEGICS ARE NOT GRACEFUL.
I'M SORRY, I...
YOU DIDN'T KNOW? SHE IS BRAIN DEAD.
YOU DIDN'T KNOW, DID YOU?

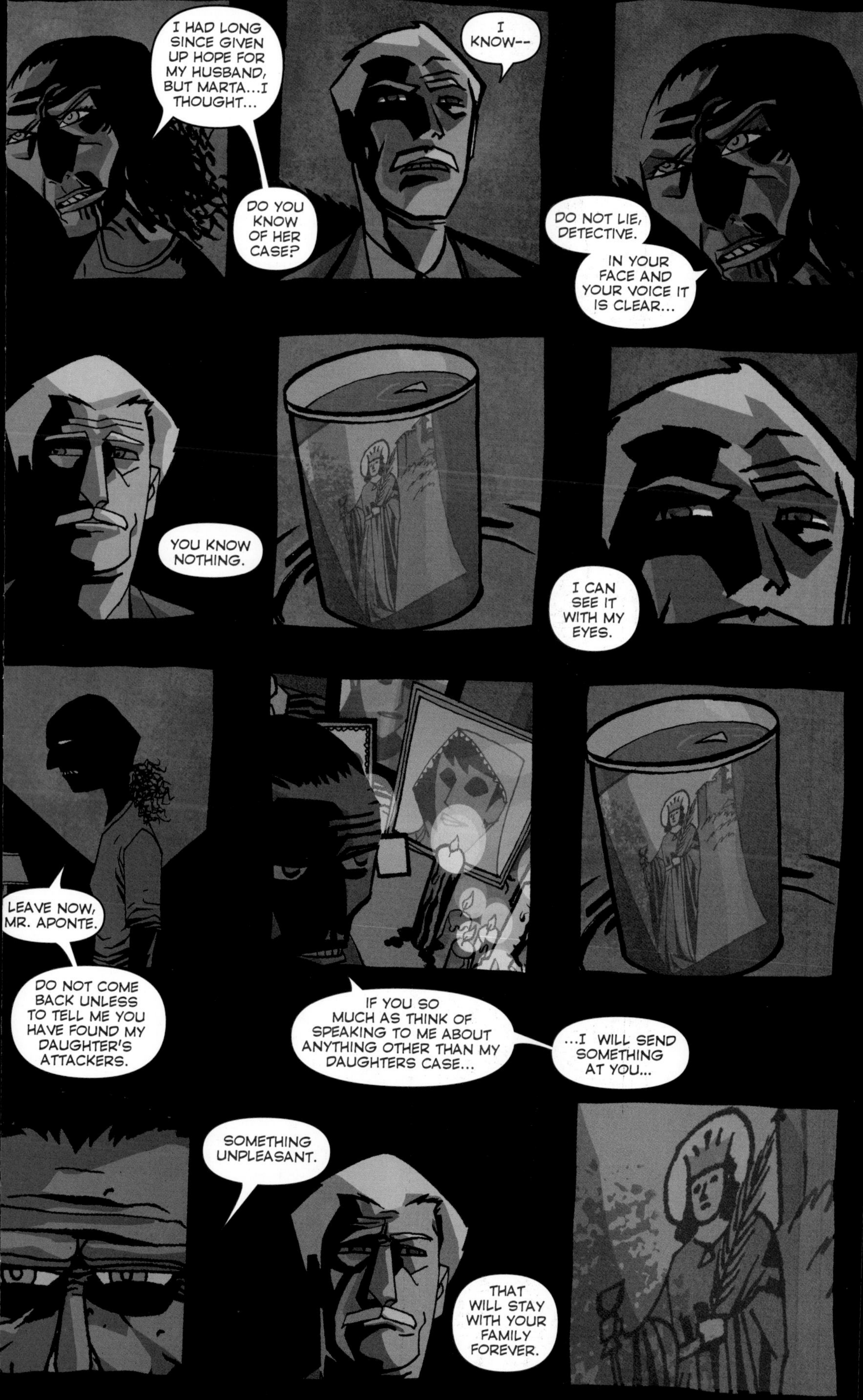
I HAD LONG SINCE GIVEN UP HOPE FOR MY HUSBAND, BUT MARTA...I THOUGHT...
DO YOU KNOW OF HER CASE?
I KNOW--
DO NOT LIE, DETECTIVE.
IN YOUR FACE AND YOUR VOICE IT IS CLEAR...
YOU KNOW NOTHING.
I CAN SEE IT WITH MY EYES.
LEAVE NOW, MR. APONTE.
DO NOT COME BACK UNLESS TO TELL ME YOU HAVE FOUND MY DAUGHTER'S ATTACKERS.
IF YOU SO MUCH AS THINK OF SPEAKING TO ME ABOUT ANYTHING OTHER THAN MY DAUGHTERS CASE...
...I WILL SEND SOMETHING AT YOU...
SOMETHING UNPLEASANT.
THAT WILL STAY WITH YOUR FAMILY FOREVER.

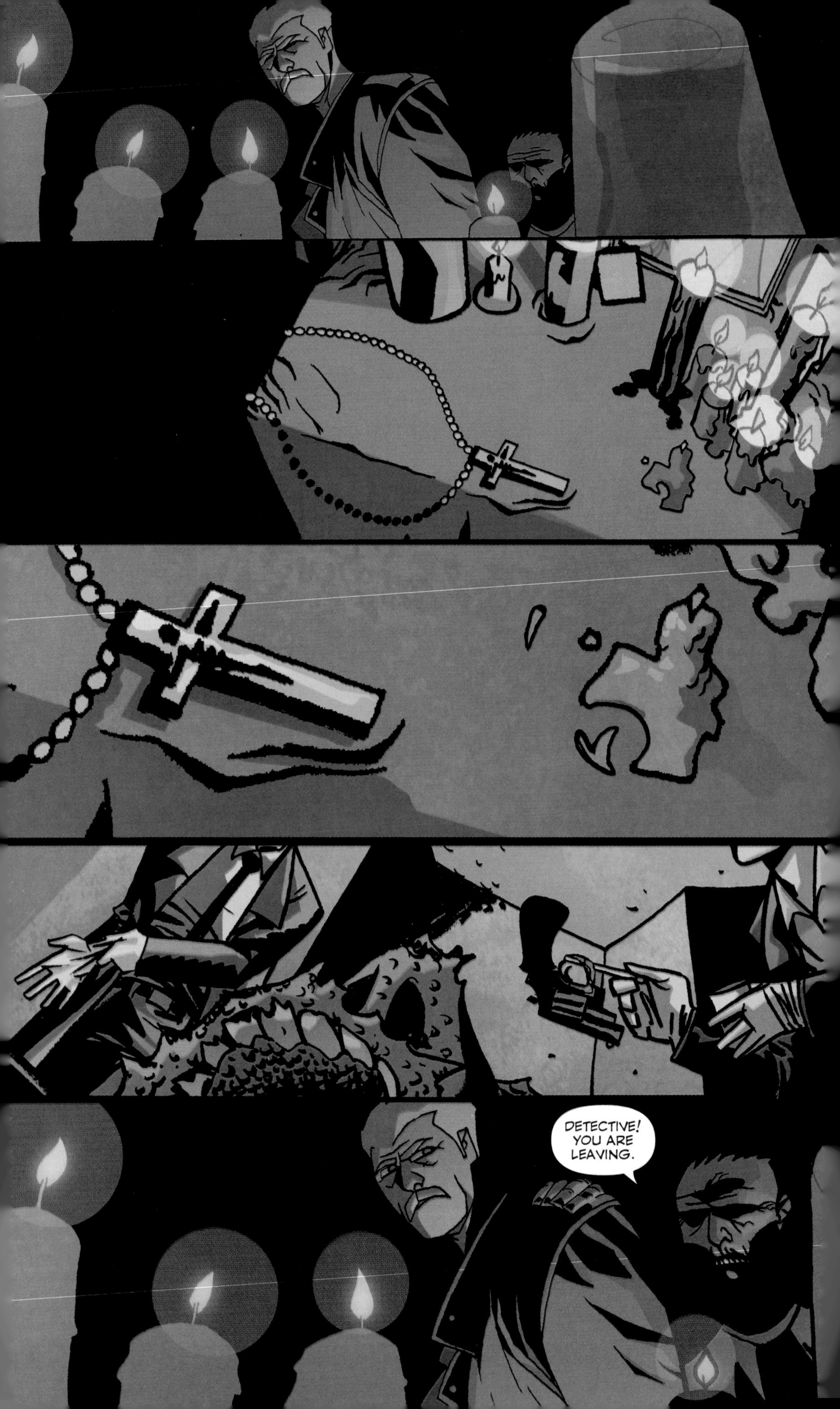
DETECTIVE! YOU ARE LEAVING.

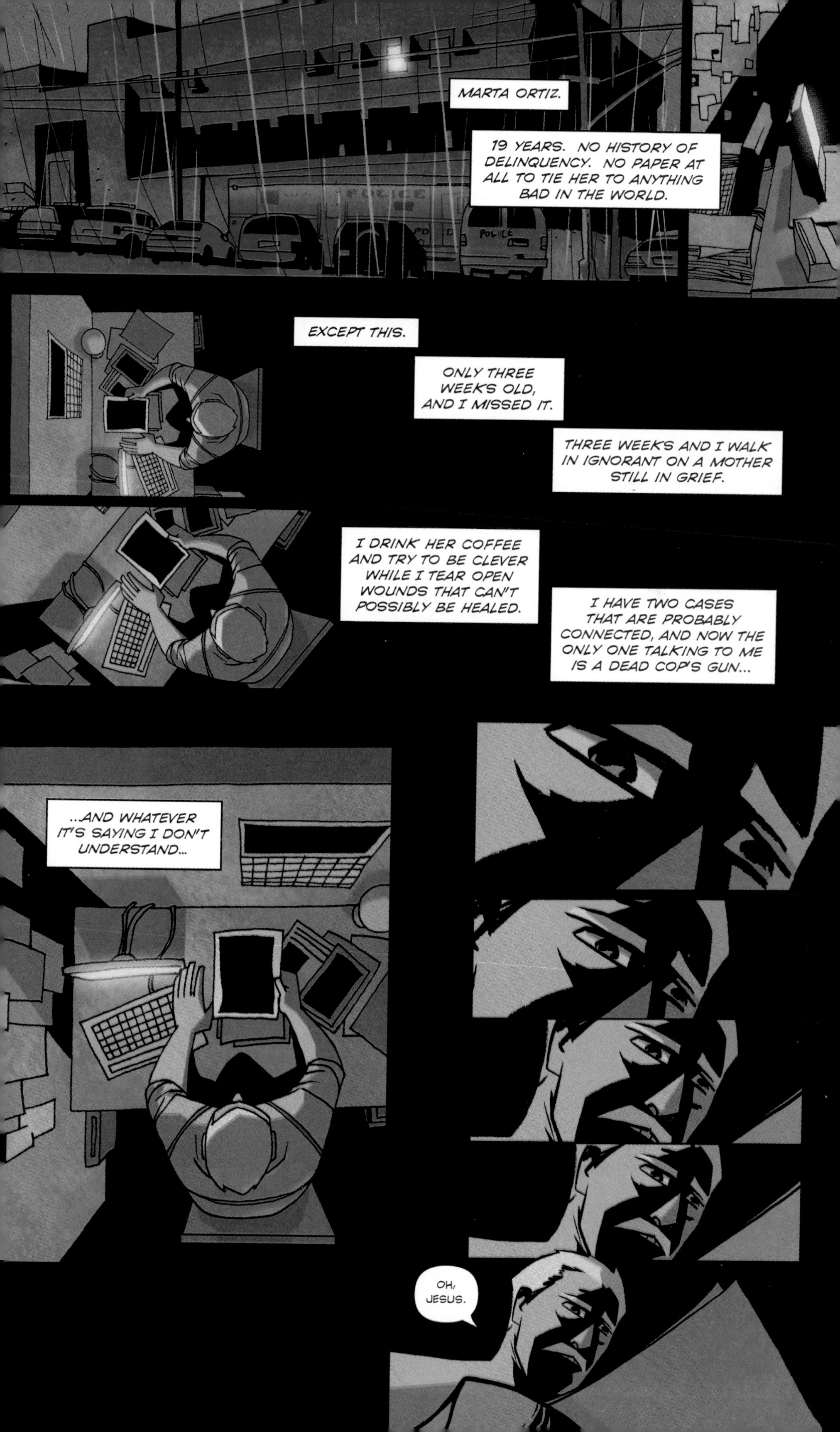
MARTA ORTIZ.
19 YEARS. NO HISTORY OF DELINQUENCY. NO PAPER AT ALL TO TIE HER TO ANYTHING BAD IN THE WORLD.
POLICE
EXCEPT THIS.
ONLY THREE WEEKS OLD, AND I MISSED IT.
THREE WEEKS AND I WALK IN IGNORANT ON A MOTHER STILL IN GRIEF.
I DRINK HER COFFEE AND TRY TO BE CLEVER WHILE I TEAR OPEN WOUNDS THAT CAN'T POSSIBLY BE HEALED.
I HAVE TWO CASES THAT ARE PROBABLY CONNECTED, AND NOW THE ONLY ONE TALKING TO ME IS A DEAD COP'S GUN...
...AND WHATEVER IT'S SAYING I DON'T UNDERSTAND...
OH, JESUS.

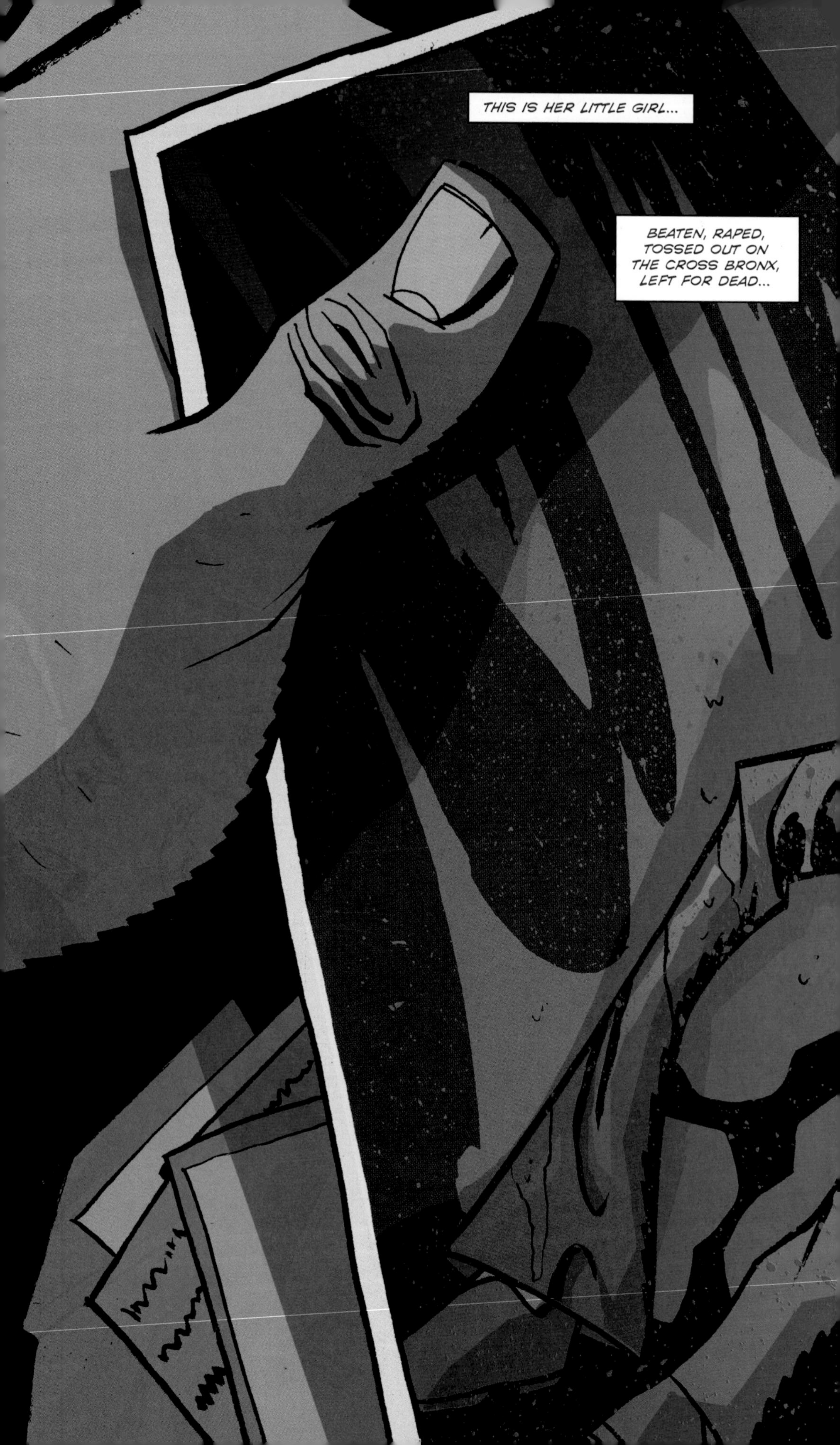
THIS IS HER LITTLE GIRL...
BEATEN, RAPED, TOSSED OUT ON THE CROSS BRONX, LEFT FOR DEAD...

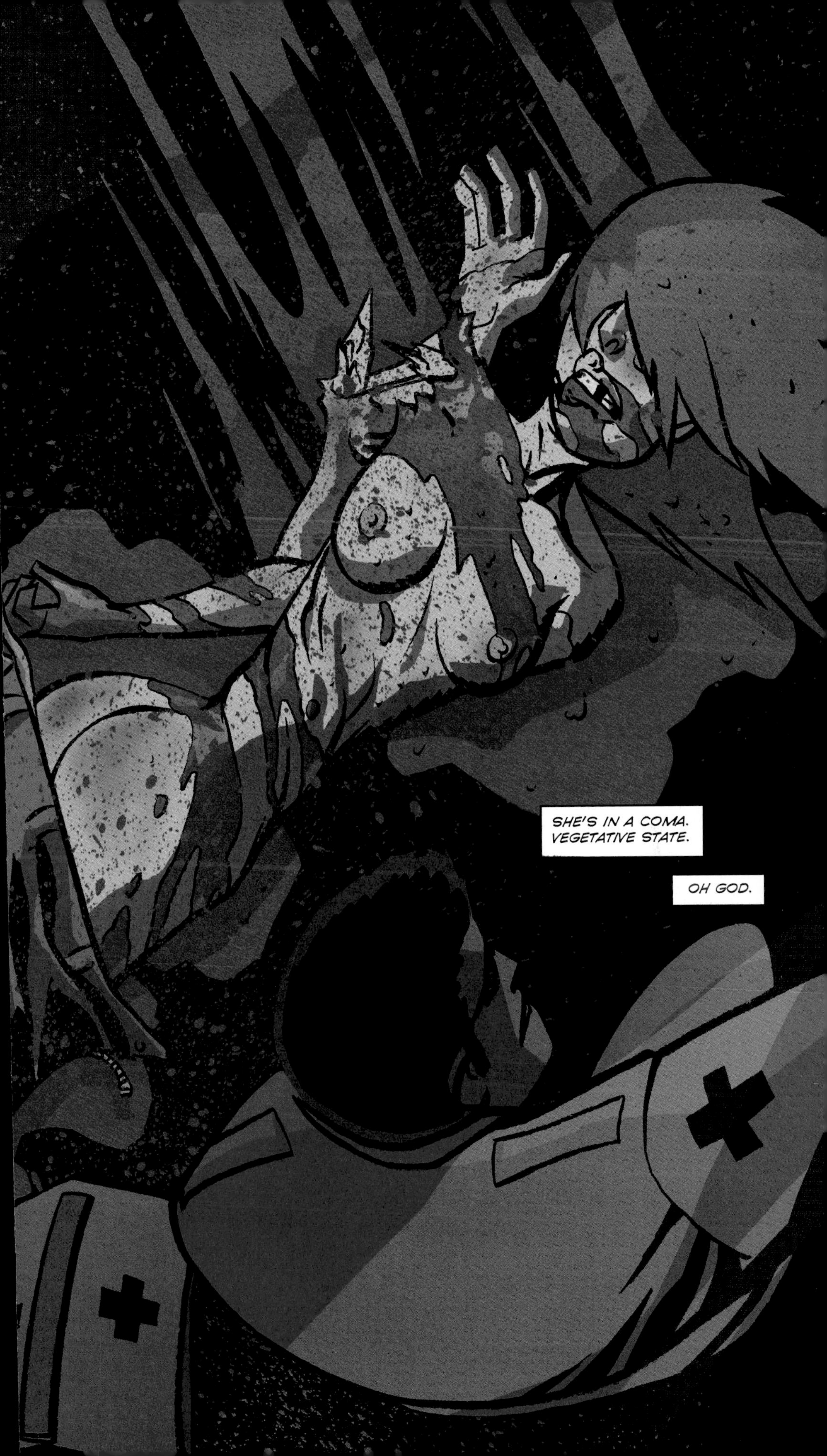
SHE'S IN A COMA. VEGETATIVE STATE.
OH GOD.

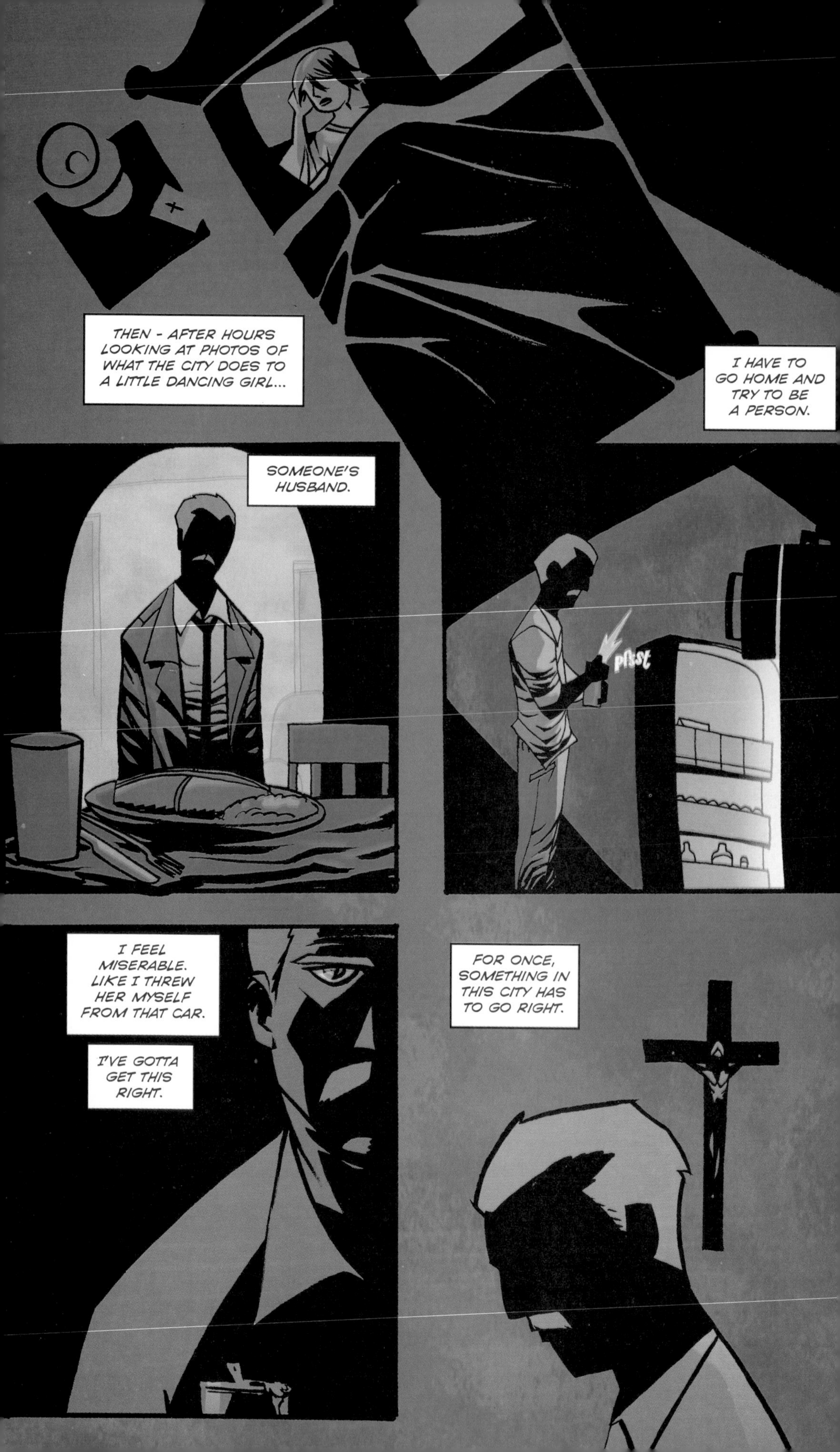
THEN - AFTER HOURS LOOKING AT PHOTOS OF WHAT THE CITY DOES TO A LITTLE DANCING GIRL...
I HAVE TO GO HOME AND TRY TO BE A PERSON.
SOMEONE'S HUSBAND.
pfsst
I FEEL MISERABLE. LIKE I THREW HER MYSELF FROM THAT CAR.
I'VE GOTTA GET THIS RIGHT.
FOR ONCE, SOMETHING IN THIS CITY HAS TO GO RIGHT.

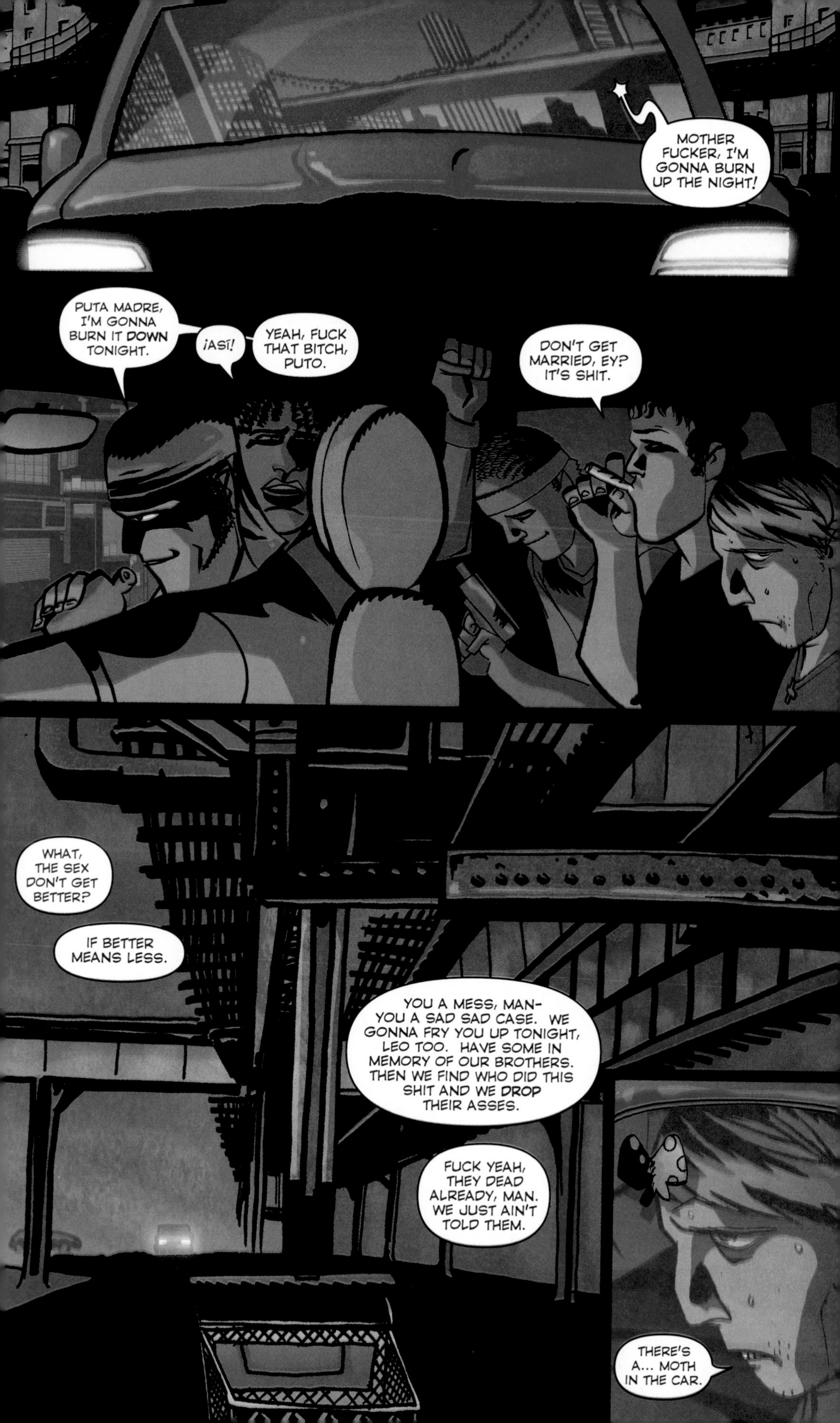
MOTHER FUCKER, I'M GONNA BURN UP THE NIGHT!
PUTA MADRE, I'M GONNA BURN IT **DOWN** TONIGHT.
¡ASÍ!
YEAH, FUCK THAT BITCH, PUTO.
DON'T GET MARRIED, EY? IT'S SHIT.
WHAT, THE SEX DON'T GET BETTER?
IF BETTER MEANS LESS.
YOU A MESS, MAN-YOU A SAD SAD CASE. WE GONNA FRY YOU UP TONIGHT, LEO TOO. HAVE SOME IN MEMORY OF OUR BROTHERS. THEN WE FIND WHO DID THIS SHIT AND WE **DROP** THEIR ASSES.
FUCK YEAH, THEY DEAD ALREADY, MAN. WE JUST AIN'T TOLD THEM.
THERE'S A... MOTH IN THE CAR.

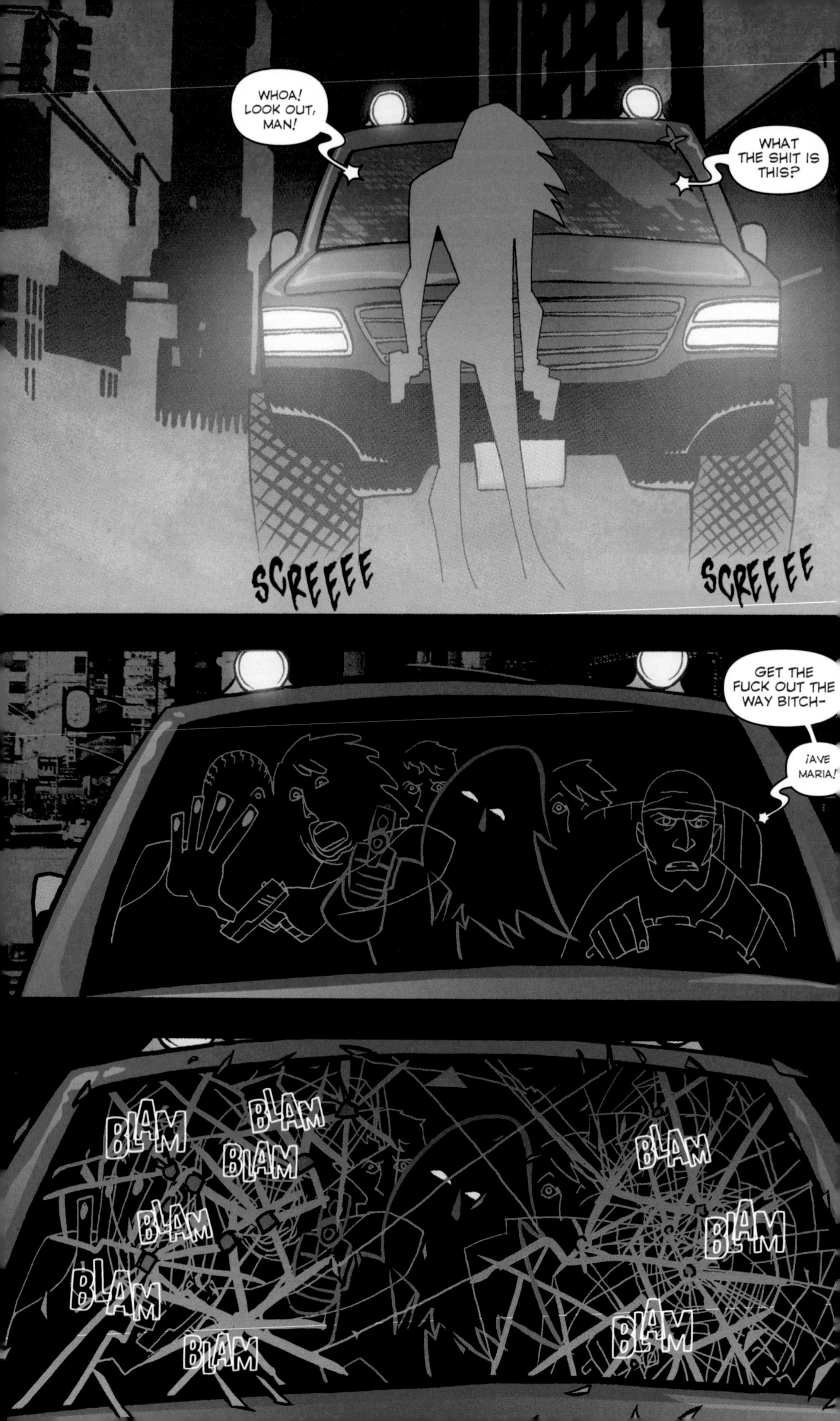
WHOA! LOOK OUT, MAN!
WHAT THE SHIT IS THIS?
SCREEEE
SCREEEE
GET THE FUCK OUT THE WAY BITCH-
¡AVE MARIA!
BLAM
BLAM
BLAM
BLAM
BLAM
BLAM
BLAM
BLAM
BLAM

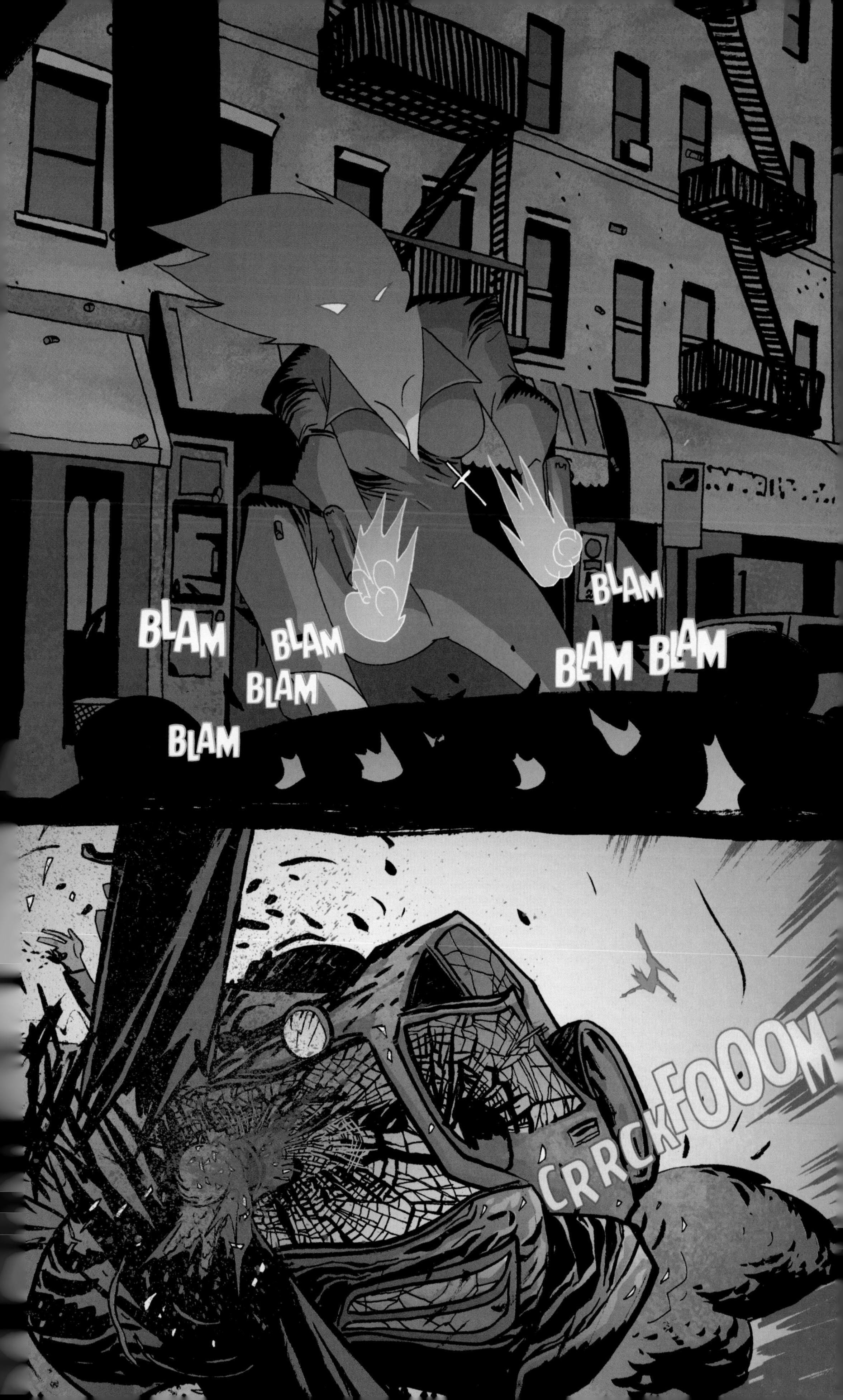
BLAM
BLAM
BLAM
BLAM
BLAM
BLAM
BLAM
CRRCKFOOOM

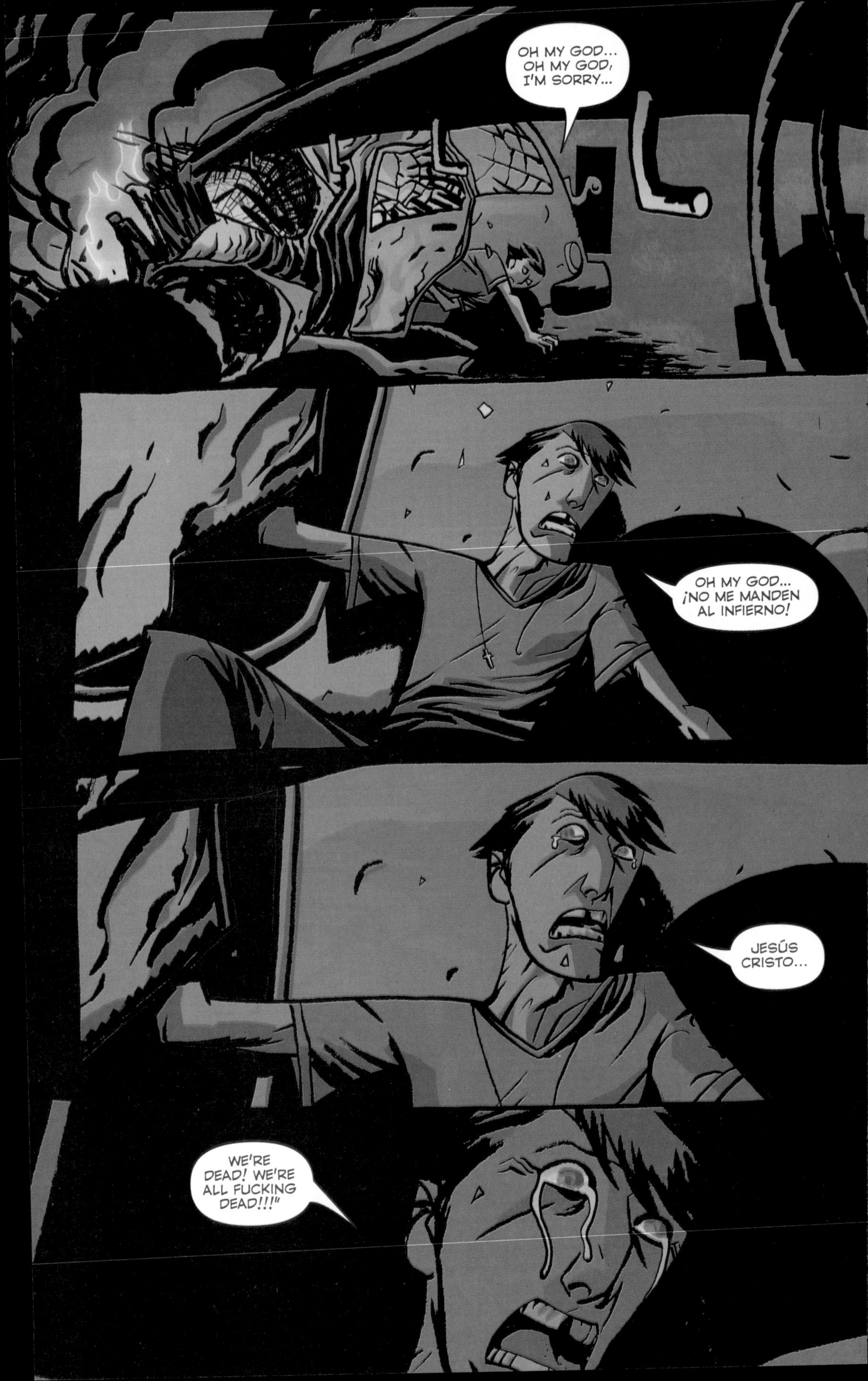

OH MY GOD... OH MY GOD, I'M SORRY...
OH MY GOD... ¡NO ME MANDEN AL INFIERNO!
JESÚS CRISTO...
WE'RE DEAD! WE'RE ALL FUCKING DEAD!!!"

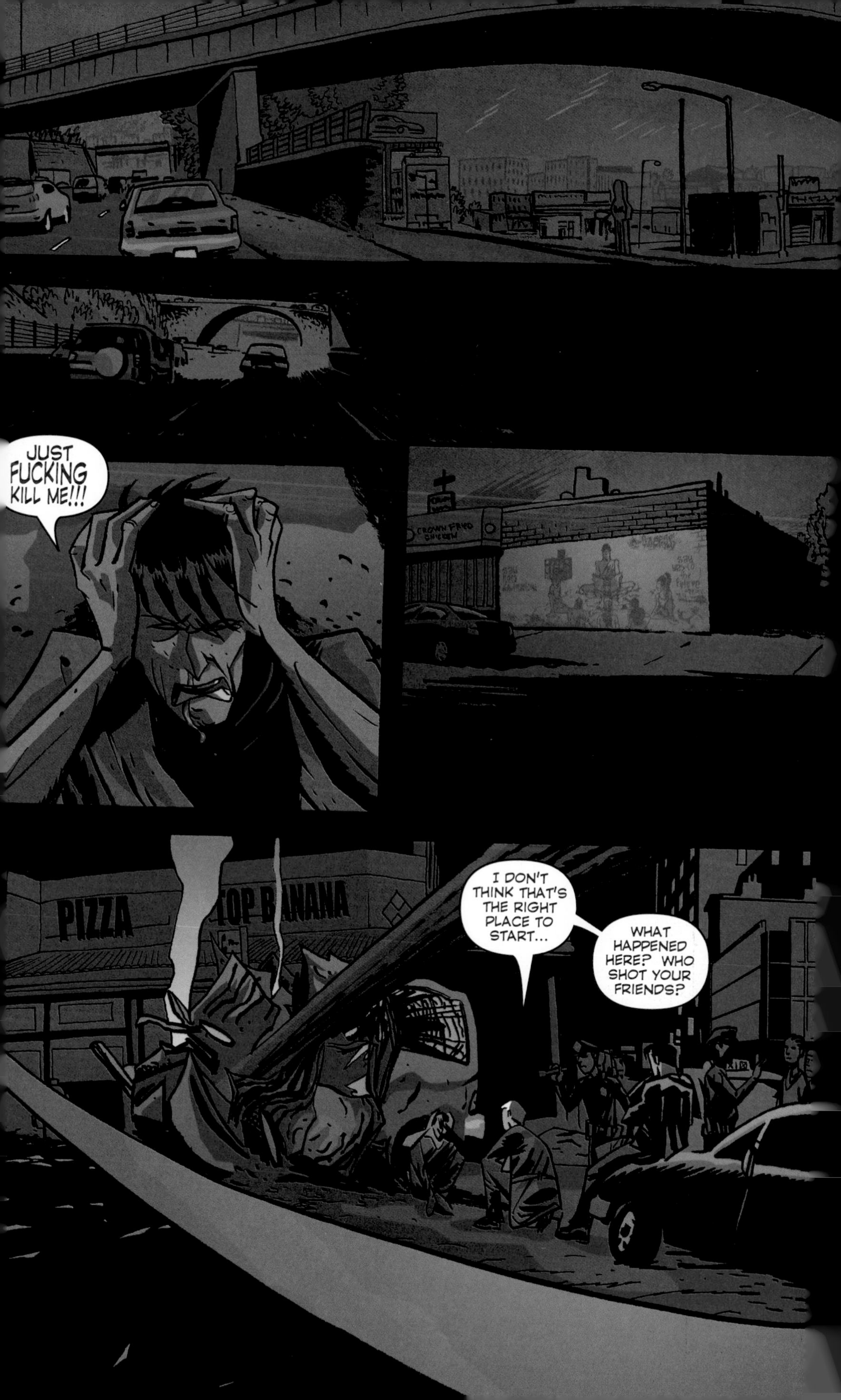

JUST FUCKING KILL ME!!!
PIZZA
TOP BANANA
I DON'T THINK THAT'S THE RIGHT PLACE TO START...
WHAT HAPPENED HERE? WHO SHOT YOUR FRIENDS?

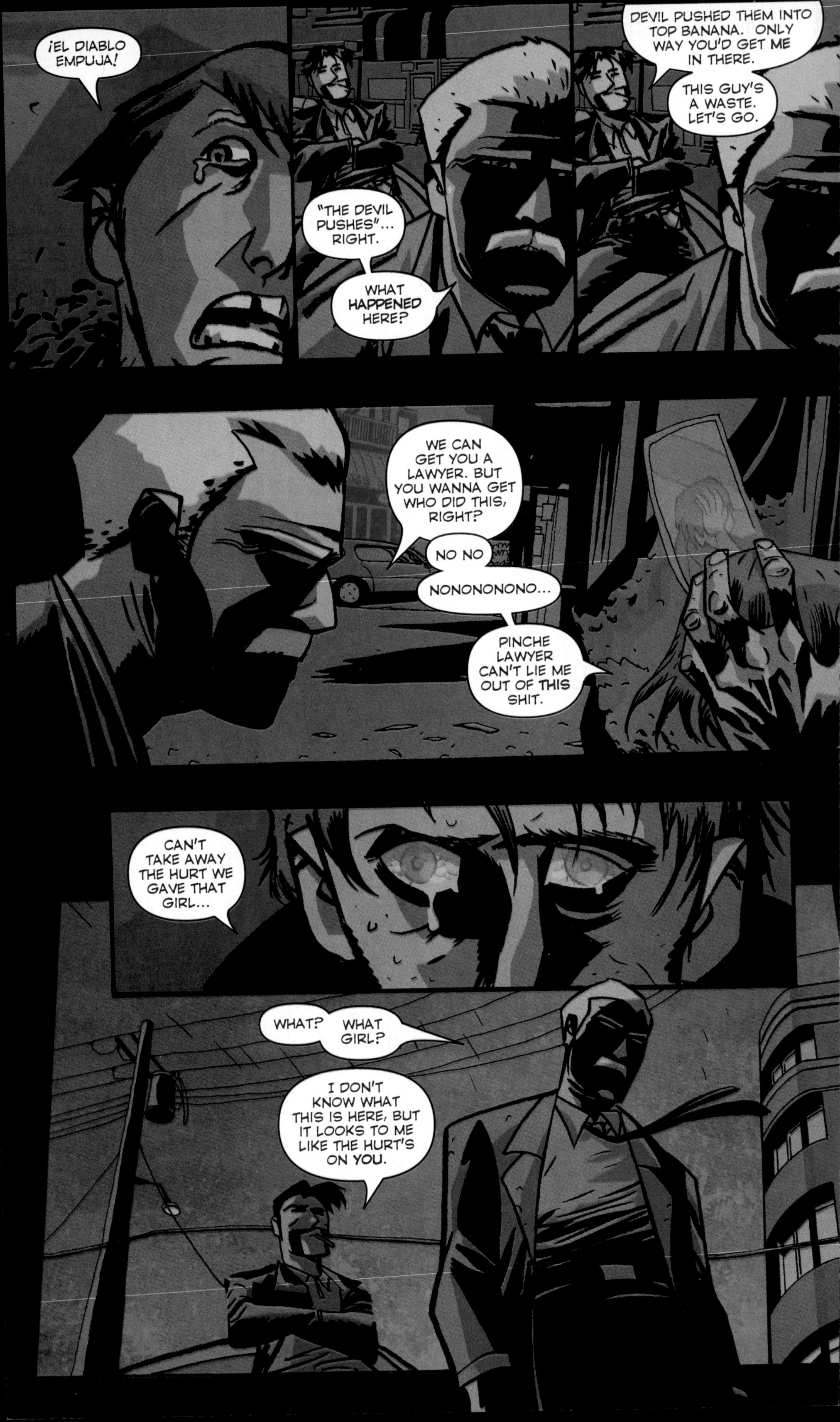
¡EL DIABLO EMPUJA!
"THE DEVIL PUSHES"... RIGHT.
WHAT HAPPENED HERE?
DEVIL PUSHED THEM INTO TOP BANANA. ONLY WAY YOU'D GET ME IN THERE.
THIS GUY'S A WASTE. LET'S GO.
WE CAN GET YOU A LAWYER. BUT YOU WANNA GET WHO DID THIS, RIGHT?
NO NO
NONONONONO...
PINCHE LAWYER CAN'T LIE ME OUT OF THIS SHIT.
CAN'T TAKE AWAY THE HURT WE GAVE THAT GIRL...
WHAT?
WHAT GIRL?
I DON'T KNOW WHAT THIS IS HERE, BUT IT LOOKS TO ME LIKE THE HURT'S ON YOU.

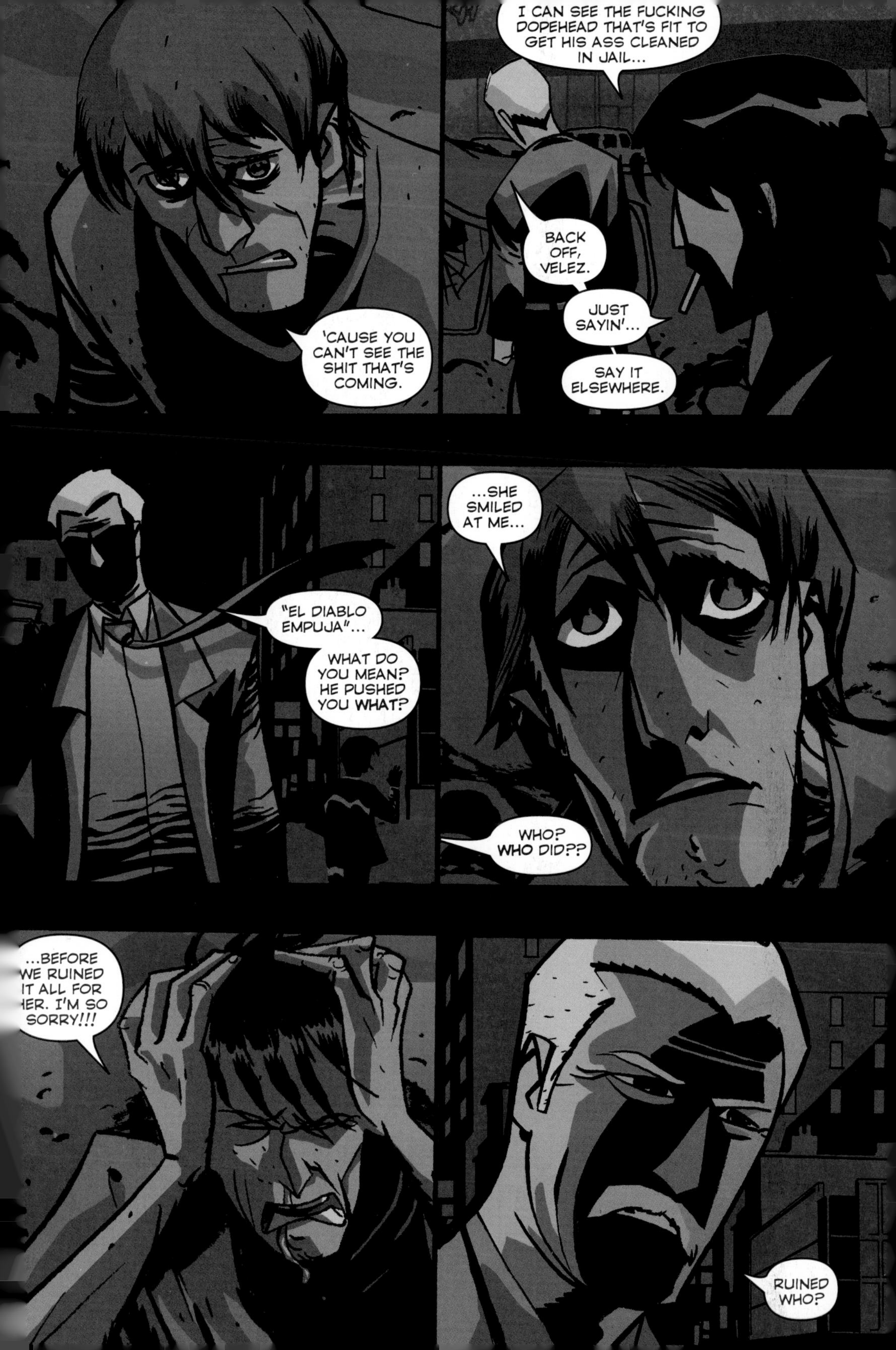
'CAUSE YOU CAN'T SEE THE SHIT THAT'S COMING.
I CAN SEE THE FUCKING DOPEHEAD THAT'S FIT TO GET HIS ASS CLEANED IN JAIL...
BACK OFF, VELEZ.
JUST SAYIN'...
SAY IT ELSEWHERE.
"EL DIABLO EMPUJA"...
WHAT DO YOU MEAN? HE PUSHED YOU WHAT?
...SHE SMILED AT ME...
WHO? WHO DID??
...BEFORE WE RUINED IT ALL FOR HER. I'M SO SORRY!!!
RUINED WHO?

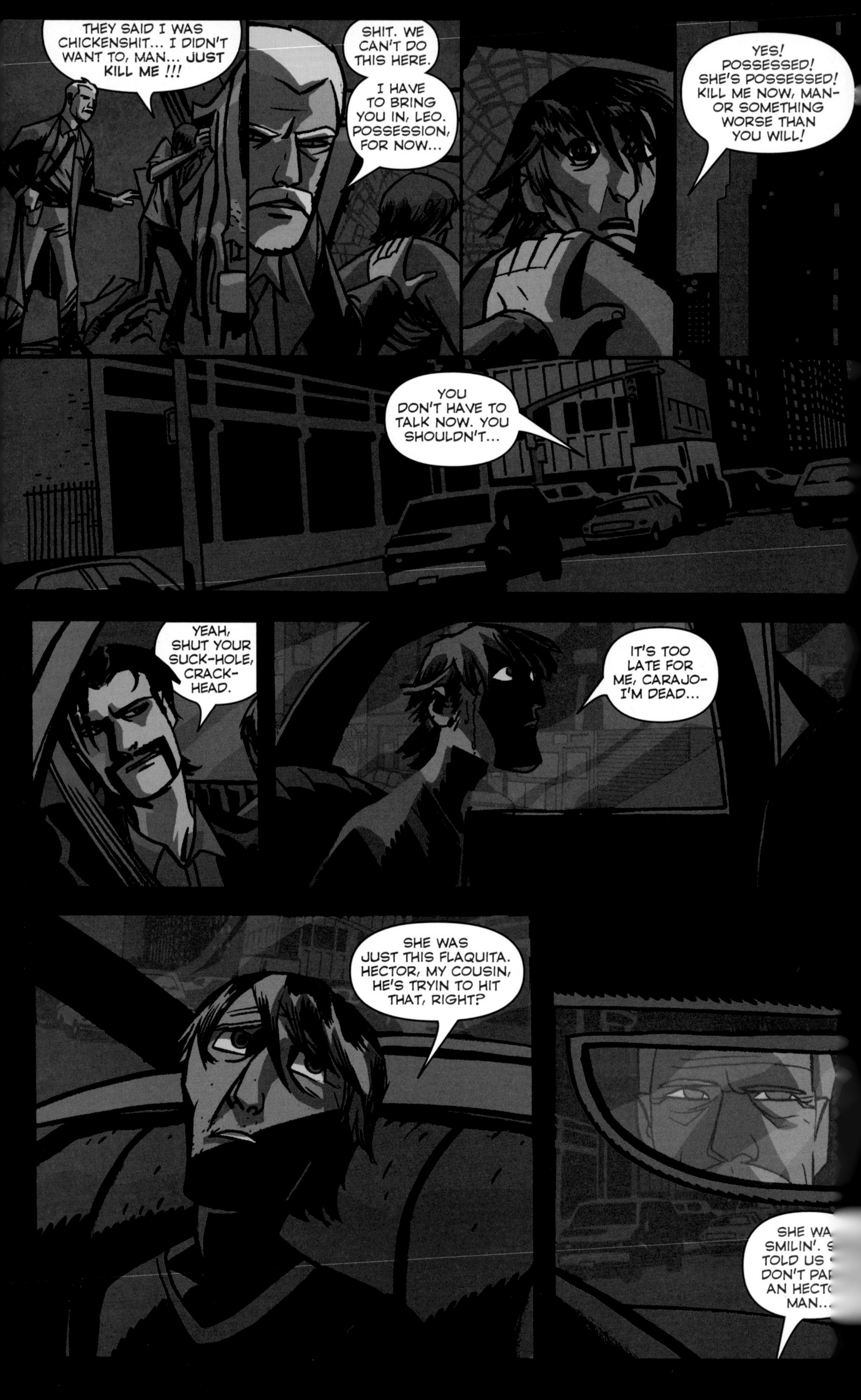
THEY SAID I WAS CHICKENSHIT... I DIDN'T WANT TO, MAN... JUST KILL ME !!!
SHIT. WE CAN'T DO THIS HERE.
I HAVE TO BRING YOU IN, LEO. POSSESSION, FOR NOW...
YES! POSSESSED! SHE'S POSSESSED! KILL ME NOW, MAN- OR SOMETHING WORSE THAN YOU WILL!
YOU DON'T HAVE TO TALK NOW. YOU SHOULDN'T...
YEAH, SHUT YOUR SUCK-HOLE, CRACK-HEAD.
IT'S TOO LATE FOR ME, CARAJO- I'M DEAD...
SHE WAS JUST THIS FLAQUITA. HECTOR, MY COUSIN, HE'S TRYIN TO HIT THAT, RIGHT?

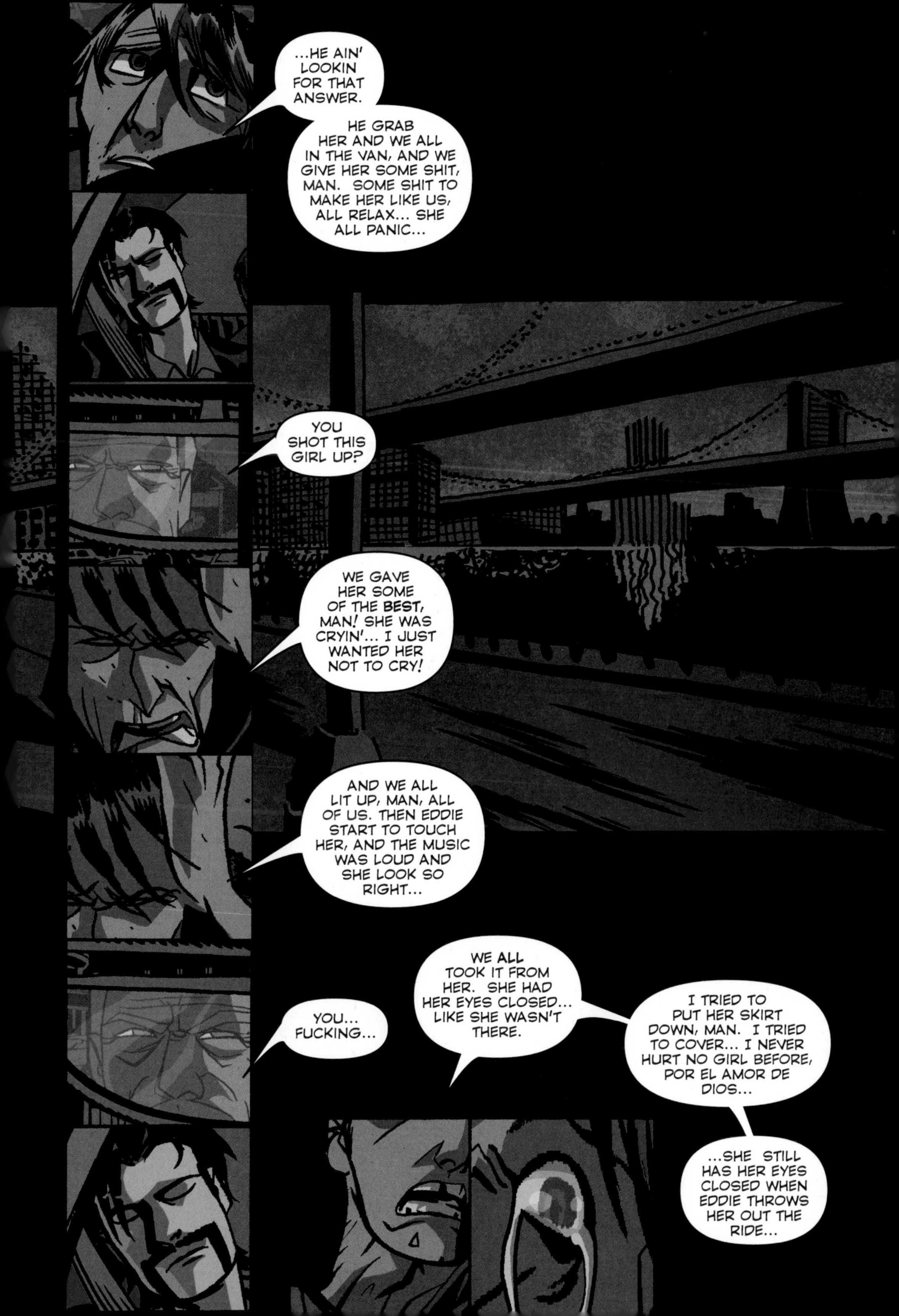
...HE AIN' LOOKIN FOR THAT ANSWER.
HE GRAB HER AND WE ALL IN THE VAN, AND WE GIVE HER SOME SHIT, MAN. SOME SHIT TO MAKE HER LIKE US, ALL RELAX... SHE ALL PANIC...
YOU SHOT THIS GIRL UP?
WE GAVE HER SOME OF THE **BEST**, MAN! SHE WAS CRYIN'... I JUST WANTED HER NOT TO CRY!
AND WE ALL LIT UP, MAN, ALL OF US. THEN EDDIE START TO TOUCH HER, AND THE MUSIC WAS LOUD AND SHE LOOK SO RIGHT...
YOU... FUCKING...
WE **ALL** TOOK IT FROM HER. SHE HAD HER EYES CLOSED... LIKE SHE WASN'T THERE.
I TRIED TO PUT HER SKIRT DOWN, MAN. I TRIED TO COVER... I NEVER HURT NO GIRL BEFORE, POR EL AMOR DE DIOS...
...SHE STILL HAS HER EYES CLOSED WHEN EDDIE THROWS HER OUT THE RIDE...

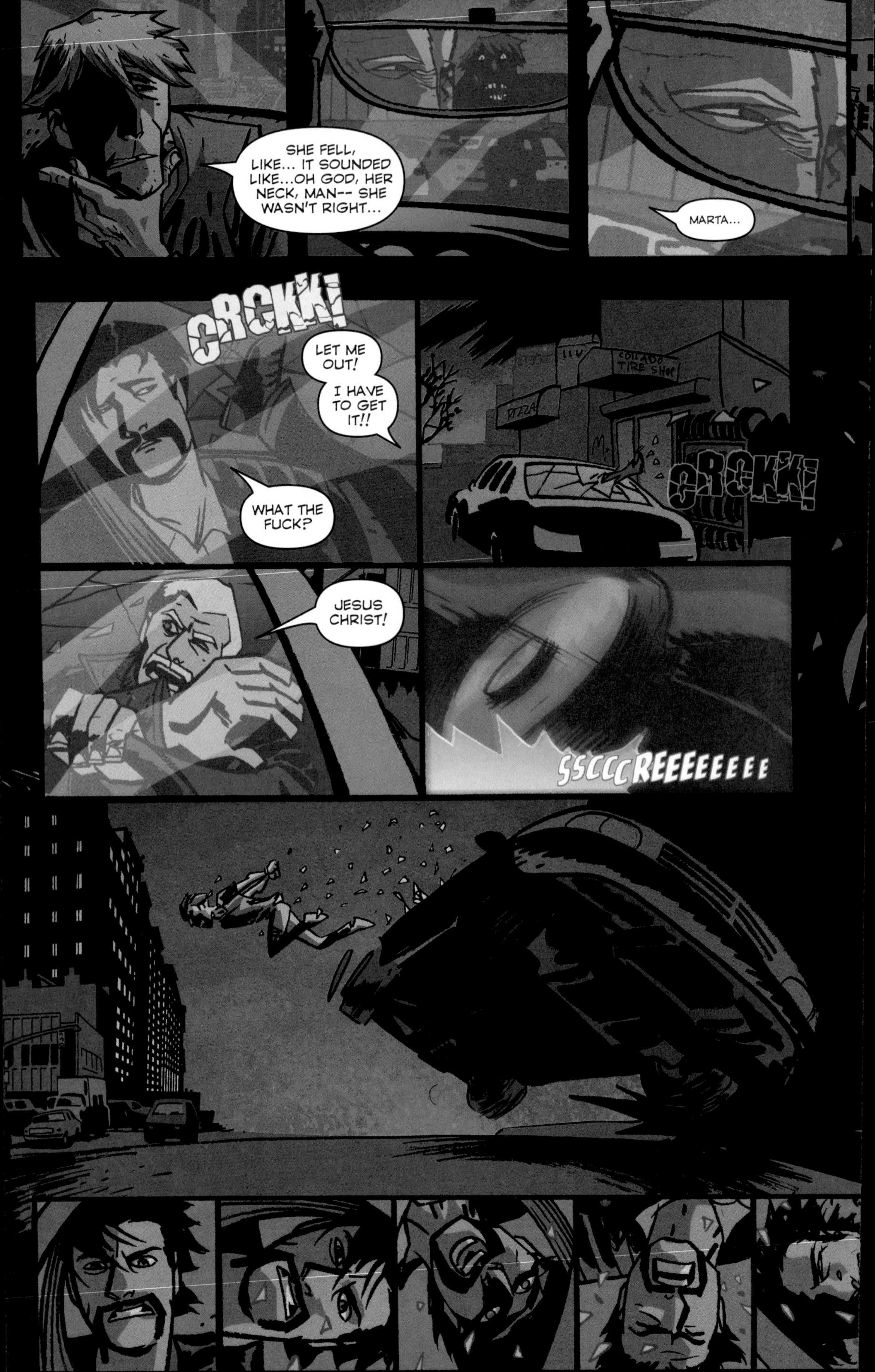
SHE FELL, LIKE... IT SOUNDED LIKE...OH GOD, HER NECK, MAN-- SHE WASN'T RIGHT...
MARTA...
CRCKK!
LET ME OUT!
I HAVE TO GET IT!!
WHAT THE FUCK?
PIZZA
COLLADO TIRE SHOP
CRCKK!
JESUS CHRIST!
SSCCCREEEEEEEE

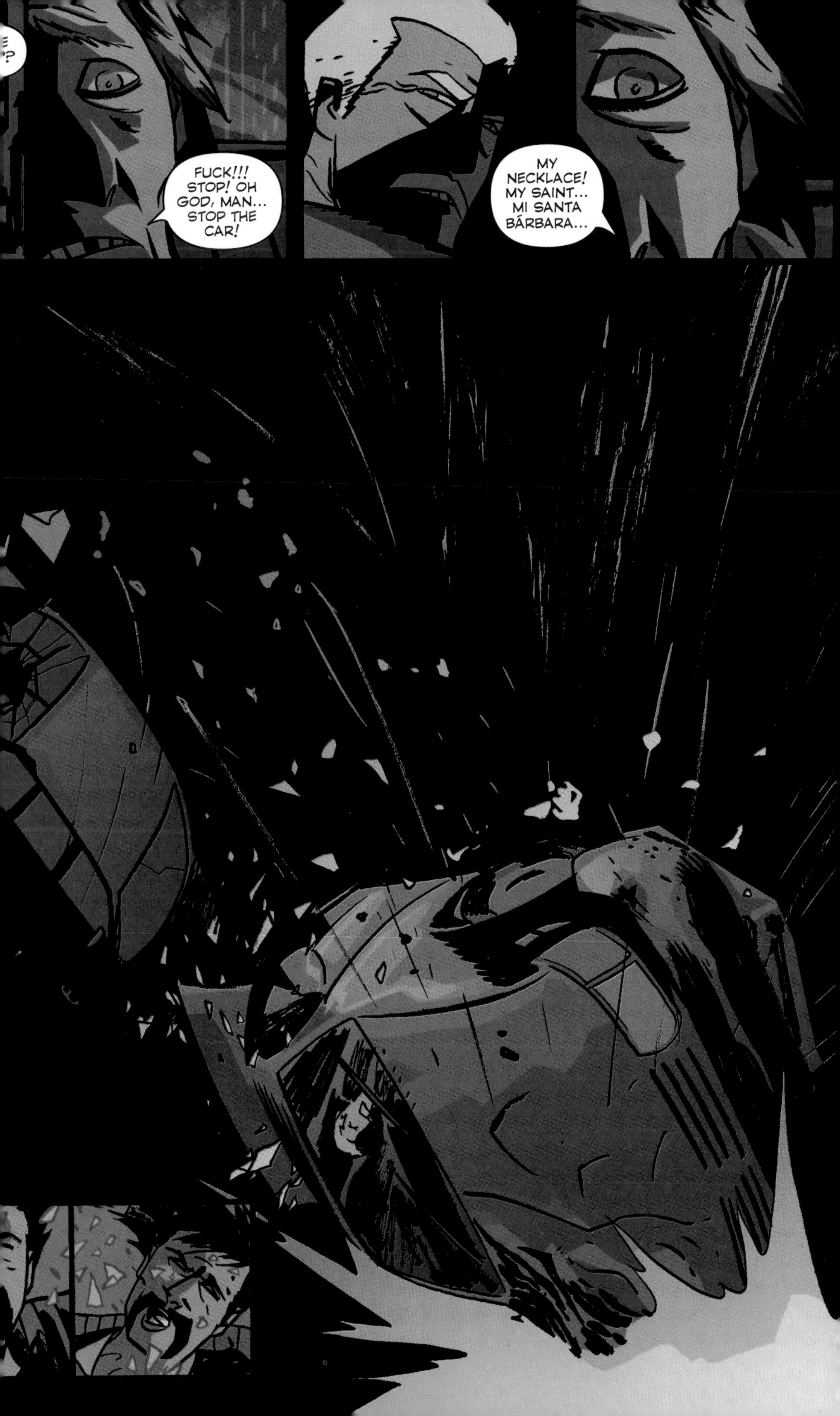
FUCK!!! STOP! OH GOD, MAN... STOP THE CAR!
MY NECKLACE! MY SAINT... MI SANTA BÁRBARA...

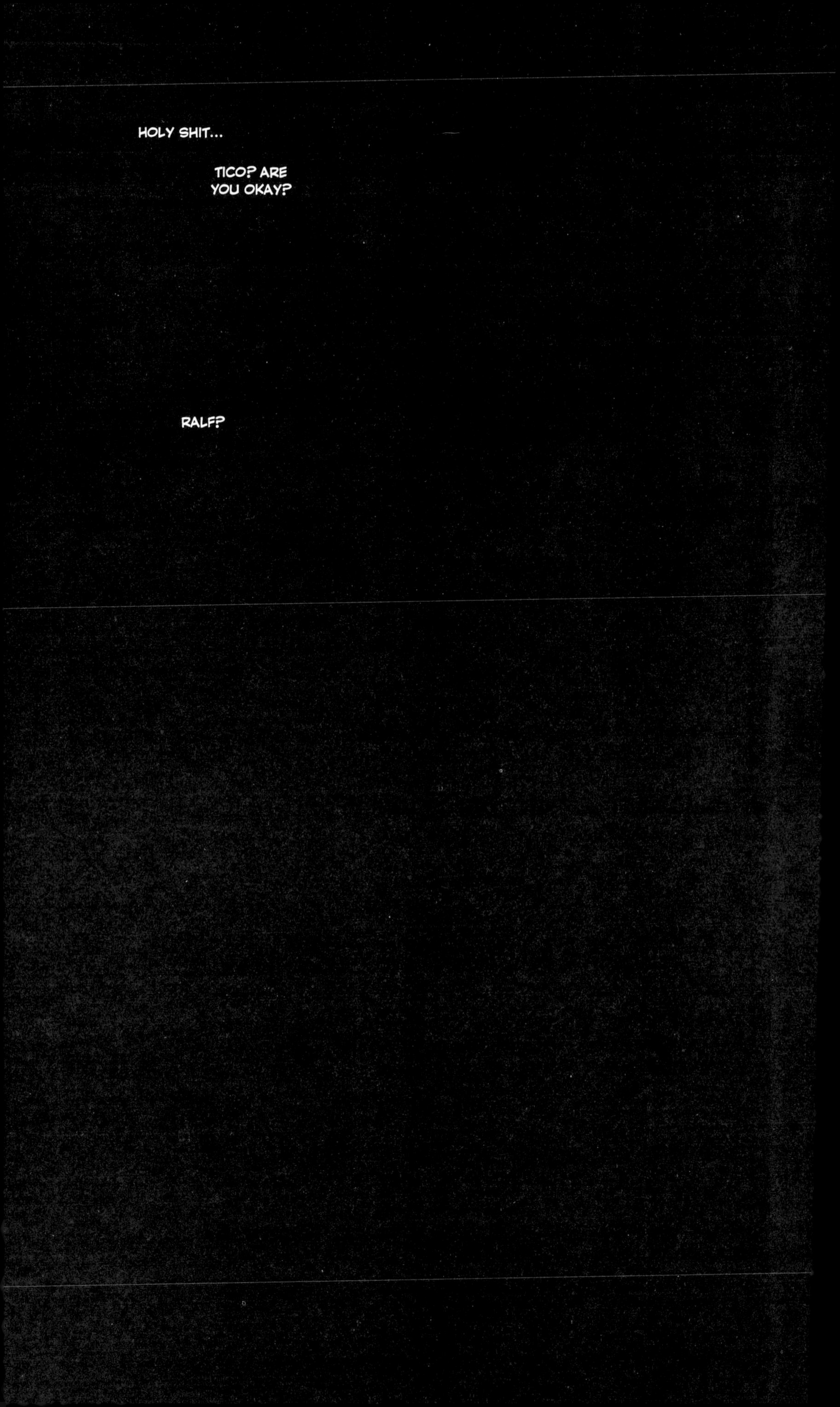
HOLY SHIT...
TICO? ARE YOU OKAY?
RALF?

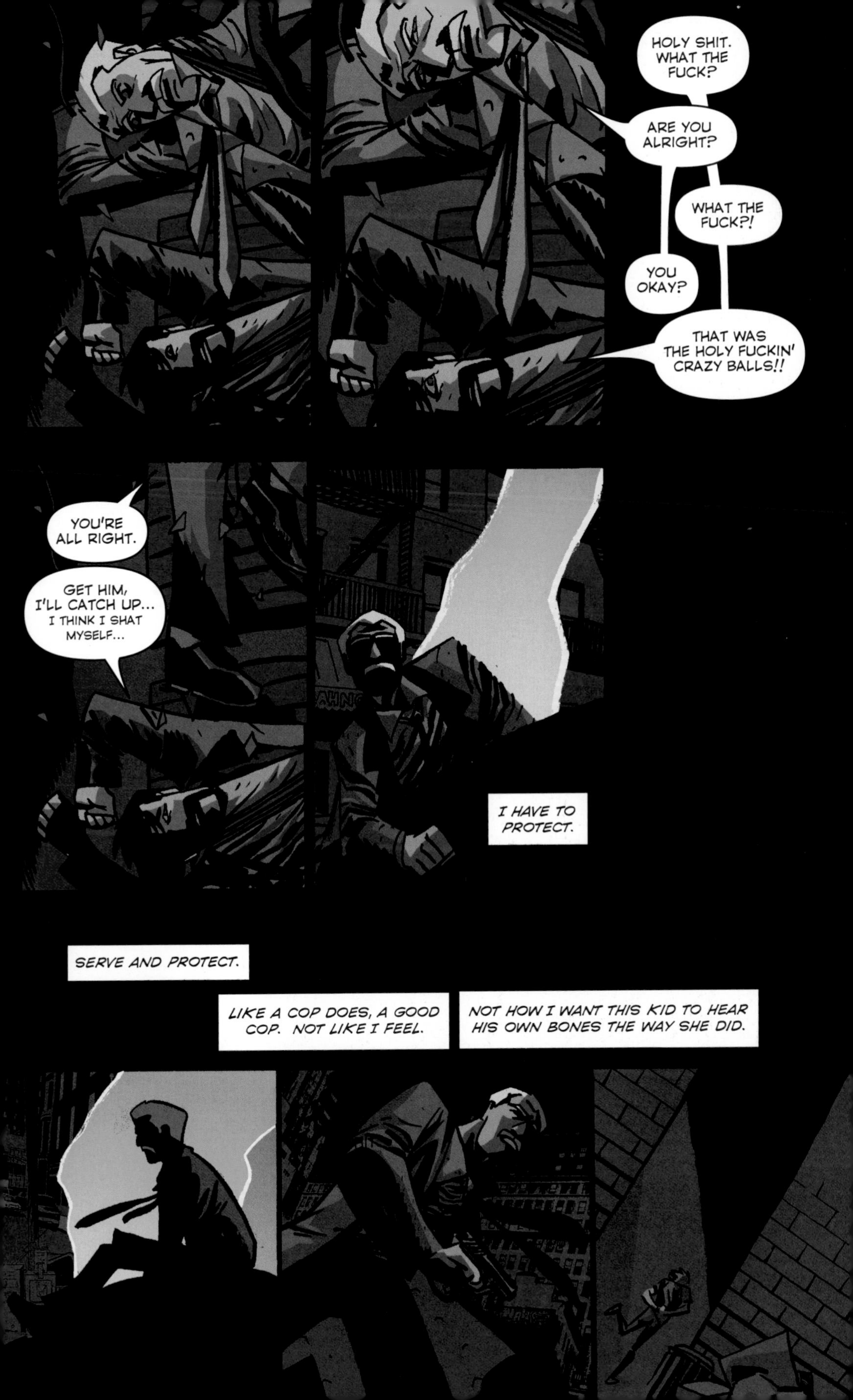
HOLY SHIT. WHAT THE FUCK?
ARE YOU ALRIGHT?
WHAT THE FUCK?!
YOU OKAY?
THAT WAS THE HOLY FUCKIN' CRAZY BALLS!!
YOU'RE ALL RIGHT.
GET HIM, I'LL CATCH UP... I THINK I SHAT MYSELF...
I HAVE TO PROTECT.
SERVE AND PROTECT.
LIKE A COP DOES, A GOOD COP. NOT LIKE I FEEL.
NOT HOW I WANT THIS KID TO HEAR HIS OWN BONES THE WAY SHE DID.

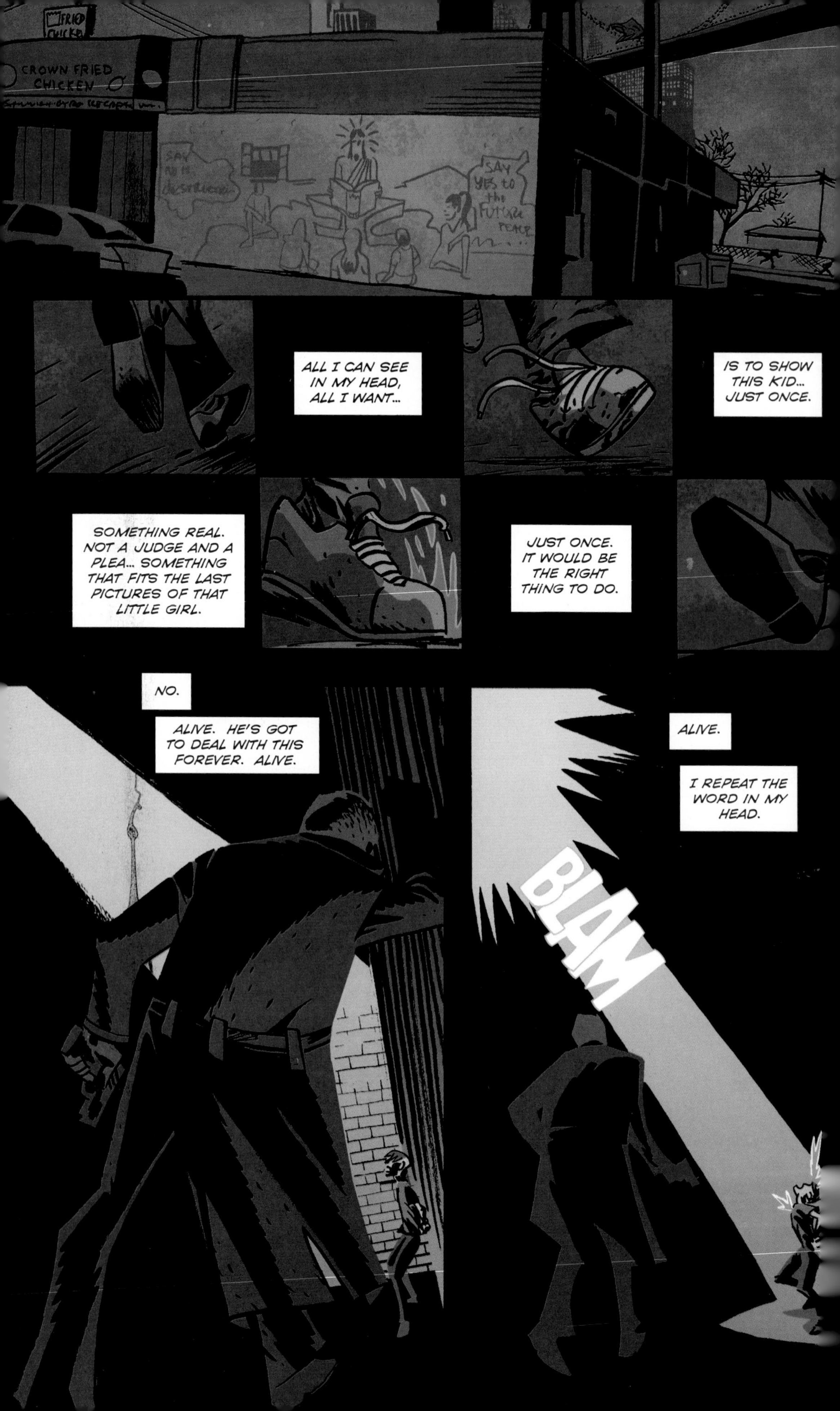
FRIED CHICKEN
CROWN FRIED CHICKEN
SAY YES to the FUTURE PEACE
ALL I CAN SEE IN MY HEAD, ALL I WANT...
IS TO SHOW THIS KID... JUST ONCE.
SOMETHING REAL. NOT A JUDGE AND A PLEA... SOMETHING THAT FITS THE LAST PICTURES OF THAT LITTLE GIRL.
JUST ONCE. IT WOULD BE THE RIGHT THING TO DO.
NO.
ALIVE. HE'S GOT TO DEAL WITH THIS FOREVER. ALIVE.
ALIVE.
I REPEAT THE WORD IN MY HEAD.
BLAM

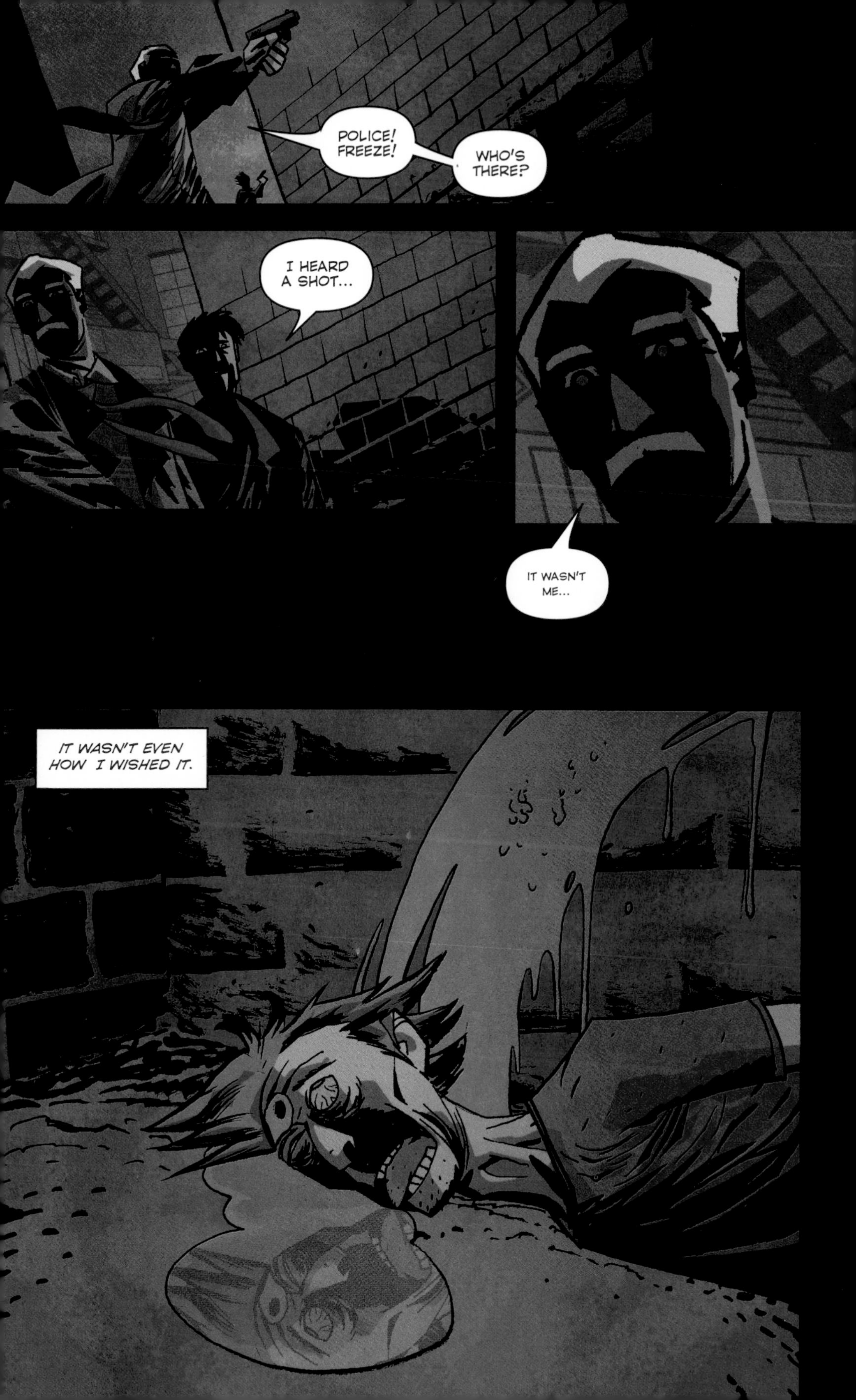
POLICE! FREEZE!
WHO'S THERE?
I HEARD A SHOT...
IT WASN'T ME...
IT WASN'T EVEN HOW I WISHED IT.

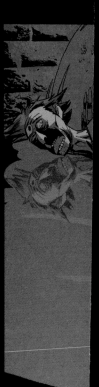

ONE SHOT, PRECISE...

NOT UGLY, LIKE MURDER --
LIKE SOMETHING ELSE.

ONE PERFECT SHOT FROM ABOVE.

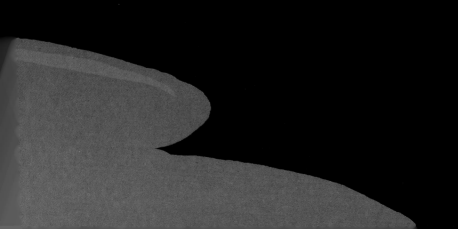

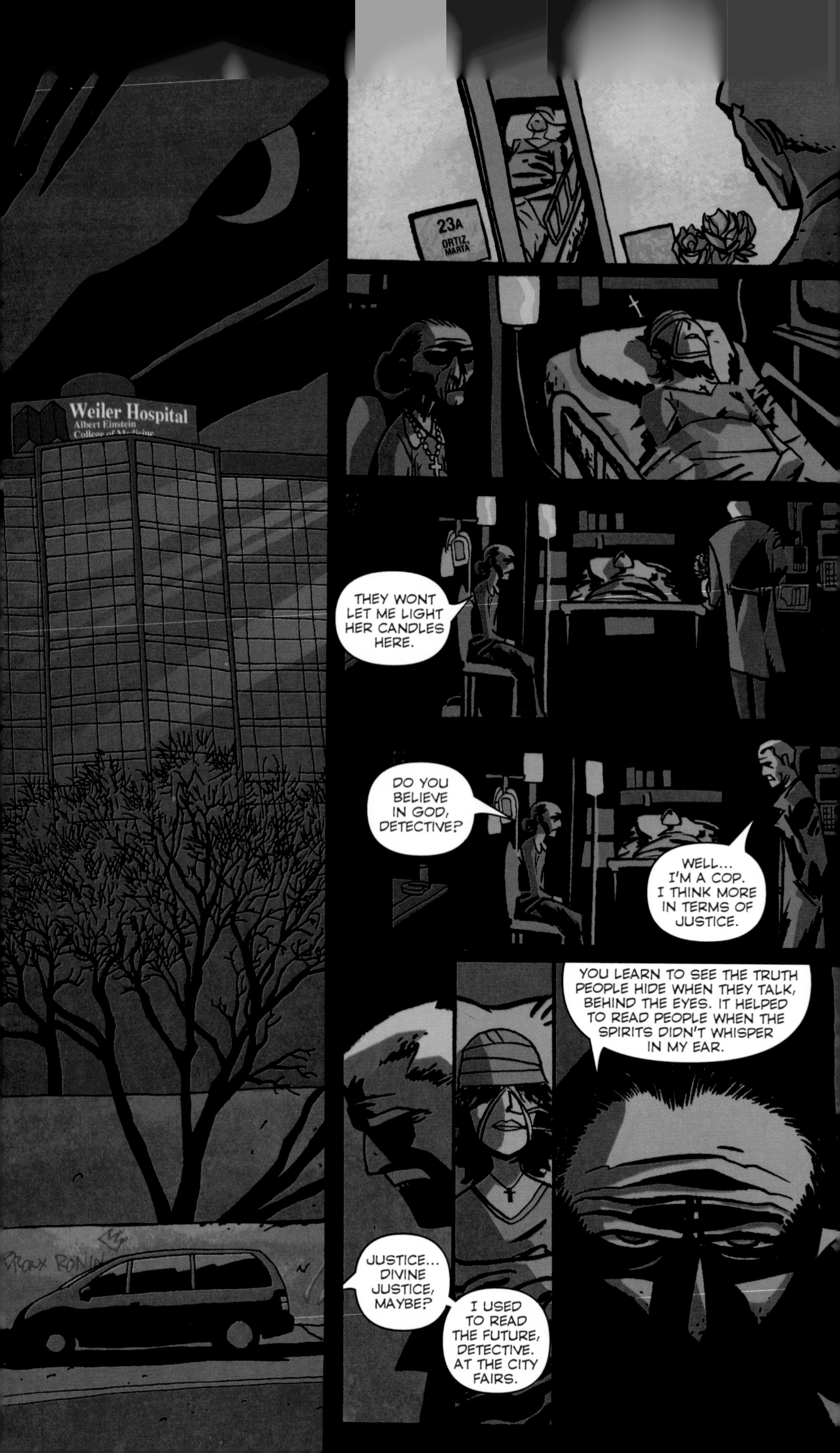
Weiler Hospital
Albert Einstein
College of Medicine
23A
ORTIZ, MARTA
THEY WONT LET ME LIGHT HER CANDLES HERE.
DO YOU BELIEVE IN GOD, DETECTIVE?
WELL... I'M A COP. I THINK MORE IN TERMS OF JUSTICE.
YOU LEARN TO SEE THE TRUTH PEOPLE HIDE WHEN THEY TALK, BEHIND THE EYES. IT HELPED TO READ PEOPLE WHEN THE SPIRITS DIDN'T WHISPER IN MY EAR.
JUSTICE... DIVINE JUSTICE, MAYBE?
I USED TO READ THE FUTURE, DETECTIVE. AT THE CITY FAIRS.

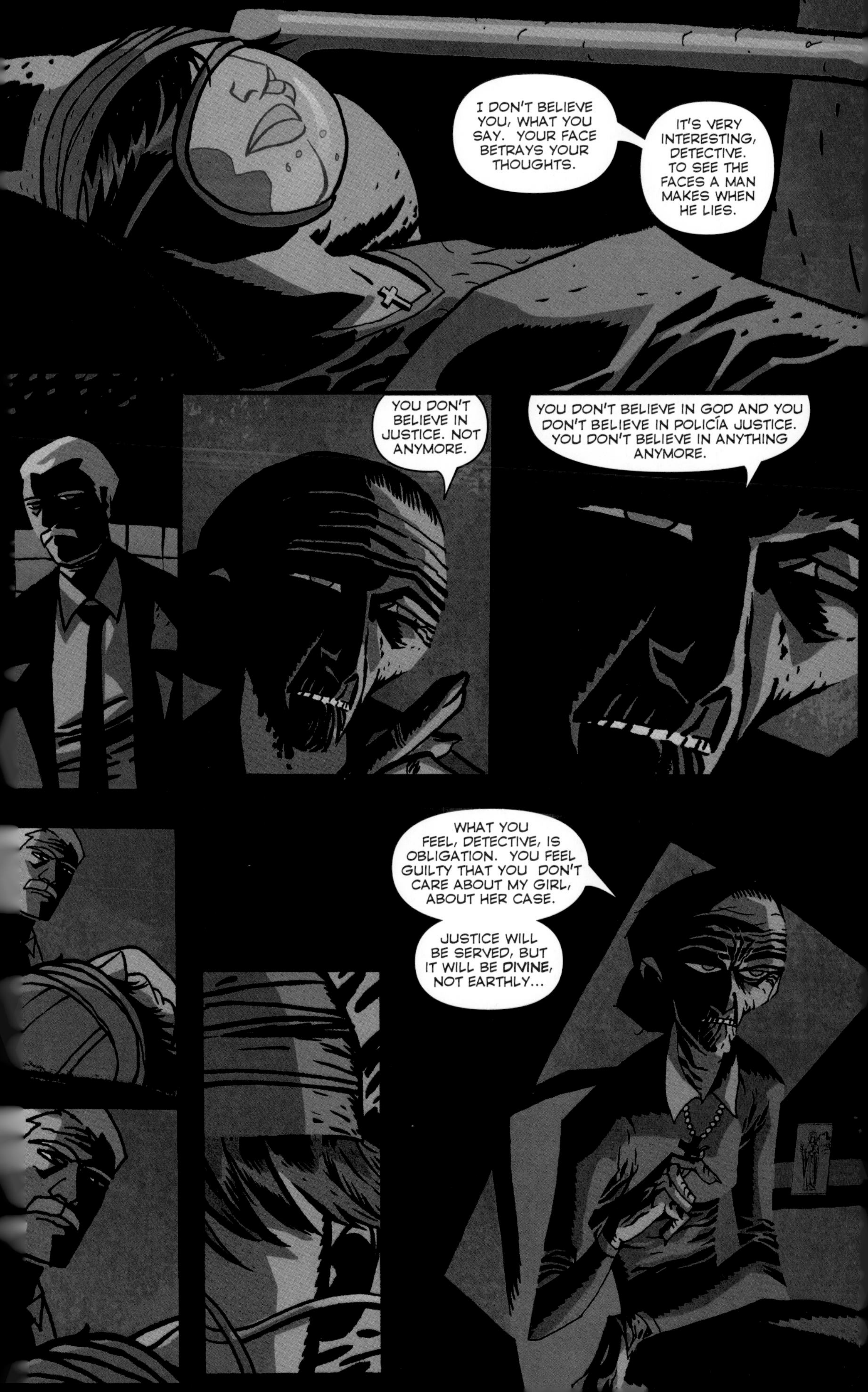
I DON'T BELIEVE YOU, WHAT YOU SAY. YOUR FACE BETRAYS YOUR THOUGHTS.
IT'S VERY INTERESTING, DETECTIVE. TO SEE THE FACES A MAN MAKES WHEN HE LIES.
YOU DON'T BELIEVE IN JUSTICE. NOT ANYMORE.
YOU DON'T BELIEVE IN GOD AND YOU DON'T BELIEVE IN POLICÍA JUSTICE. YOU DON'T BELIEVE IN ANYTHING ANYMORE.
WHAT YOU FEEL, DETECTIVE, IS OBLIGATION. YOU FEEL GUILTY THAT YOU DON'T CARE ABOUT MY GIRL, ABOUT HER CASE.
JUSTICE WILL BE SERVED, BUT IT WILL BE **DIVINE**, NOT EARTHLY...

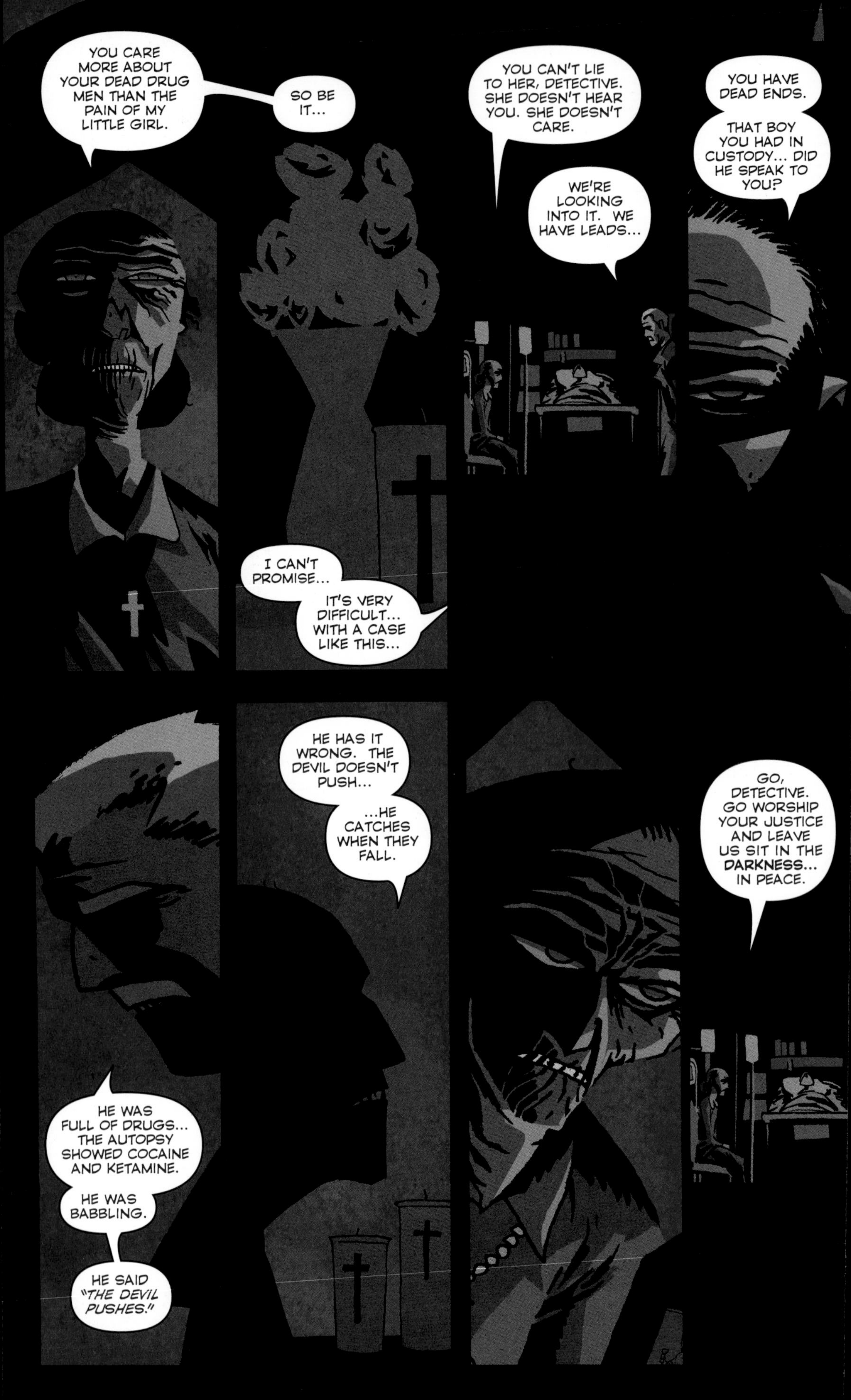

YOU CARE MORE ABOUT YOUR DEAD DRUG MEN THAN THE PAIN OF MY LITTLE GIRL.
SO BE IT...
I CAN'T PROMISE...
IT'S VERY DIFFICULT... WITH A CASE LIKE THIS...
YOU CAN'T LIE TO HER, DETECTIVE. SHE DOESN'T HEAR YOU. SHE DOESN'T CARE.
WE'RE LOOKING INTO IT. WE HAVE LEADS...
YOU HAVE DEAD ENDS.
THAT BOY YOU HAD IN CUSTODY... DID HE SPEAK TO YOU?
HE WAS FULL OF DRUGS... THE AUTOPSY SHOWED COCAINE AND KETAMINE.
HE WAS BABBLING.
HE SAID *"THE DEVIL PUSHES."*
HE HAS IT WRONG. THE DEVIL DOESN'T PUSH...
...HE CATCHES WHEN THEY FALL.
GO, DETECTIVE. GO WORSHIP YOUR JUSTICE AND LEAVE US SIT IN THE **DARKNESS...** IN PEACE.

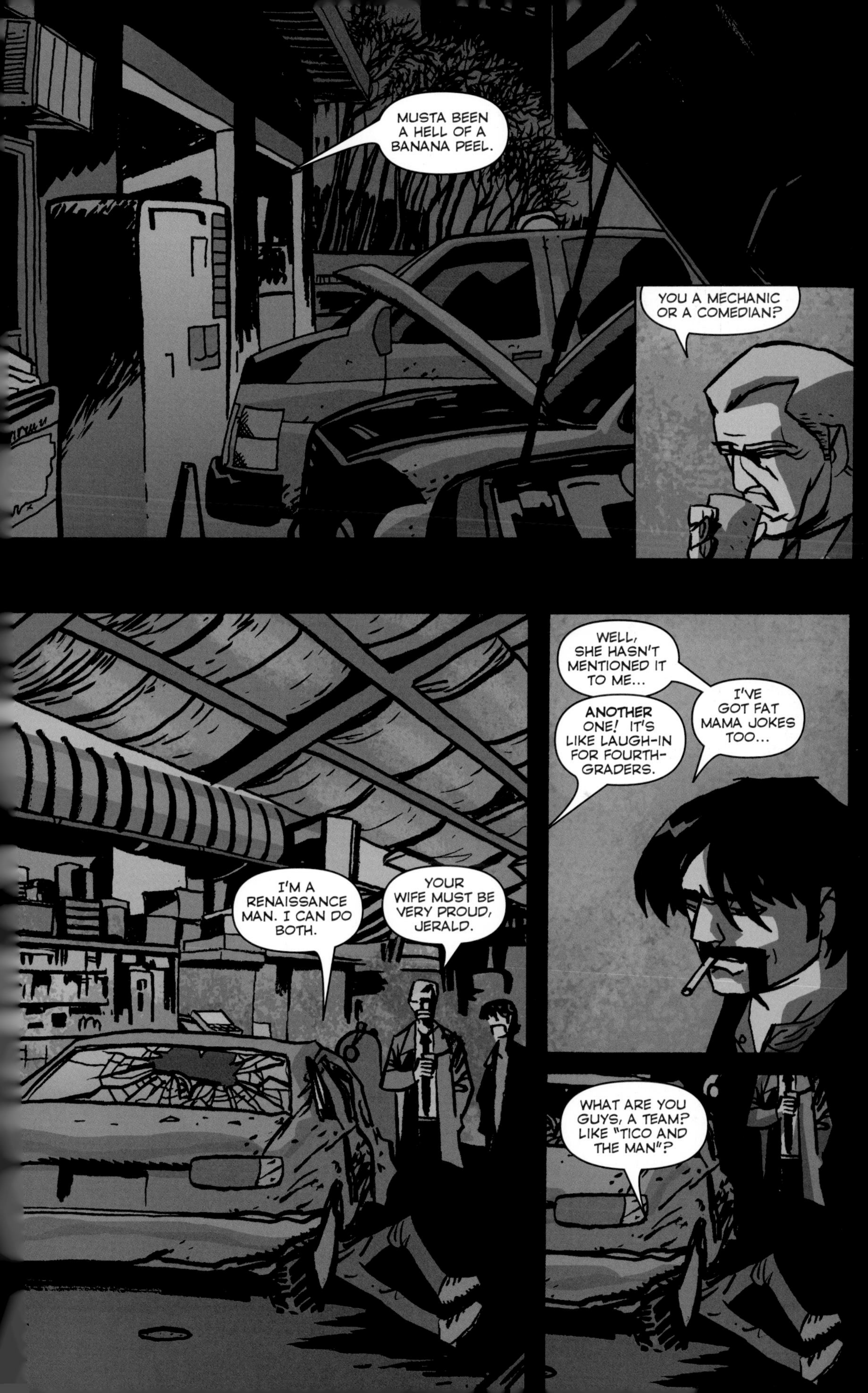
MUSTA BEEN A HELL OF A BANANA PEEL.
YOU A MECHANIC OR A COMEDIAN?
I'M A RENAISSANCE MAN. I CAN DO BOTH.
YOUR WIFE MUST BE VERY PROUD, JERALD.
WELL, SHE HASN'T MENTIONED IT TO ME...
I'VE GOT FAT MAMA JOKES TOO...
ANOTHER ONE! IT'S LIKE LAUGH-IN FOR FOURTH-GRADERS.
WHAT ARE YOU GUYS, A TEAM? LIKE "TICO AND THE MAN"?

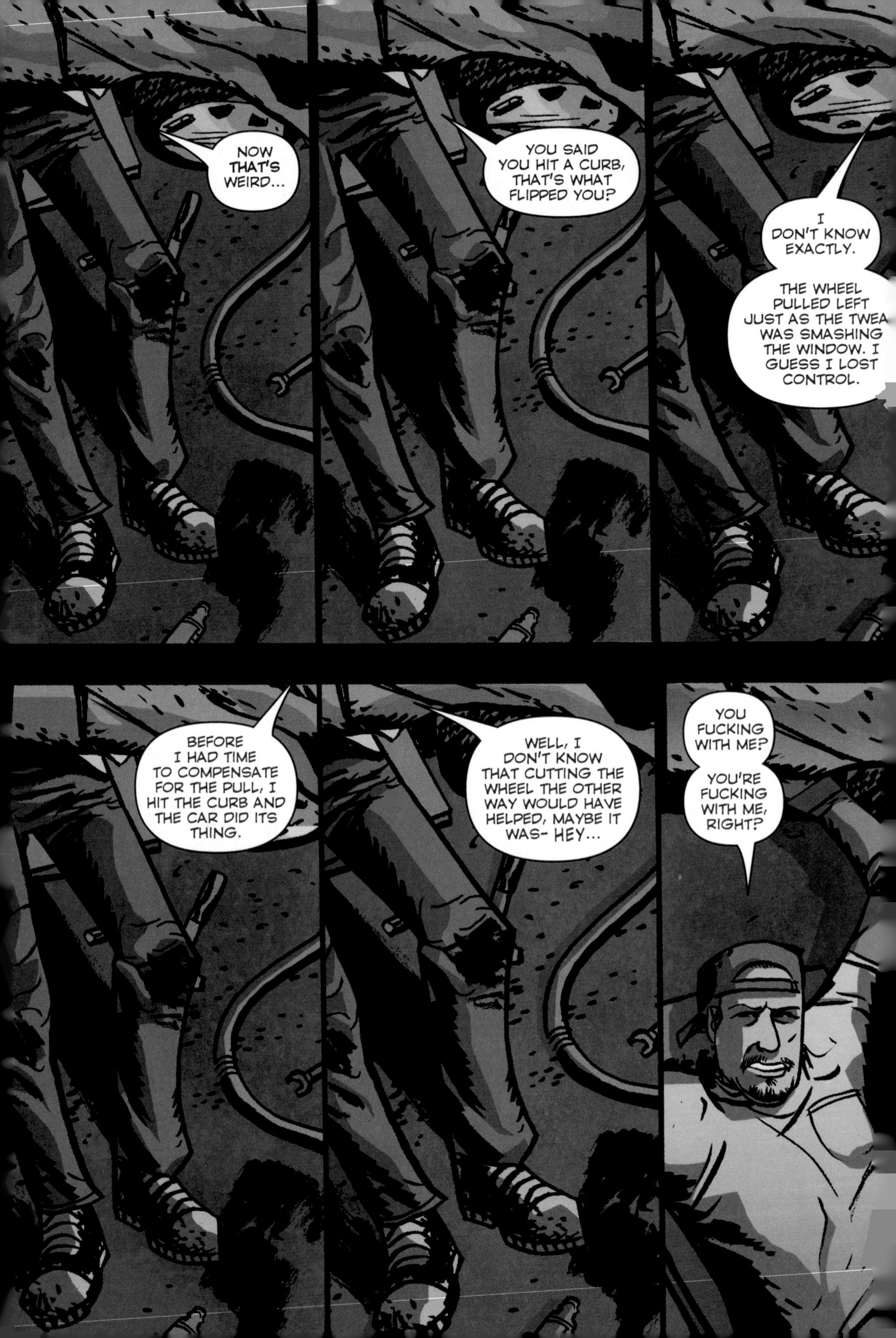
NOW THAT'S WEIRD...
YOU SAID YOU HIT A CURB, THAT'S WHAT FLIPPED YOU?
I DON'T KNOW EXACTLY.
THE WHEEL PULLED LEFT JUST AS THE TWEA WAS SMASHING THE WINDOW. I GUESS I LOST CONTROL.
BEFORE I HAD TIME TO COMPENSATE FOR THE PULL, I HIT THE CURB AND THE CAR DID ITS THING.
WELL, I DON'T KNOW THAT CUTTING THE WHEEL THE OTHER WAY WOULD HAVE HELPED, MAYBE IT WAS- HEY...
YOU FUCKING WITH ME?
YOU'RE FUCKING WITH ME, RIGHT?

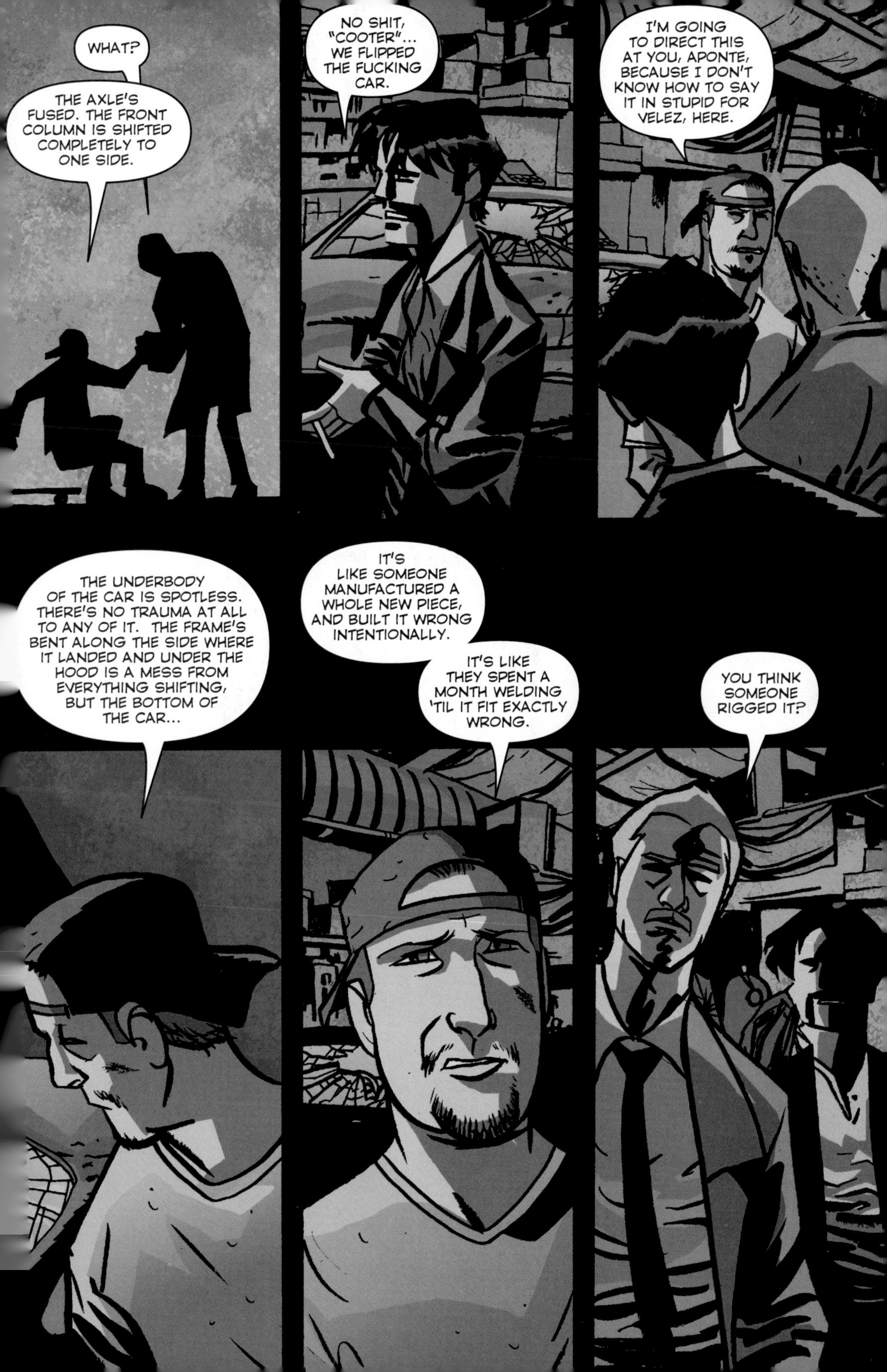
WHAT?
THE AXLE'S FUSED. THE FRONT COLUMN IS SHIFTED COMPLETELY TO ONE SIDE.
NO SHIT, "COOTER"... WE FLIPPED THE FUCKING CAR.
I'M GOING TO DIRECT THIS AT YOU, APONTE, BECAUSE I DON'T KNOW HOW TO SAY IT IN STUPID FOR VELEZ, HERE.
THE UNDERBODY OF THE CAR IS SPOTLESS. THERE'S NO TRAUMA AT ALL TO ANY OF IT. THE FRAME'S BENT ALONG THE SIDE WHERE IT LANDED AND UNDER THE HOOD IS A MESS FROM EVERYTHING SHIFTING, BUT THE BOTTOM OF THE CAR...
IT'S LIKE SOMEONE MANUFACTURED A WHOLE NEW PIECE, AND BUILT IT WRONG INTENTIONALLY.
IT'S LIKE THEY SPENT A MONTH WELDING 'TIL IT FIT EXACTLY WRONG.
YOU THINK SOMEONE RIGGED IT?

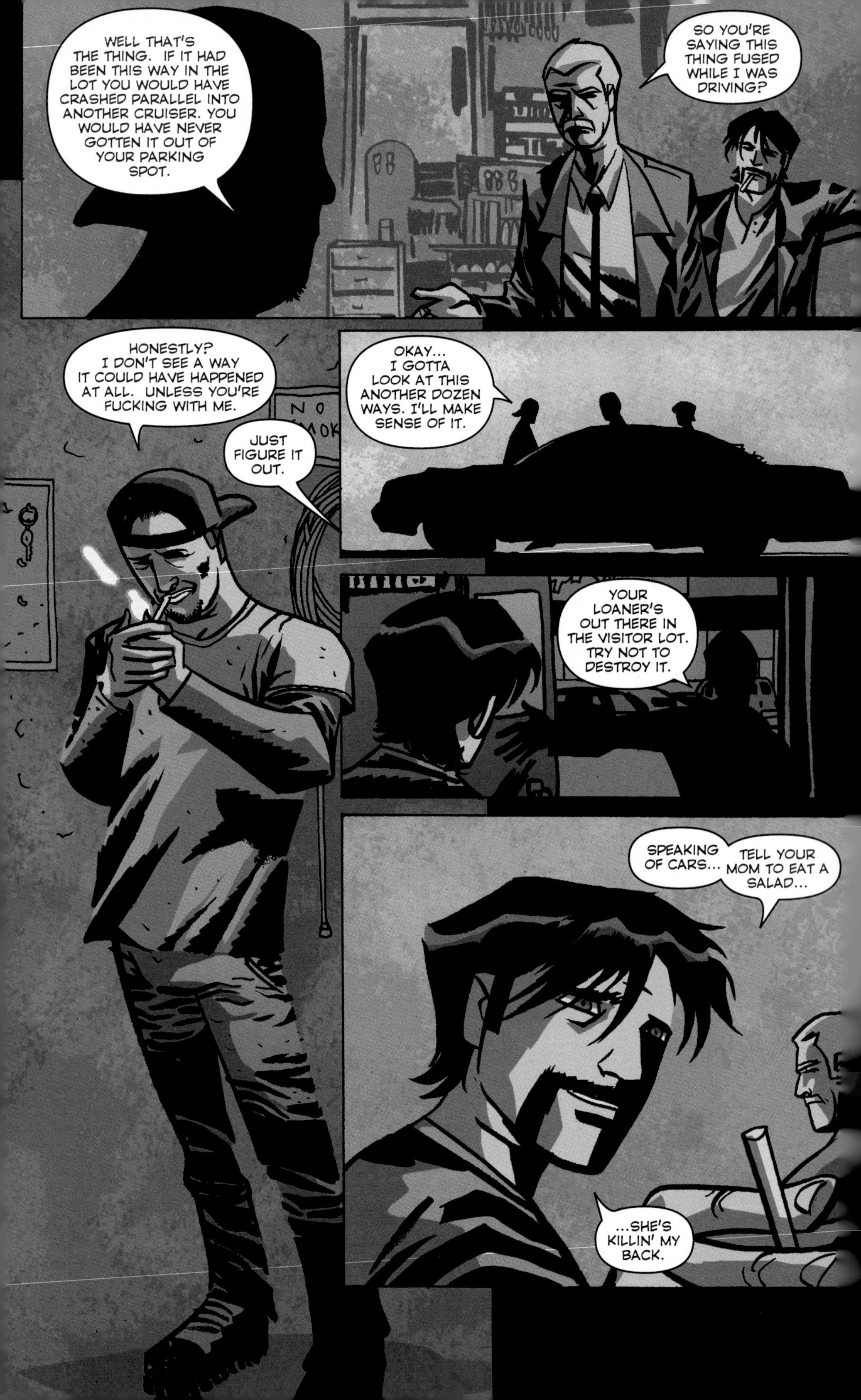

WELL THAT'S THE THING. IF IT HAD BEEN THIS WAY IN THE LOT YOU WOULD HAVE CRASHED PARALLEL INTO ANOTHER CRUISER. YOU WOULD HAVE NEVER GOTTEN IT OUT OF YOUR PARKING SPOT.
SO YOU'RE SAYING THIS THING FUSED WHILE I WAS DRIVING?
HONESTLY? I DON'T SEE A WAY IT COULD HAVE HAPPENED AT ALL. UNLESS YOU'RE FUCKING WITH ME.
JUST FIGURE IT OUT.
OKAY... I GOTTA LOOK AT THIS ANOTHER DOZEN WAYS. I'LL MAKE SENSE OF IT.
YOUR LOANER'S OUT THERE IN THE VISITOR LOT. TRY NOT TO DESTROY IT.
SPEAKING OF CARS...
TELL YOUR MOM TO EAT A SALAD...
...SHE'S KILLIN' MY BACK.

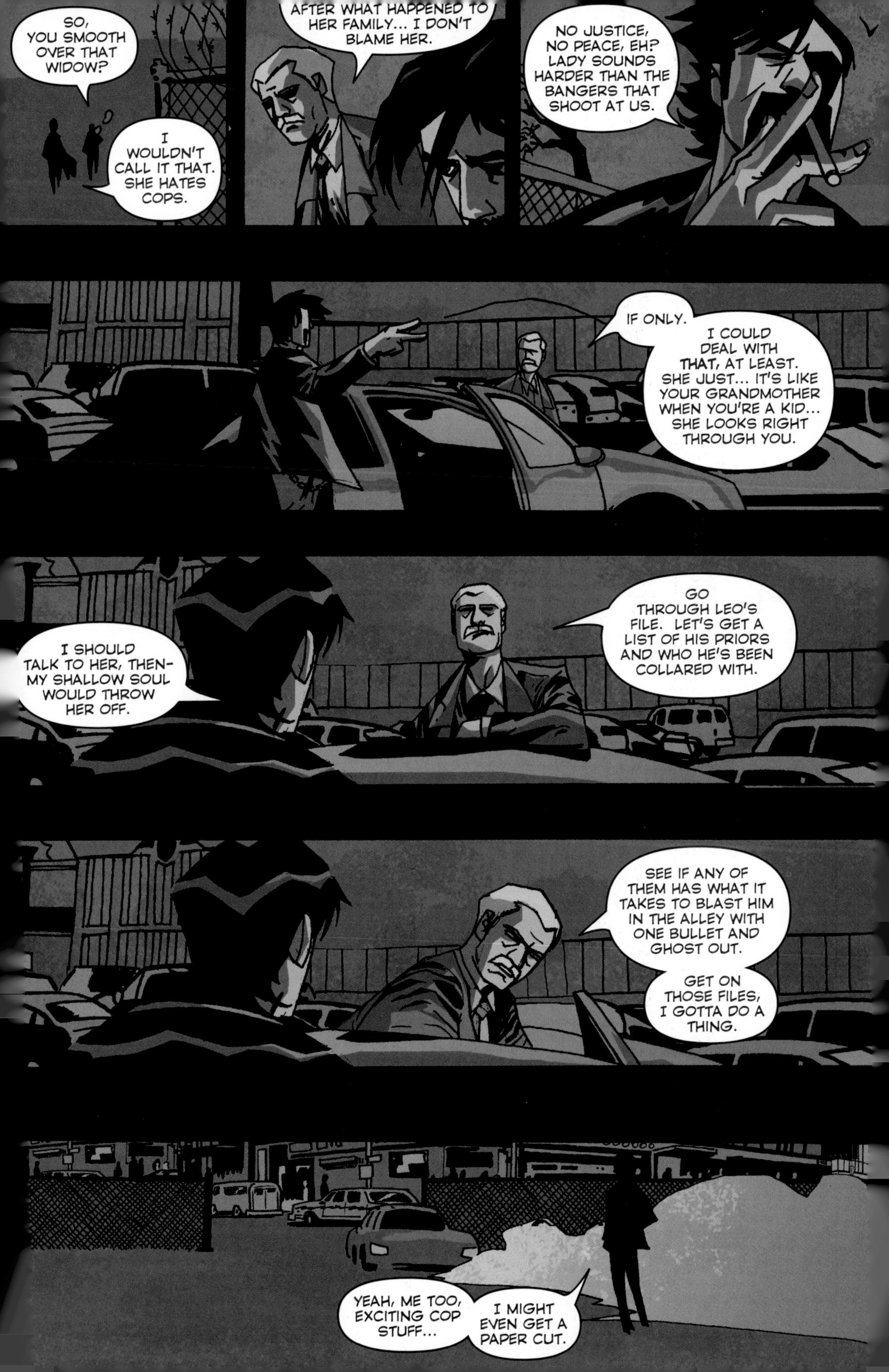
SO, YOU SMOOTH OVER THAT WIDOW?
I WOULDN'T CALL IT THAT. SHE HATES COPS.
AFTER WHAT HAPPENED TO HER FAMILY... I DON'T BLAME HER.
NO JUSTICE, NO PEACE, EH? LADY SOUNDS HARDER THAN THE BANGERS THAT SHOOT AT US.
IF ONLY.
I COULD DEAL WITH **THAT**, AT LEAST. SHE JUST... IT'S LIKE YOUR GRANDMOTHER WHEN YOU'RE A KID... SHE LOOKS RIGHT THROUGH YOU.
I SHOULD TALK TO HER, THEN- MY SHALLOW SOUL WOULD THROW HER OFF.
GO THROUGH LEO'S FILE. LET'S GET A LIST OF HIS PRIORS AND WHO HE'S BEEN COLLARED WITH.
SEE IF ANY OF THEM HAS WHAT IT TAKES TO BLAST HIM IN THE ALLEY WITH ONE BULLET AND GHOST OUT.
GET ON THOSE FILES, I GOTTA DO A THING.
YEAH, ME TOO, EXCITING COP STUFF...
I MIGHT EVEN GET A PAPER CUT.

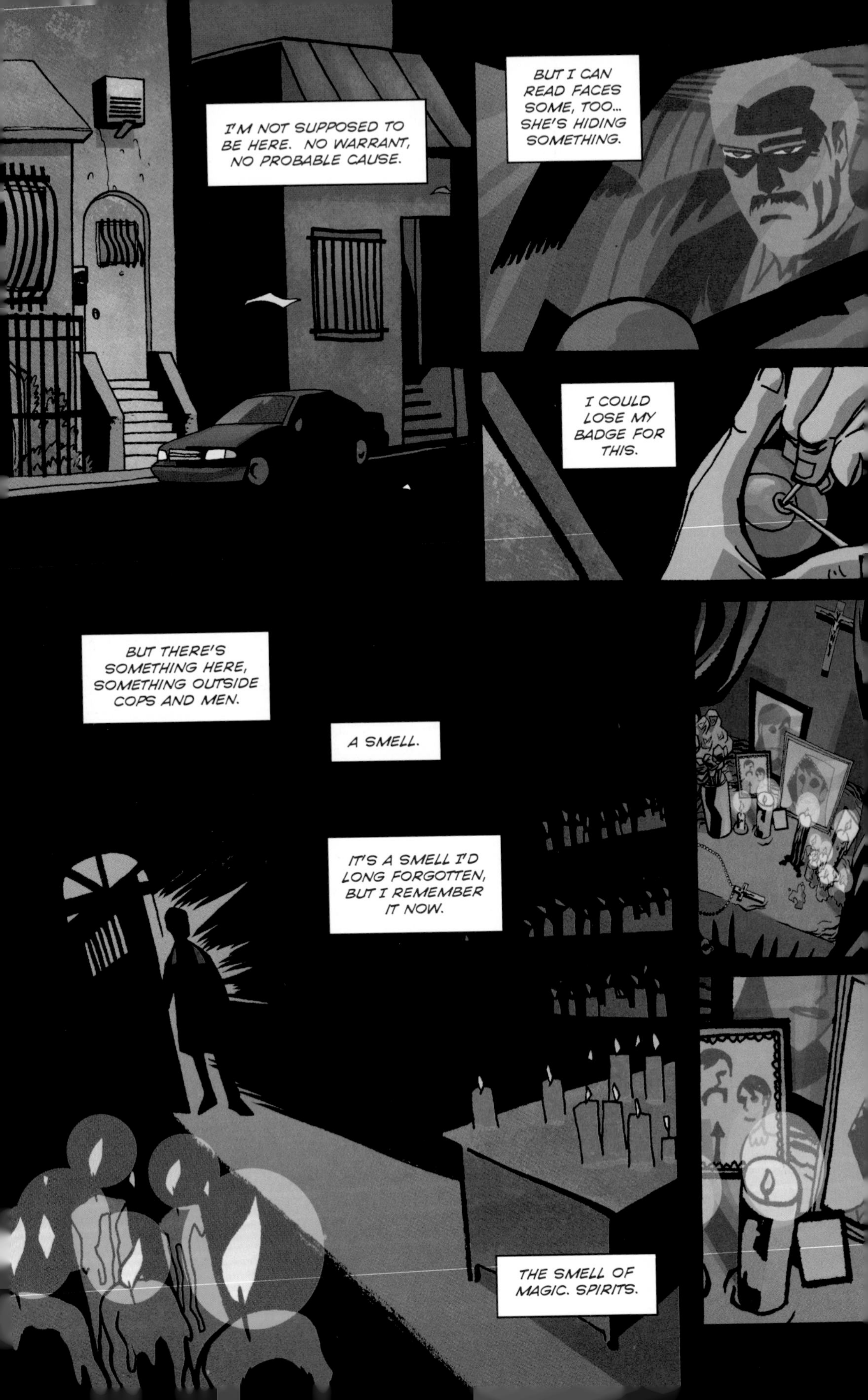
I'M NOT SUPPOSED TO BE HERE. NO WARRANT, NO PROBABLE CAUSE.
BUT I CAN READ FACES SOME, TOO... SHE'S HIDING SOMETHING.
I COULD LOSE MY BADGE FOR THIS.
BUT THERE'S SOMETHING HERE, SOMETHING OUTSIDE COPS AND MEN.
A SMELL.
IT'S A SMELL I'D LONG FORGOTTEN, BUT I REMEMBER IT NOW.
THE SMELL OF MAGIC. SPIRITS.

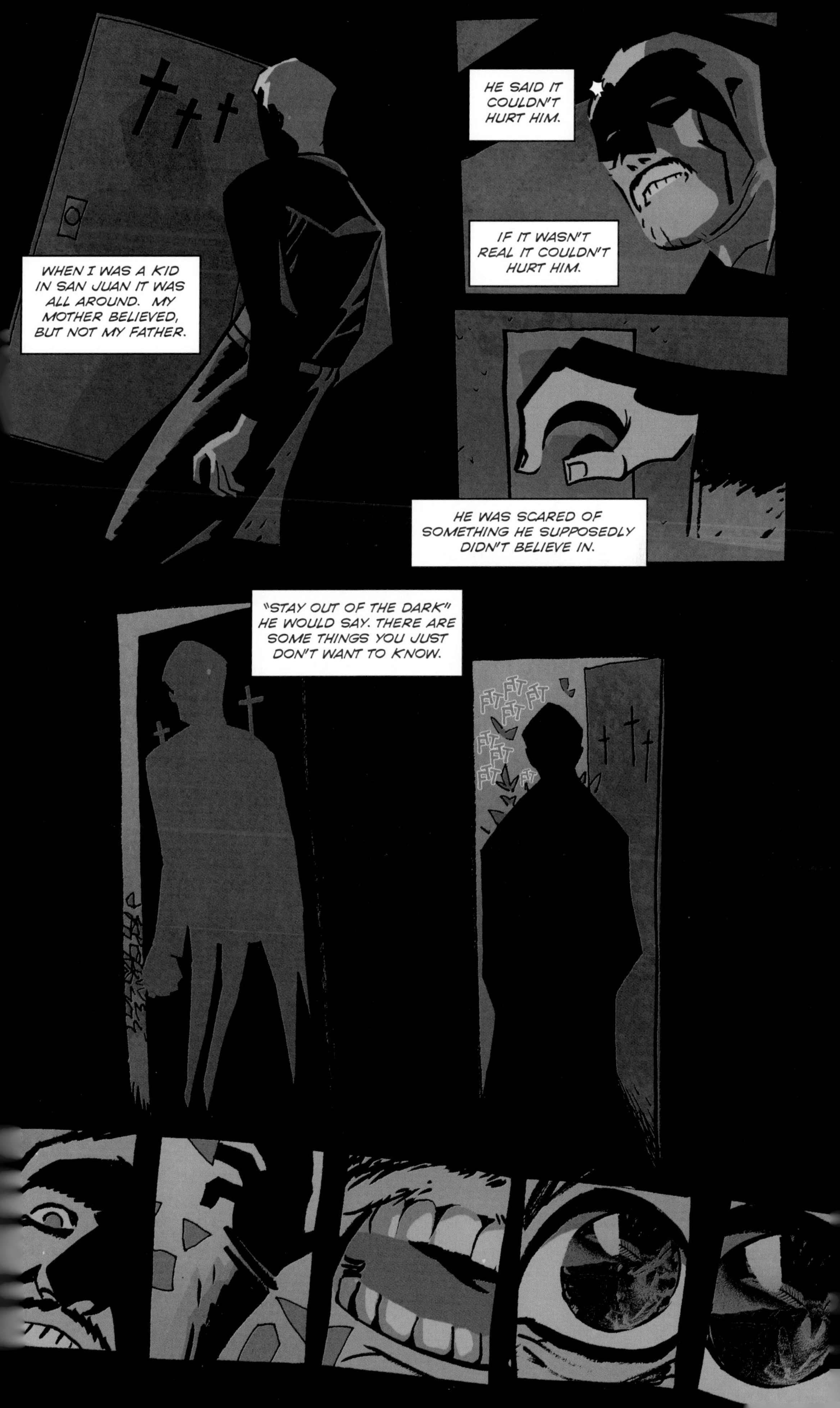
WHEN I WAS A KID IN SAN JUAN IT WAS ALL AROUND. MY MOTHER BELIEVED, BUT NOT MY FATHER.
HE SAID IT COULDN'T HURT HIM.
IF IT WASN'T REAL IT COULDN'T HURT HIM.
HE WAS SCARED OF SOMETHING HE SUPPOSEDLY DIDN'T BELIEVE IN.
"STAY OUT OF THE DARK" HE WOULD SAY. THERE ARE SOME THINGS YOU JUST DON'T WANT TO KNOW.
FT FT FT FT
FT FT FT FT

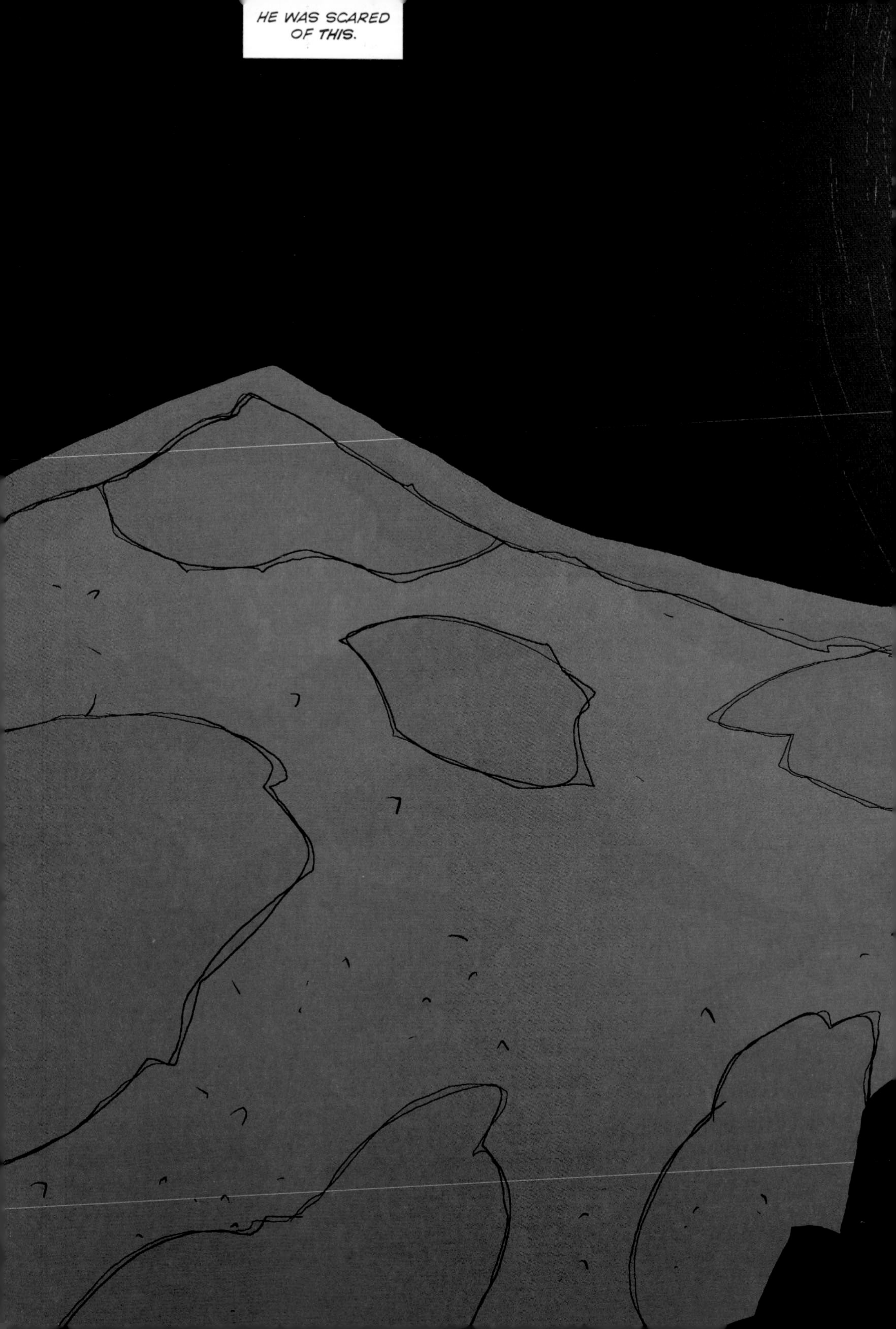
HE WAS SCARED OF THIS.

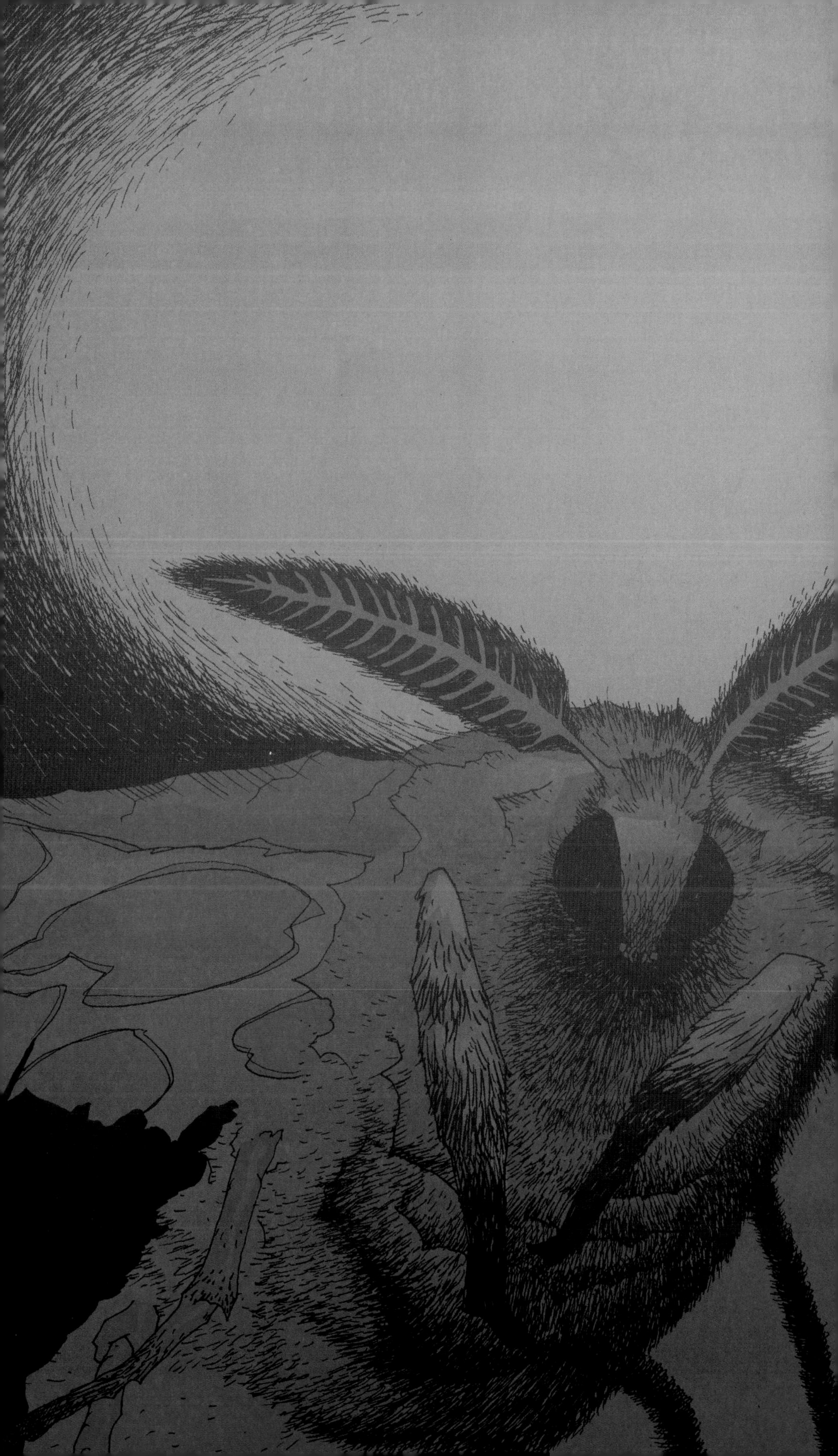

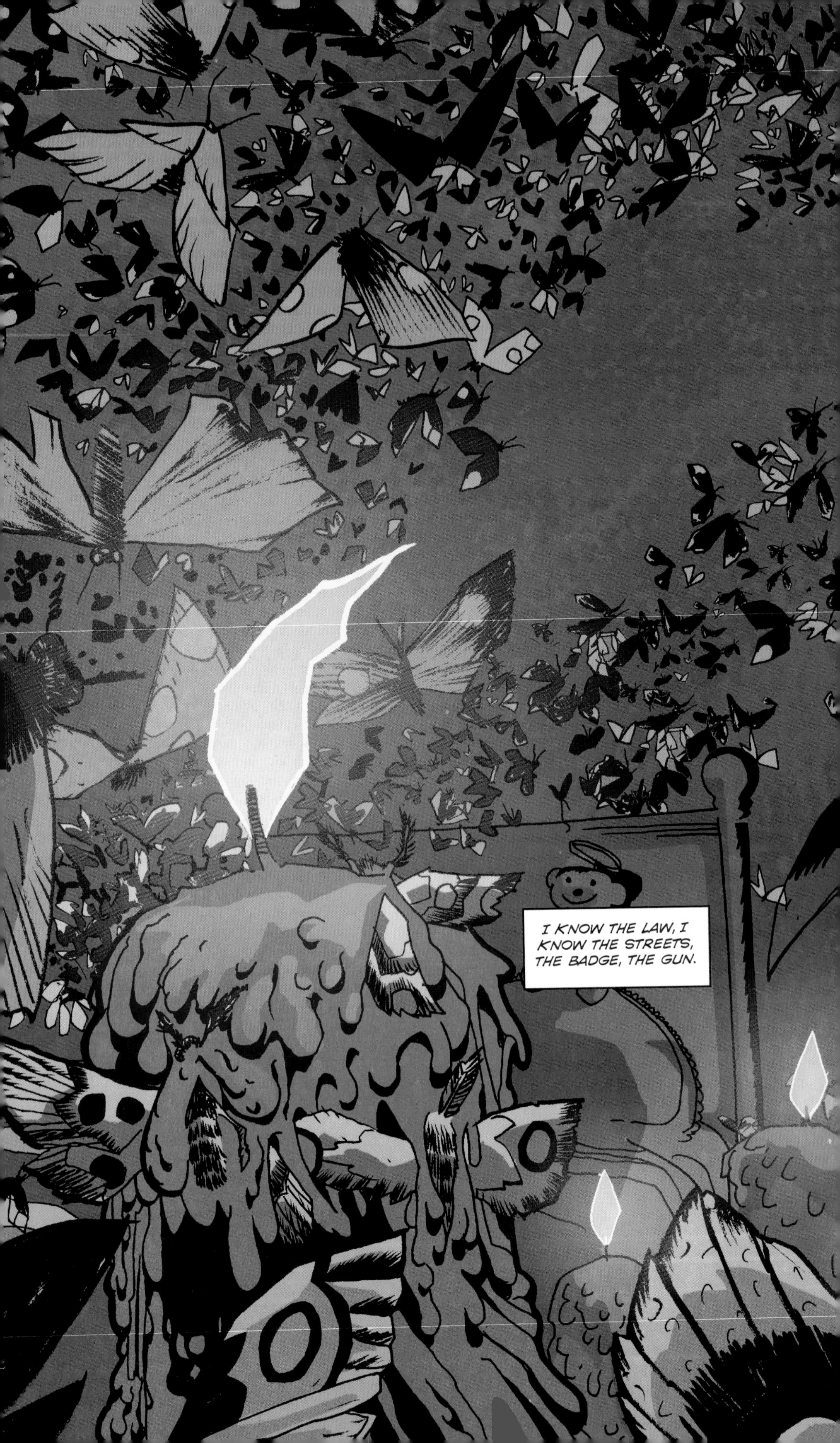
I KNOW THE LAW, I KNOW THE STREETS, THE BADGE, THE GUN.

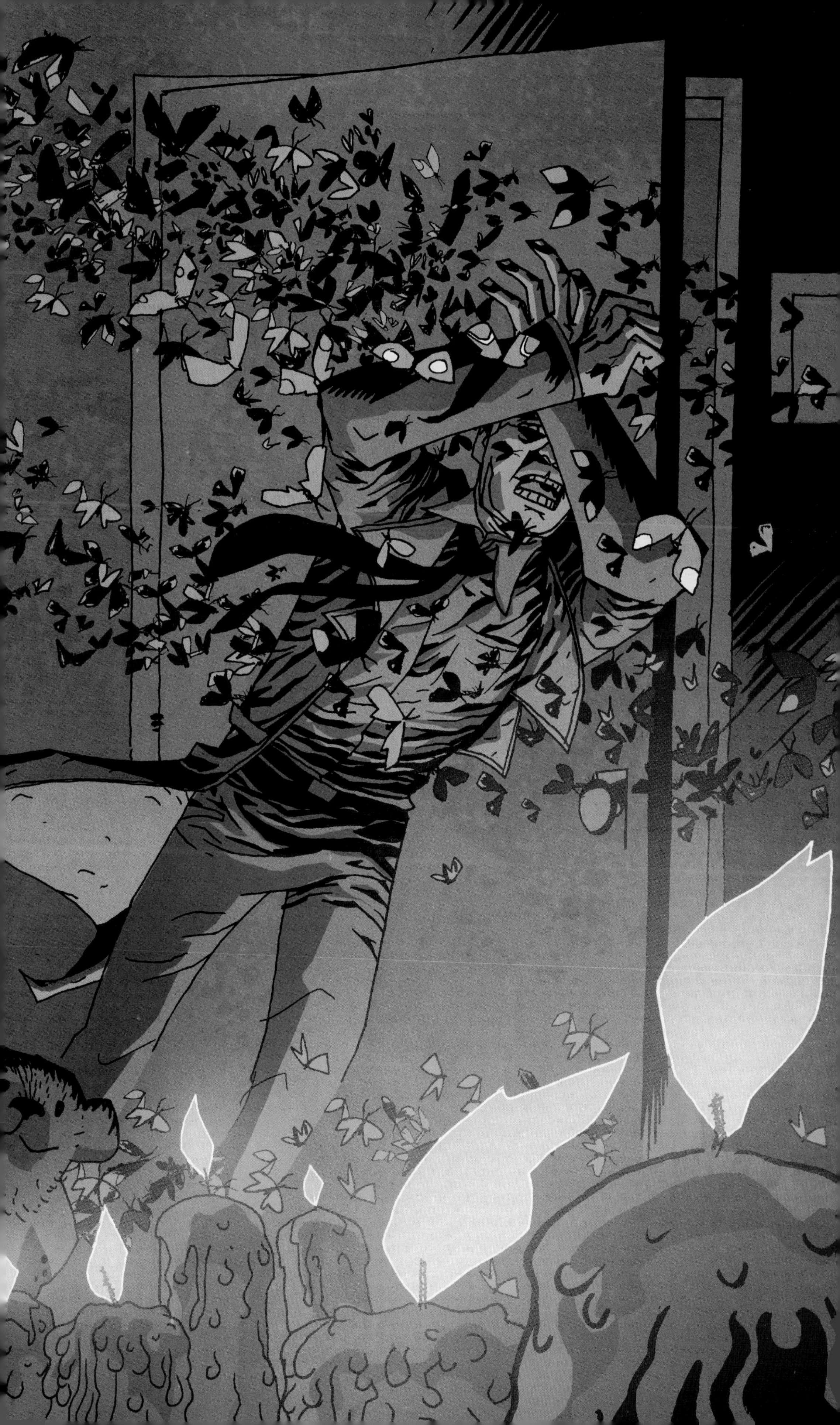

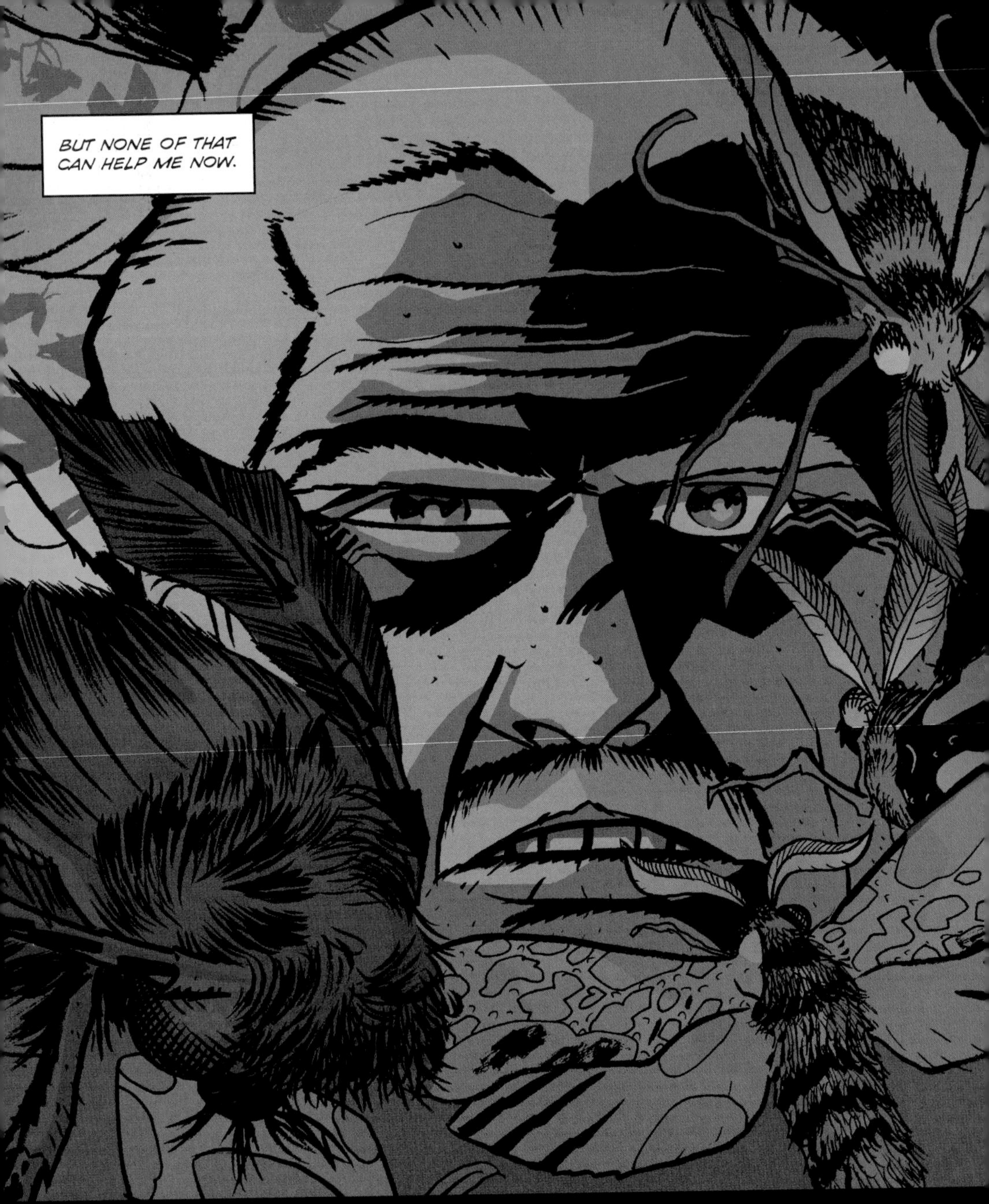
BUT NONE OF THAT CAN HELP ME NOW.

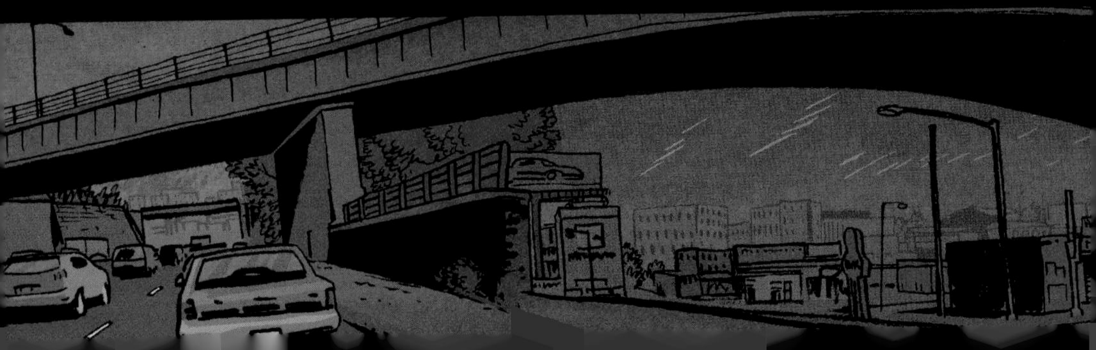

3

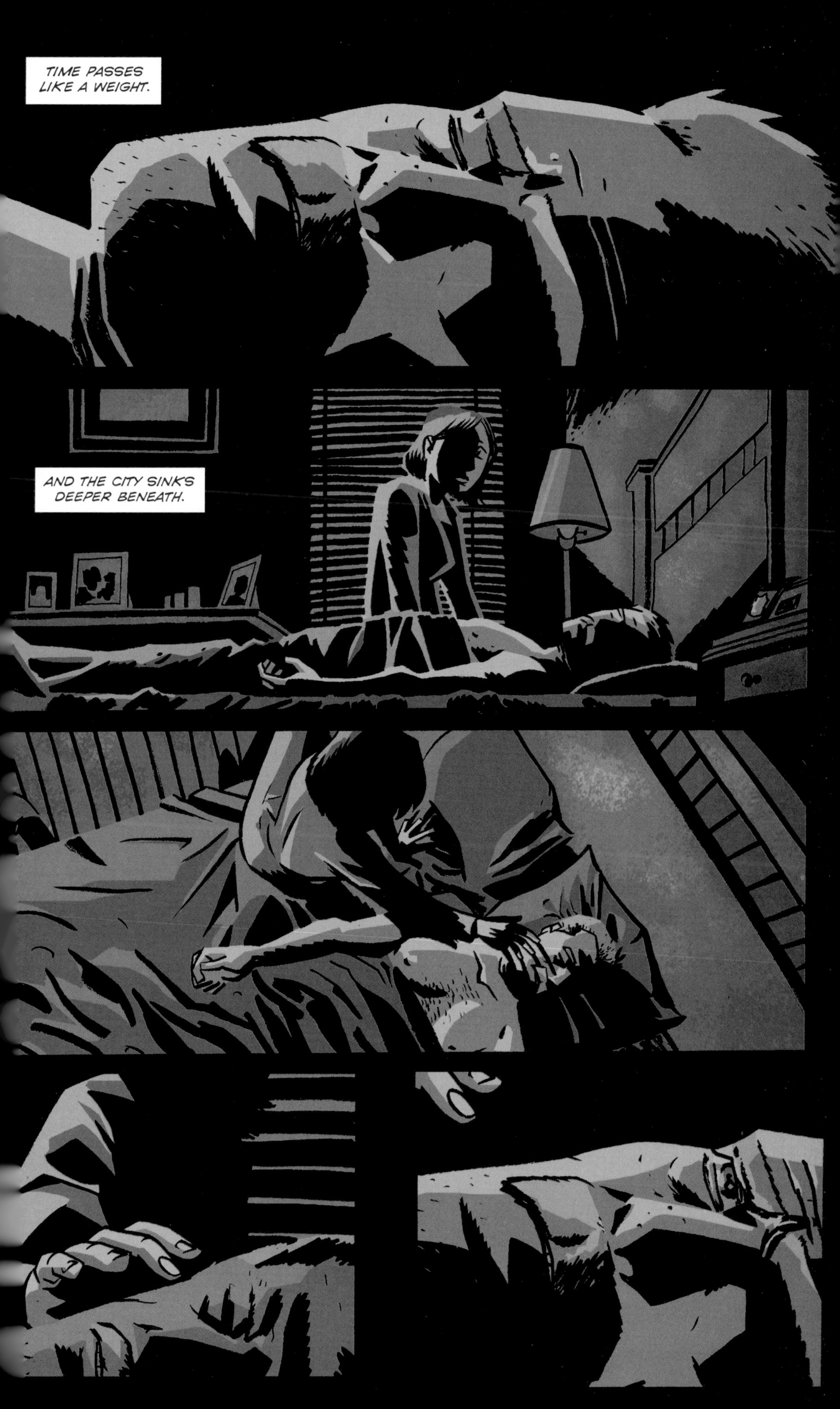
TIME PASSES LIKE A WEIGHT.
AND THE CITY SINKS DEEPER BENEATH.

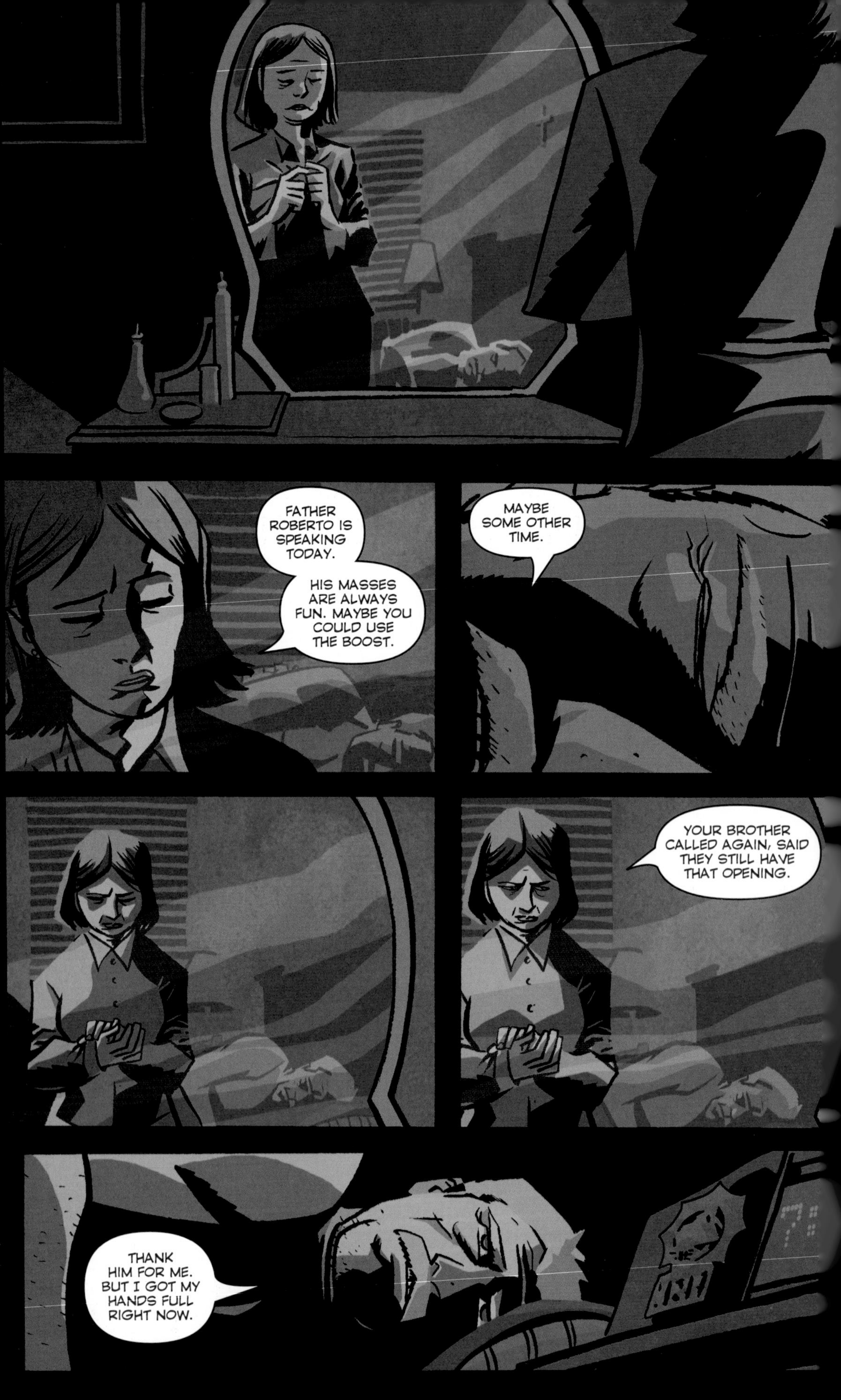
FATHER ROBERTO IS SPEAKING TODAY.
HIS MASSES ARE ALWAYS FUN. MAYBE YOU COULD USE THE BOOST.
MAYBE SOME OTHER TIME.
YOUR BROTHER CALLED AGAIN, SAID THEY STILL HAVE THAT OPENING.
THANK HIM FOR ME. BUT I GOT MY HANDS FULL RIGHT NOW.

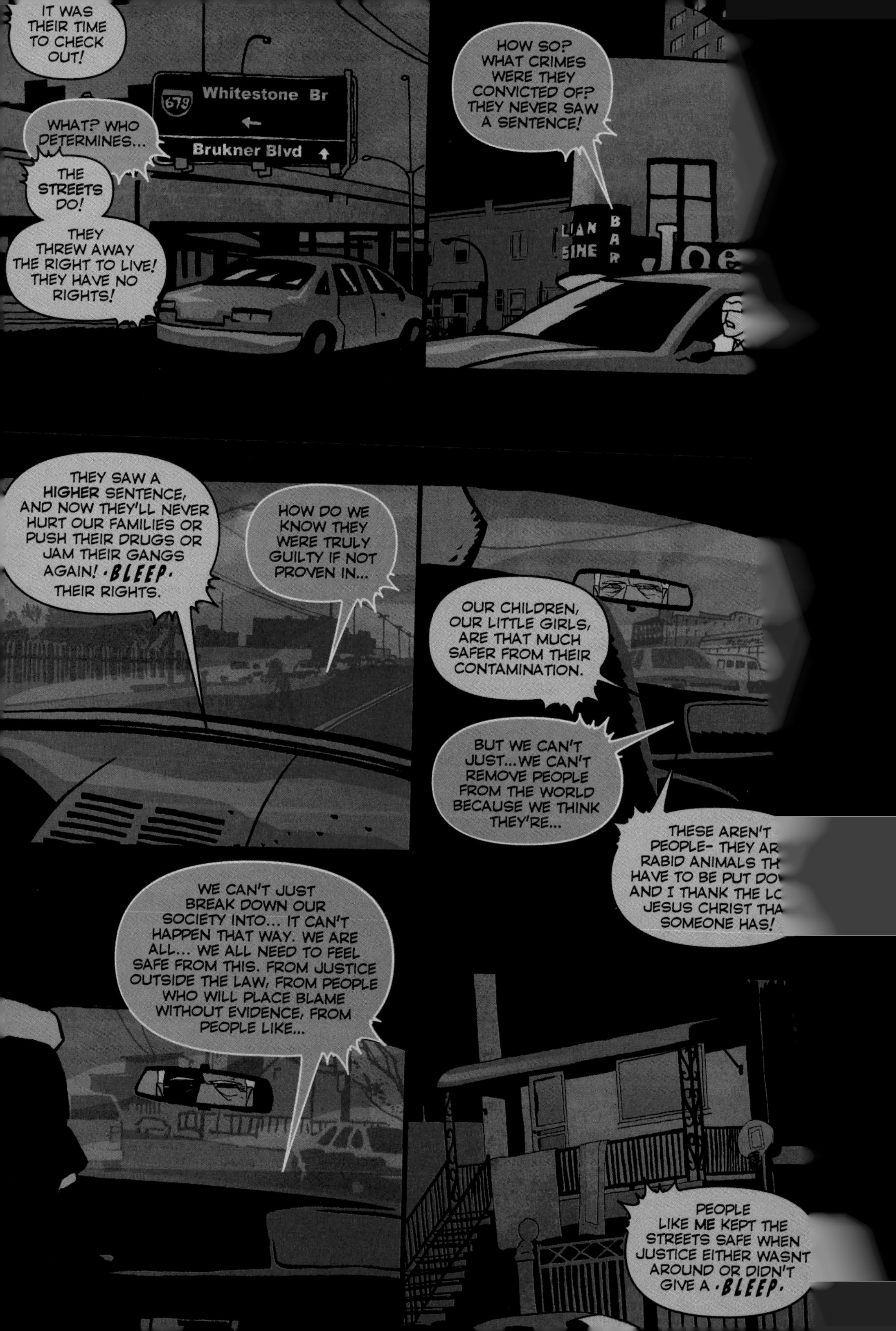
IT WAS THEIR TIME TO CHECK OUT!
Whitestone Br
679
Brukner Blvd
WHAT? WHO DETERMINES...
THE STREETS DO!
THEY THREW AWAY THE RIGHT TO LIVE! THEY HAVE NO RIGHTS!
HOW SO? WHAT CRIMES WERE THEY CONVICTED OF? THEY NEVER SAW A SENTENCE!
BAR
Joe
THEY SAW A HIGHER SENTENCE, AND NOW THEY'LL NEVER HURT OUR FAMILIES OR PUSH THEIR DRUGS OR JAM THEIR GANGS AGAIN! ·BLEEP· THEIR RIGHTS.
HOW DO WE KNOW THEY WERE TRULY GUILTY IF NOT PROVEN IN...
OUR CHILDREN, OUR LITTLE GIRLS, ARE THAT MUCH SAFER FROM THEIR CONTAMINATION.
BUT WE CAN'T JUST...WE CAN'T REMOVE PEOPLE FROM THE WORLD BECAUSE WE THINK THEY'RE...
THESE AREN'T PEOPLE- THEY AR RABID ANIMALS TH HAVE TO BE PUT DO AND I THANK THE LO JESUS CHRIST THA SOMEONE HAS!
WE CAN'T JUST BREAK DOWN OUR SOCIETY INTO... IT CAN'T HAPPEN THAT WAY. WE ARE ALL... WE ALL NEED TO FEEL SAFE FROM THIS. FROM JUSTICE OUTSIDE THE LAW, FROM PEOPLE WHO WILL PLACE BLAME WITHOUT EVIDENCE, FROM PEOPLE LIKE...
PEOPLE LIKE ME KEPT THE STREETS SAFE WHEN JUSTICE EITHER WASNT AROUND OR DIDN'T GIVE A ·BLEEP·

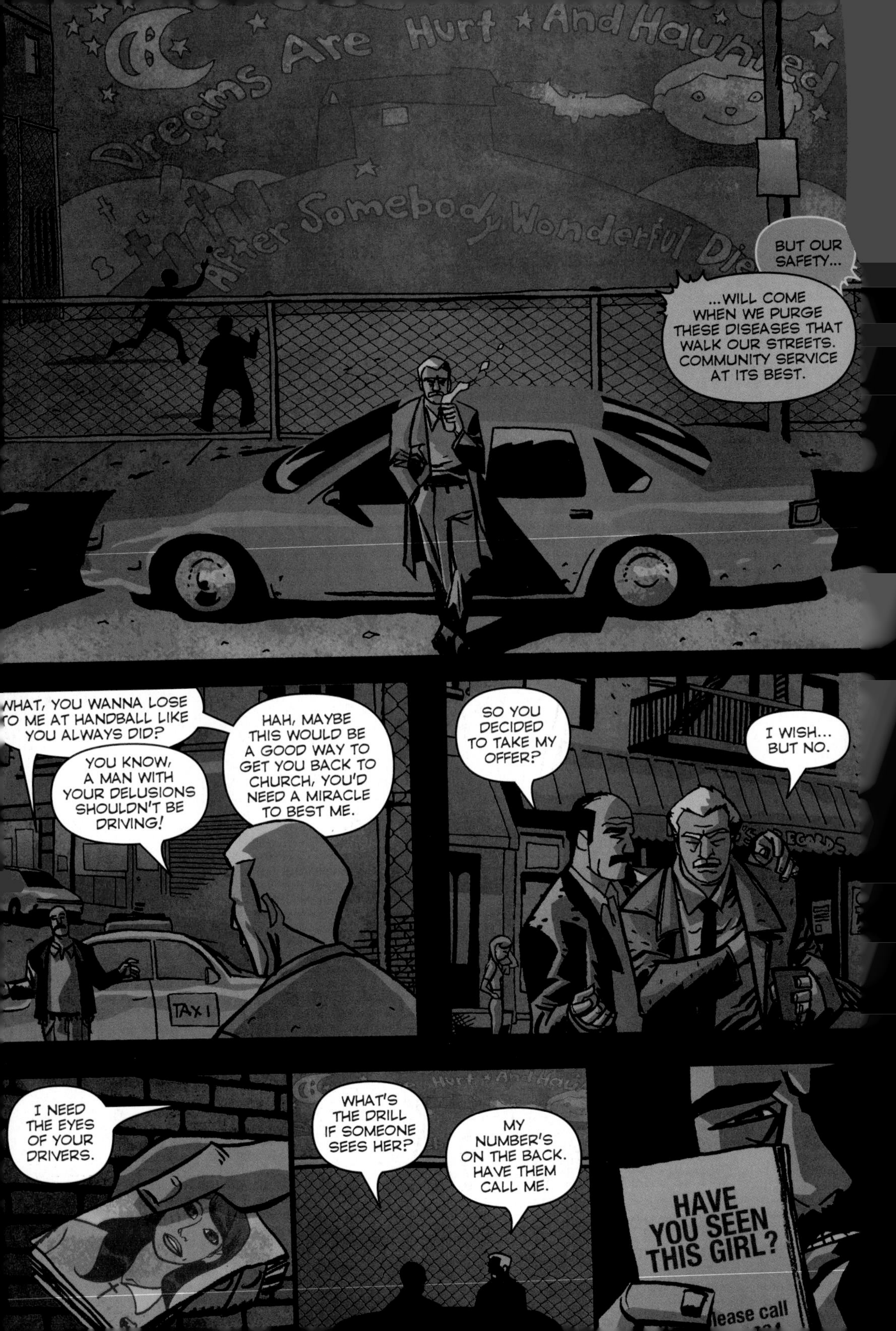
Dreams Are Hurt And Haunted After Somebody Wonderful Dies
BUT OUR SAFETY...
...WILL COME WHEN WE PURGE THESE DISEASES THAT WALK OUR STREETS. COMMUNITY SERVICE AT ITS BEST.
WHAT, YOU WANNA LOSE TO ME AT HANDBALL LIKE YOU ALWAYS DID?
YOU KNOW, A MAN WITH YOUR DELUSIONS SHOULDN'T BE DRIVING!
HAH, MAYBE THIS WOULD BE A GOOD WAY TO GET YOU BACK TO CHURCH, YOU'D NEED A MIRACLE TO BEST ME.
TAXI
SO YOU DECIDED TO TAKE MY OFFER?
I WISH... BUT NO.
I NEED THE EYES OF YOUR DRIVERS.
WHAT'S THE DRILL IF SOMEONE SEES HER?
MY NUMBER'S ON THE BACK. HAVE THEM CALL ME.
HAVE YOU SEEN THIS GIRL?

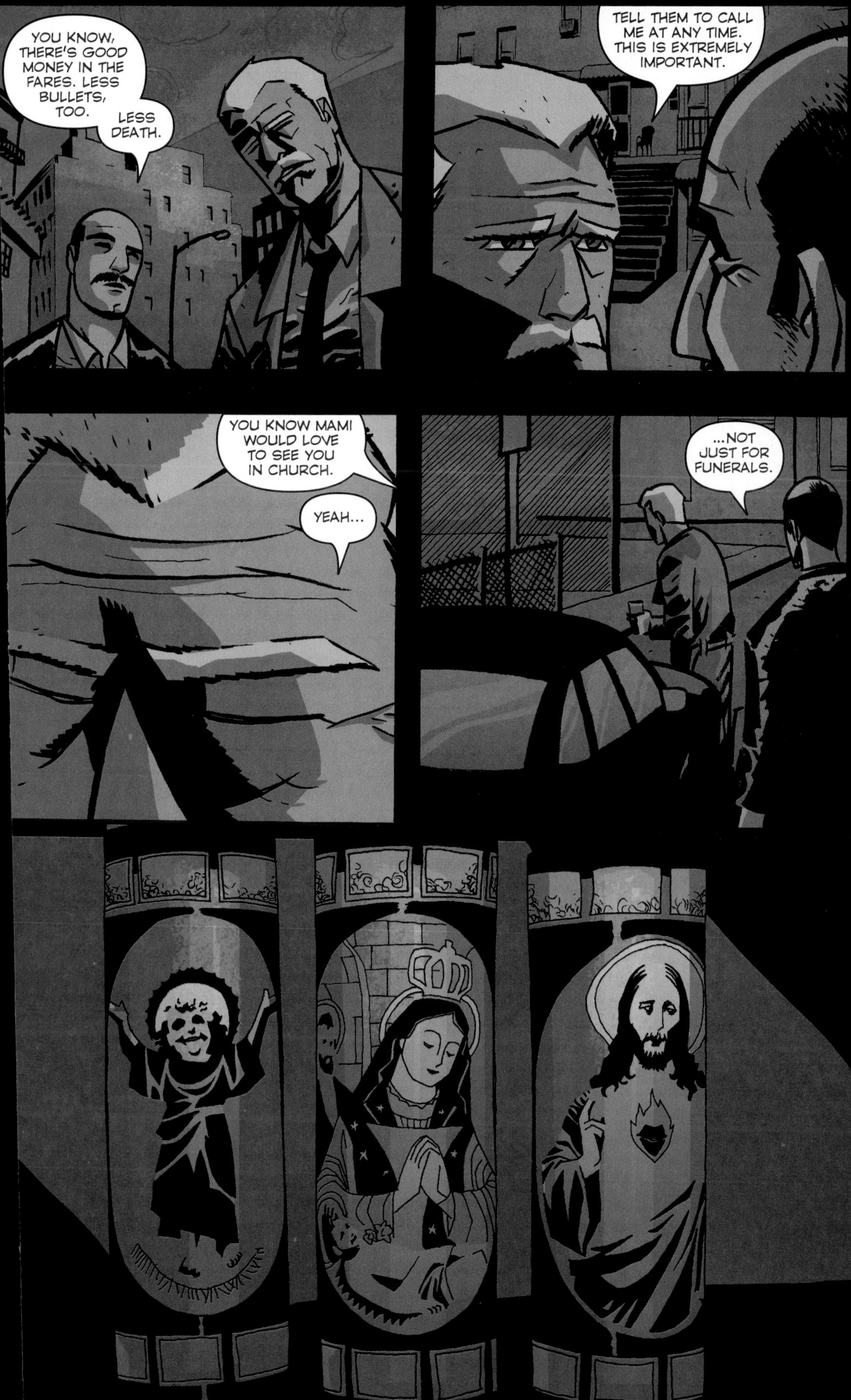

YOU KNOW, THERE'S GOOD MONEY IN THE FARES. LESS BULLETS, TOO.
LESS DEATH.
TELL THEM TO CALL ME AT ANY TIME. THIS IS EXTREMELY IMPORTANT.
YOU KNOW MAMI WOULD LOVE TO SEE YOU IN CHURCH.
YEAH...
...NOT JUST FOR FUNERALS.

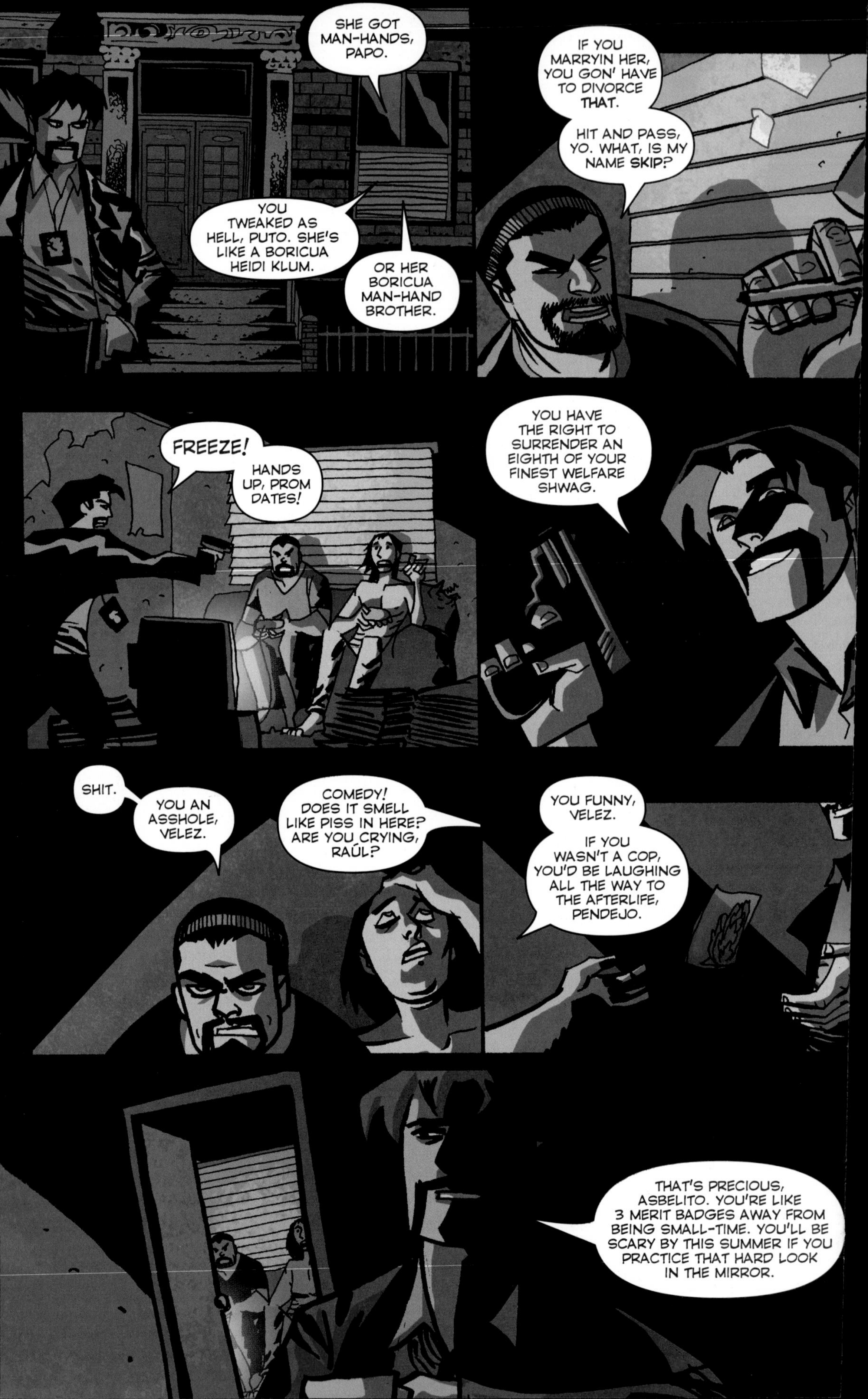

SHE GOT MAN-HANDS, PAPO.
YOU TWEAKED AS HELL, PUTO. SHE'S LIKE A BORICUA HEIDI KLUM.
OR HER BORICUA MAN-HAND BROTHER.
IF YOU MARRYIN HER, YOU GON' HAVE TO DIVORCE THAT.
HIT AND PASS, YO. WHAT, IS MY NAME SKIP?
FREEZE!
HANDS UP, PROM DATES!
YOU HAVE THE RIGHT TO SURRENDER AN EIGHTH OF YOUR FINEST WELFARE SHWAG.
SHIT.
YOU AN ASSHOLE, VELEZ.
COMEDY! DOES IT SMELL LIKE PISS IN HERE? ARE YOU CRYING, RAÚL?
YOU FUNNY, VELEZ.
IF YOU WASN'T A COP, YOU'D BE LAUGHING ALL THE WAY TO THE AFTERLIFE, PENDEJO.
THAT'S PRECIOUS, ASBELITO. YOU'RE LIKE 3 MERIT BADGES AWAY FROM BEING SMALL-TIME. YOU'LL BE SCARY BY THIS SUMMER IF YOU PRACTICE THAT HARD LOOK IN THE MIRROR.

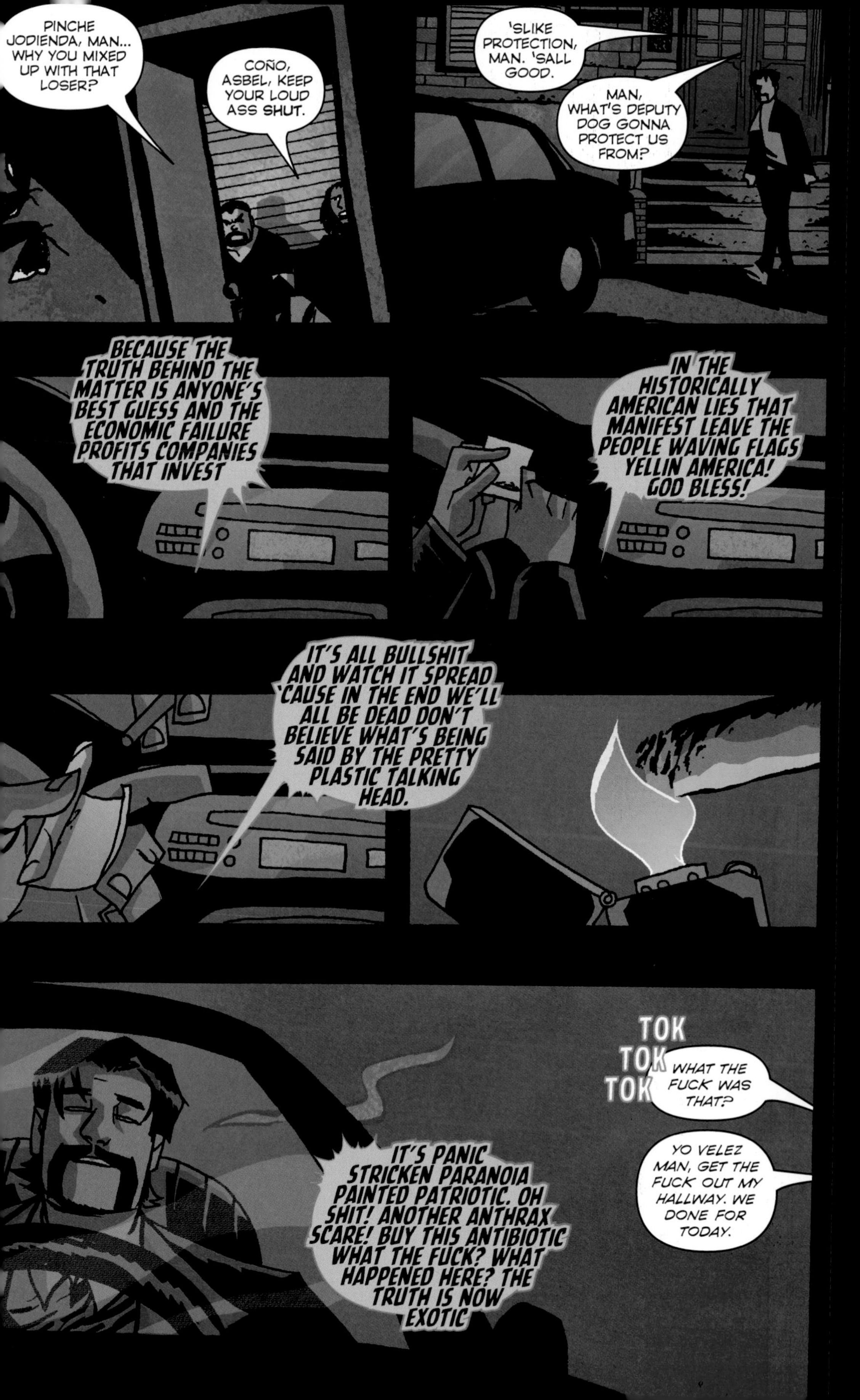
PINCHE JODIENDA, MAN... WHY YOU MIXED UP WITH THAT LOSER?
COÑO, ASBEL, KEEP YOUR LOUD ASS SHUT.
'SLIKE PROTECTION, MAN. 'SALL GOOD.
MAN, WHAT'S DEPUTY DOG GONNA PROTECT US FROM?
BECAUSE THE TRUTH BEHIND THE MATTER IS ANYONE'S BEST GUESS AND THE ECONOMIC FAILURE PROFITS COMPANIES THAT INVEST
IN THE HISTORICALLY AMERICAN LIES THAT MANIFEST LEAVE THE PEOPLE WAVING FLAGS YELLIN AMERICA! GOD BLESS!
IT'S ALL BULLSHIT AND WATCH IT SPREAD 'CAUSE IN THE END WE'LL ALL BE DEAD DON'T BELIEVE WHAT'S BEING SAID BY THE PRETTY PLASTIC TALKING HEAD.
IT'S PANIC STRICKEN PARANOIA PAINTED PATRIOTIC. OH SHIT! ANOTHER ANTHRAX SCARE! BUY THIS ANTIBIOTIC WHAT THE FUCK? WHAT HAPPENED HERE? THE TRUTH IS NOW EXOTIC
TOK TOK TOK
WHAT THE FUCK WAS THAT?
YO VELEZ MAN, GET THE FUCK OUT MY HALLWAY. WE DONE FOR TODAY.

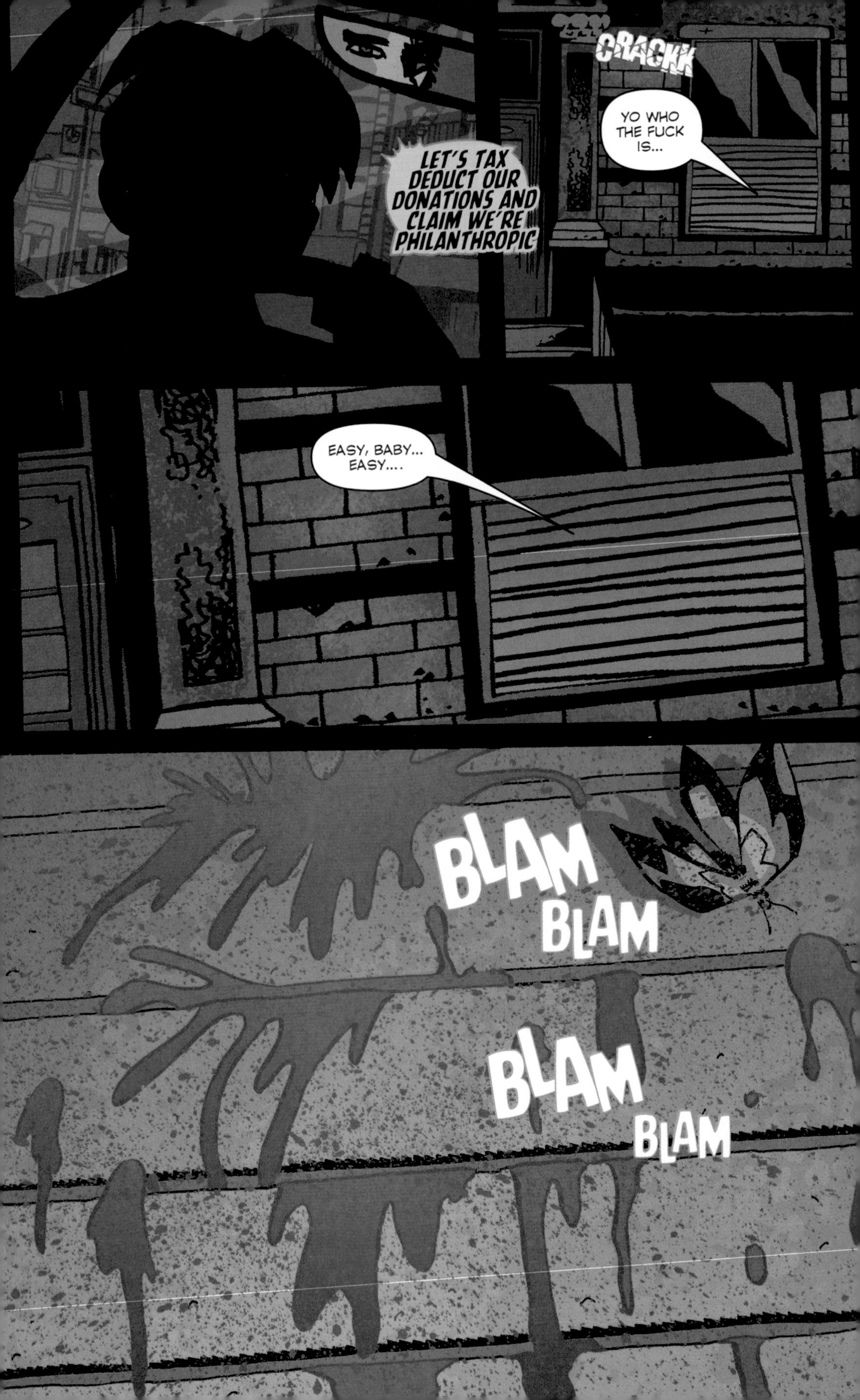
CRACKK
LET'S TAX DEDUCT OUR DONATIONS AND CLAIM WE'RE PHILANTHROPIC
YO WHO THE FUCK IS...
EASY, BABY... EASY....
BLAM
BLAM
BLAM
BLAM

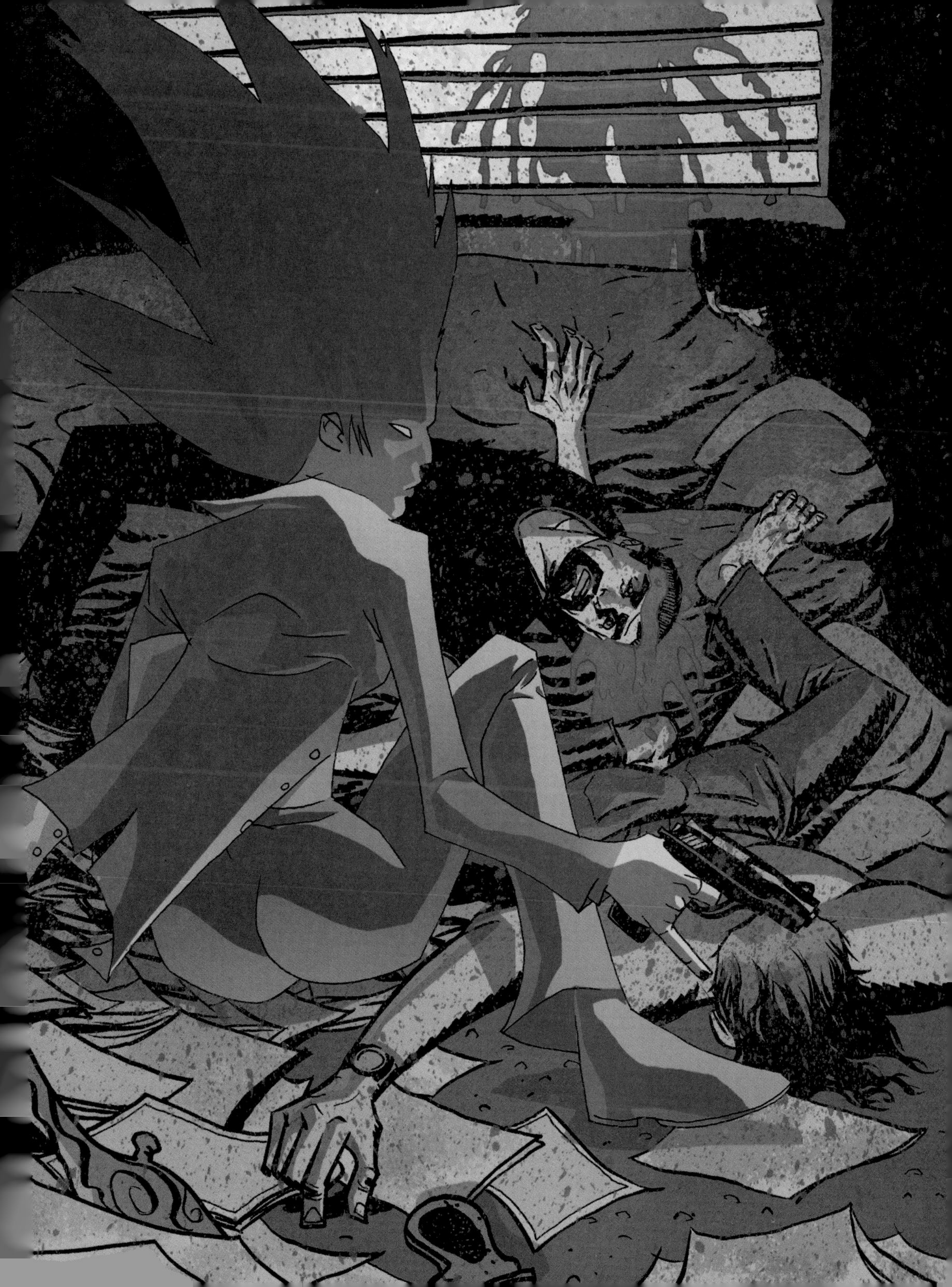

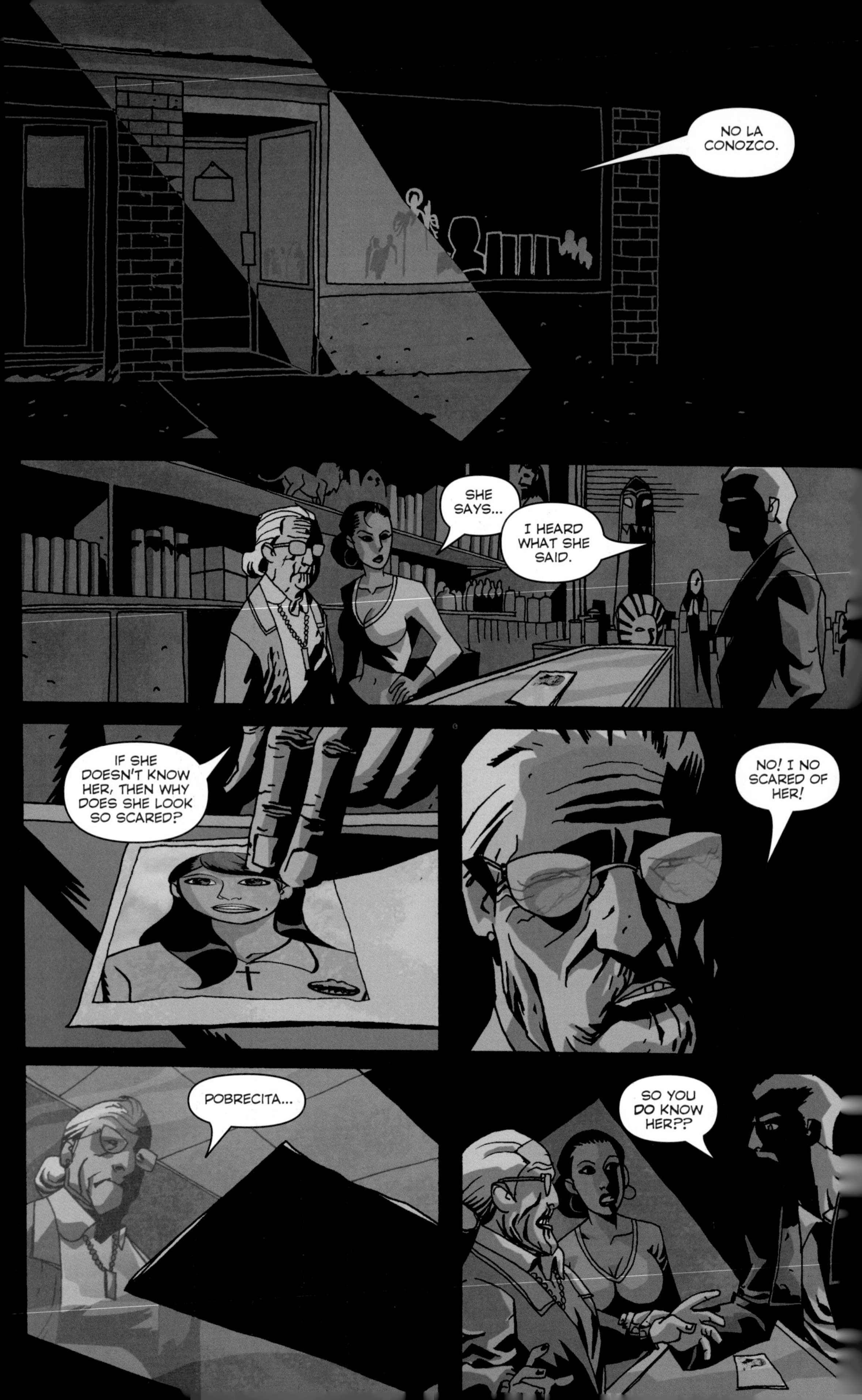
NO LA CONOZCO.
SHE SAYS...
I HEARD WHAT SHE SAID.
IF SHE DOESN'T KNOW HER, THEN WHY DOES SHE LOOK SO SCARED?
NO! I NO SCARED OF HER!
POBRECITA...
SO YOU DO KNOW HER??

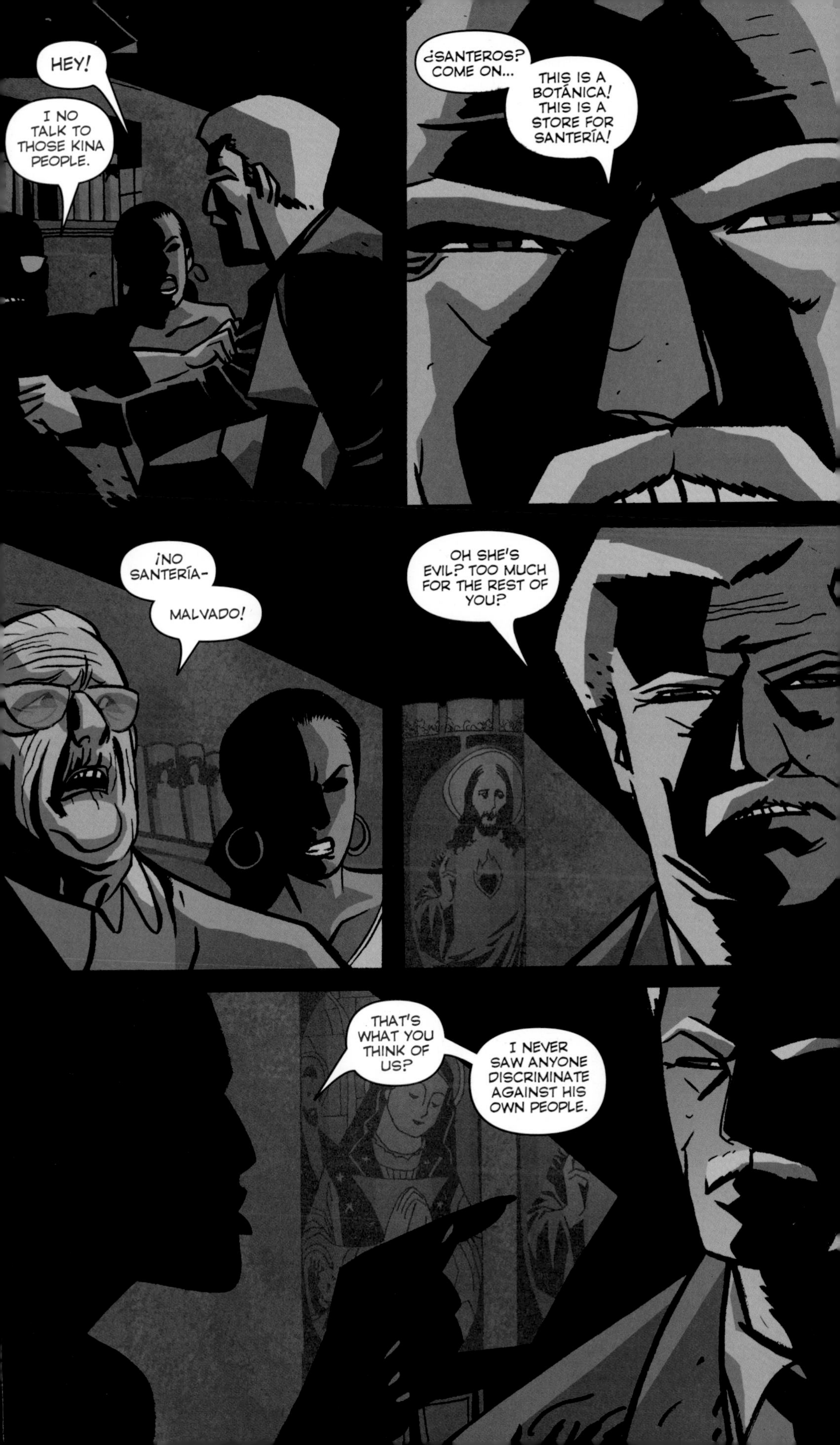
HEY!
I NO TALK TO THOSE KINA PEOPLE.
¿SANTEROS? COME ON...
THIS IS A BOTÁNICA! THIS IS A STORE FOR SANTERÍA!
¡NO SANTERÍA-
MALVADO!
OH SHE'S EVIL? TOO MUCH FOR THE REST OF YOU?
THAT'S WHAT YOU THINK OF US?
I NEVER SAW ANYONE DISCRIMINATE AGAINST HIS OWN PEOPLE.

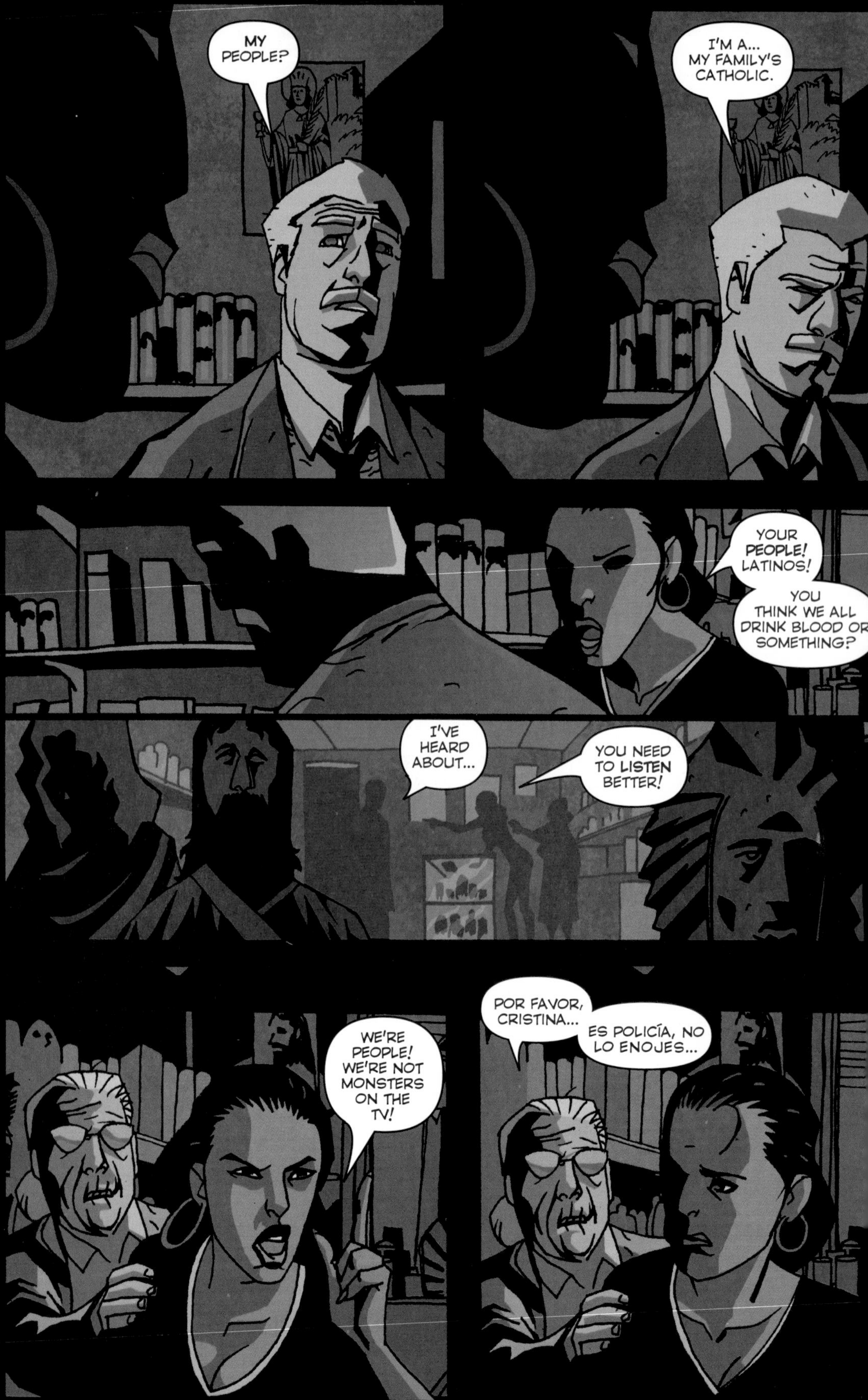
MY PEOPLE?
I'M A... MY FAMILY'S CATHOLIC.
YOUR PEOPLE! LATINOS!
YOU THINK WE ALL DRINK BLOOD OR SOMETHING?
I'VE HEARD ABOUT...
YOU NEED TO LISTEN BETTER!
WE'RE PEOPLE! WE'RE NOT MONSTERS ON THE TV!
POR FAVOR, CRISTINA...
ES POLICÍA, NO LO ENOJES...

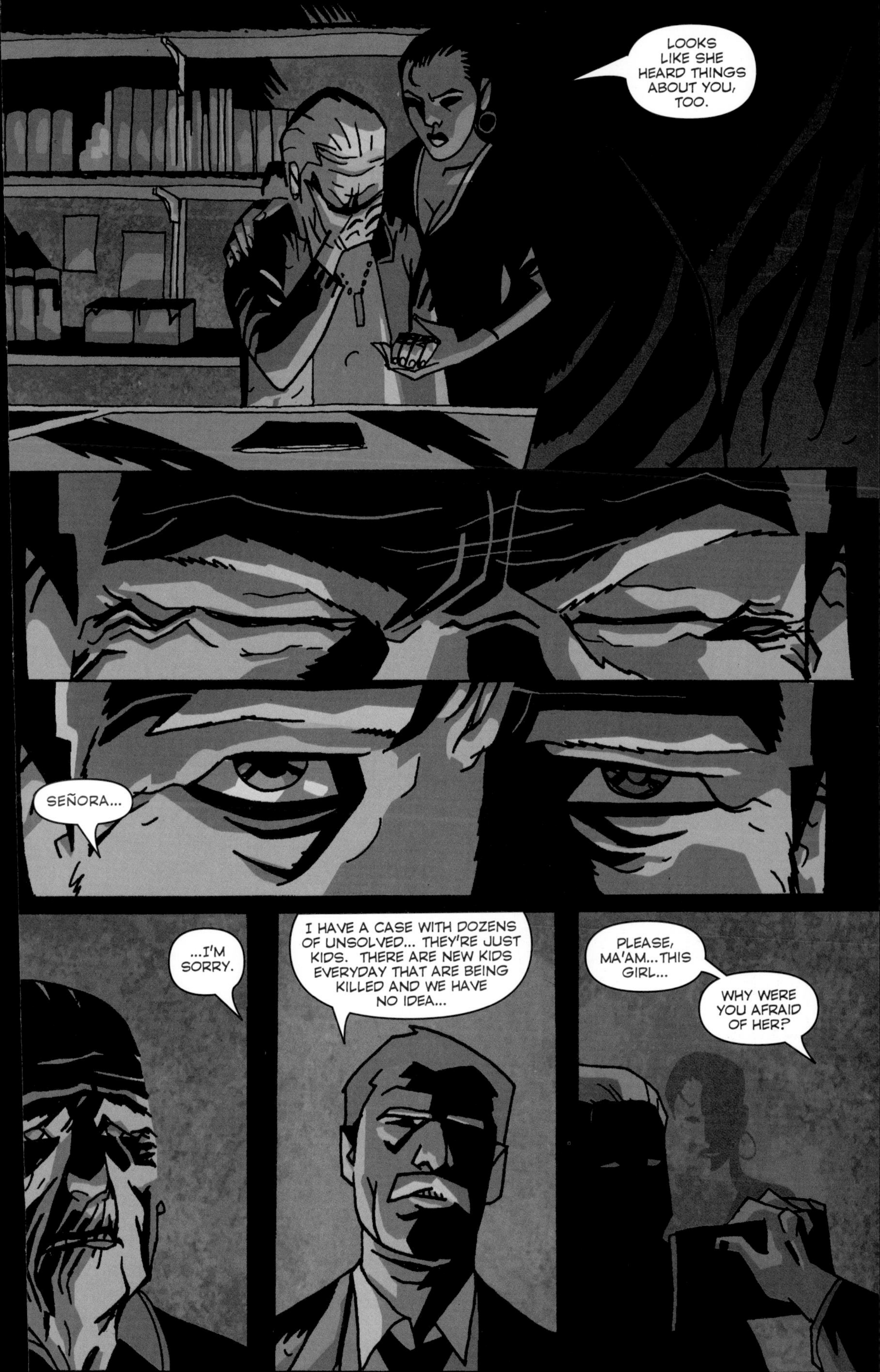
LOOKS LIKE SHE HEARD THINGS ABOUT YOU, TOO.
SEÑORA...
...I'M SORRY.
I HAVE A CASE WITH DOZENS OF UNSOLVED... THEY'RE JUST KIDS. THERE ARE NEW KIDS EVERYDAY THAT ARE BEING KILLED AND WE HAVE NO IDEA...
PLEASE, MA'AM...THIS GIRL...
WHY WERE YOU AFRAID OF HER?

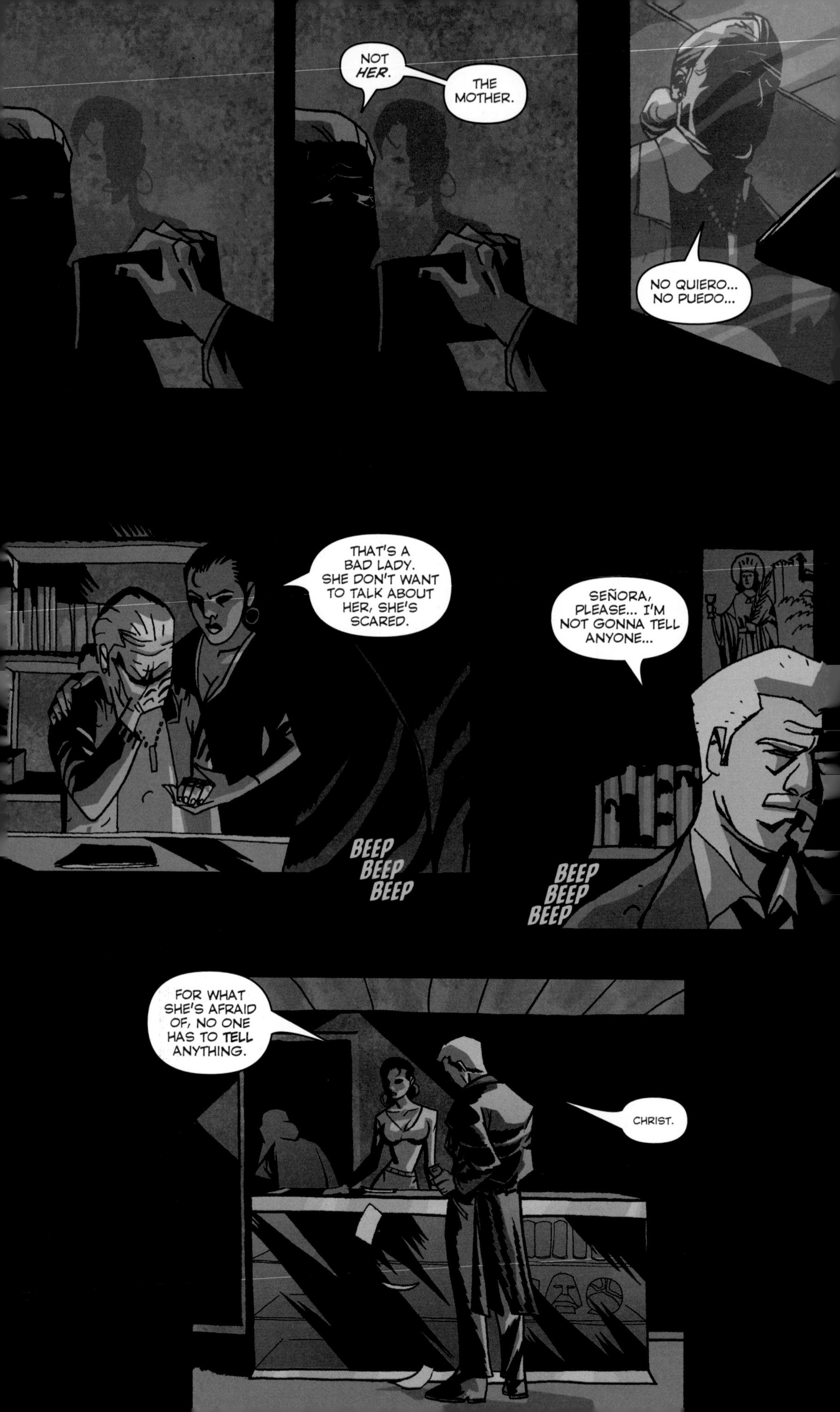
NOT *HER*.
THE MOTHER.
NO QUIERO... NO PUEDO...
THAT'S A BAD LADY. SHE DON'T WANT TO TALK ABOUT HER, SHE'S SCARED.
BEEP BEEP BEEP
SEÑORA, PLEASE... I'M NOT GONNA TELL ANYONE...
BEEP BEEP BEEP
FOR WHAT SHE'S AFRAID OF, NO ONE HAS TO **TELL** ANYTHING.
CHRIST.

NOT COPING SO WELL, EH?

BENDICIÓN.

WHAT?

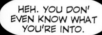

HEH. YOU DON' EVEN KNOW WHAT YOU'RE INTO.

HOW DO YOU KNOW WHAT I'M INTO?

WHAT DO YOU KNOW ABOUT ME?

I KNOW YOU STINK OF AN EGGUN.

YOU SIR... ARE DEALING WITH PEOPLE OF A DIFFERENT CLOTH.

I GOT IN TROUBLE IN THERE FOR CALLING PEOPLE DIFFERENT.

YOU GOT TROUBLE FOR CALLING THEM BAD.

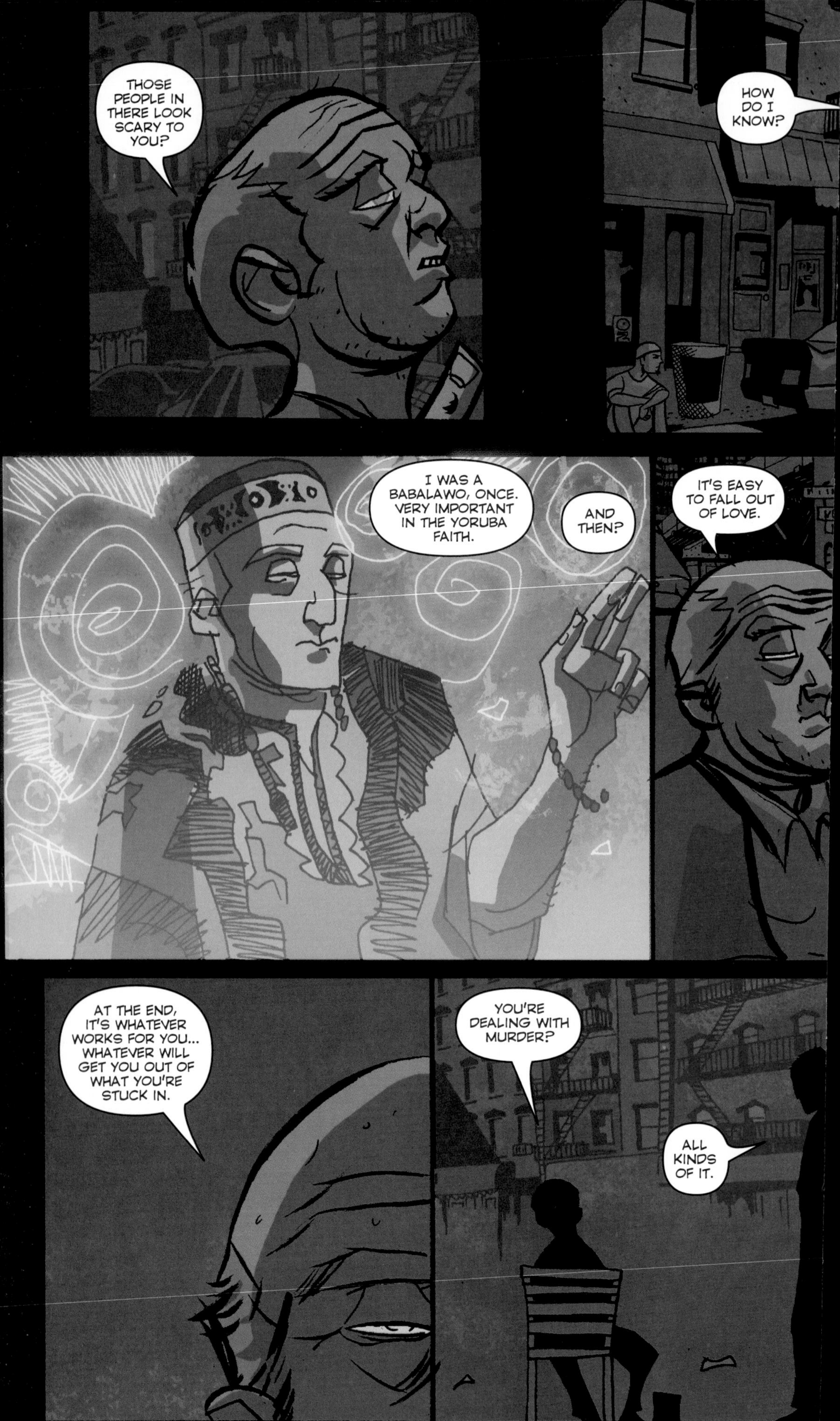
THOSE PEOPLE IN THERE LOOK SCARY TO YOU?
HOW DO I KNOW?
I WAS A BABALAWO, ONCE. VERY IMPORTANT IN THE YORUBA FAITH.
AND THEN?
IT'S EASY TO FALL OUT OF LOVE.
AT THE END, IT'S WHATEVER WORKS FOR YOU... WHATEVER WILL GET YOU OUT OF WHAT YOU'RE STUCK IN.
YOU'RE DEALING WITH MURDER?
ALL KINDS OF IT.

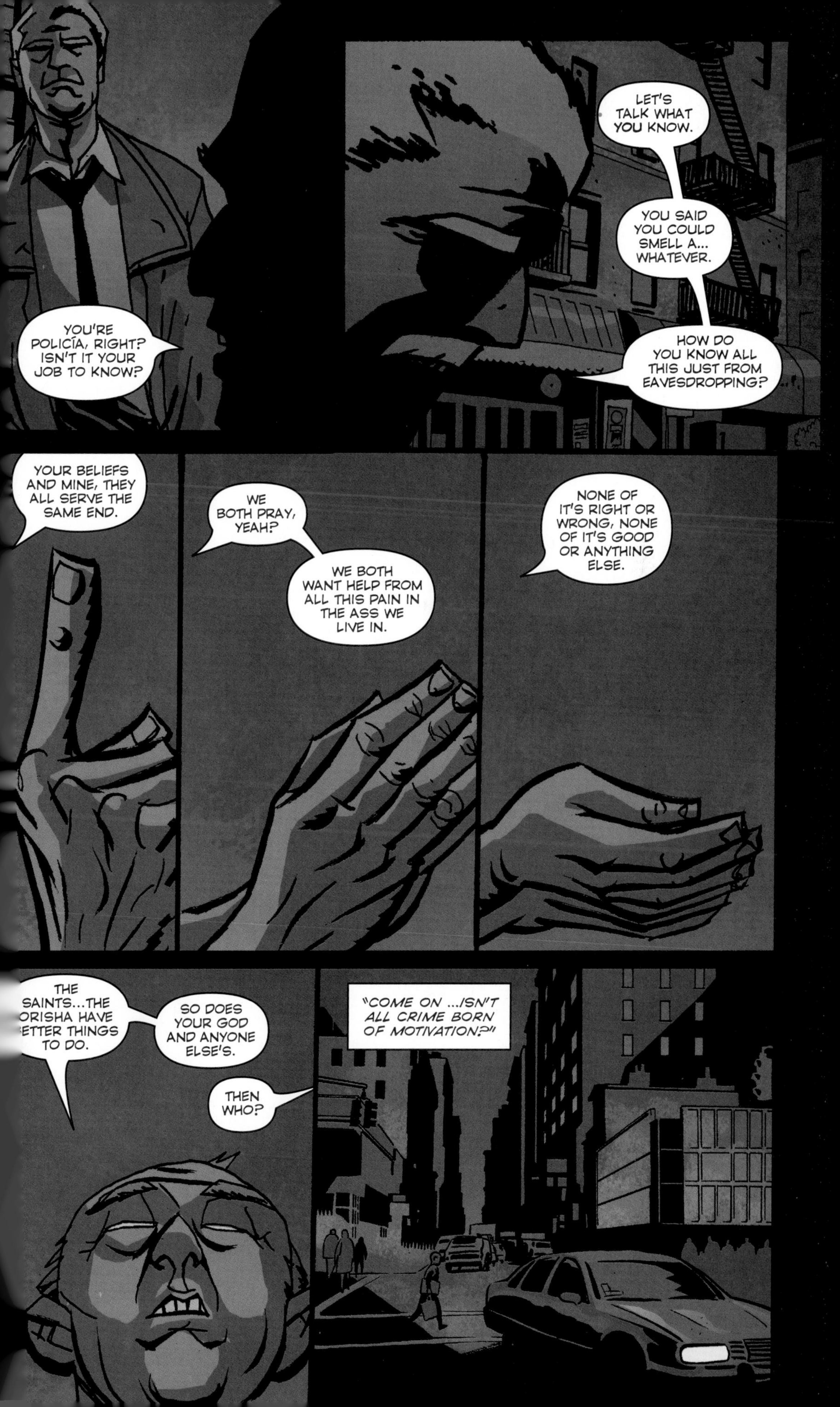
YOU'RE POLICÍA, RIGHT? ISN'T IT YOUR JOB TO KNOW?
LET'S TALK WHAT YOU KNOW.
YOU SAID YOU COULD SMELL A... WHATEVER.
HOW DO YOU KNOW ALL THIS JUST FROM EAVESDROPPING?
YOUR BELIEFS AND MINE, THEY ALL SERVE THE SAME END.
WE BOTH PRAY, YEAH?
WE BOTH WANT HELP FROM ALL THIS PAIN IN THE ASS WE LIVE IN.
NONE OF IT'S RIGHT OR WRONG, NONE OF IT'S GOOD OR ANYTHING ELSE.
THE SAINTS...THE ORISHA HAVE BETTER THINGS TO DO.
SO DOES YOUR GOD AND ANYONE ELSE'S.
THEN WHO?
"COME ON ...ISN'T ALL CRIME BORN OF MOTIVATION?"

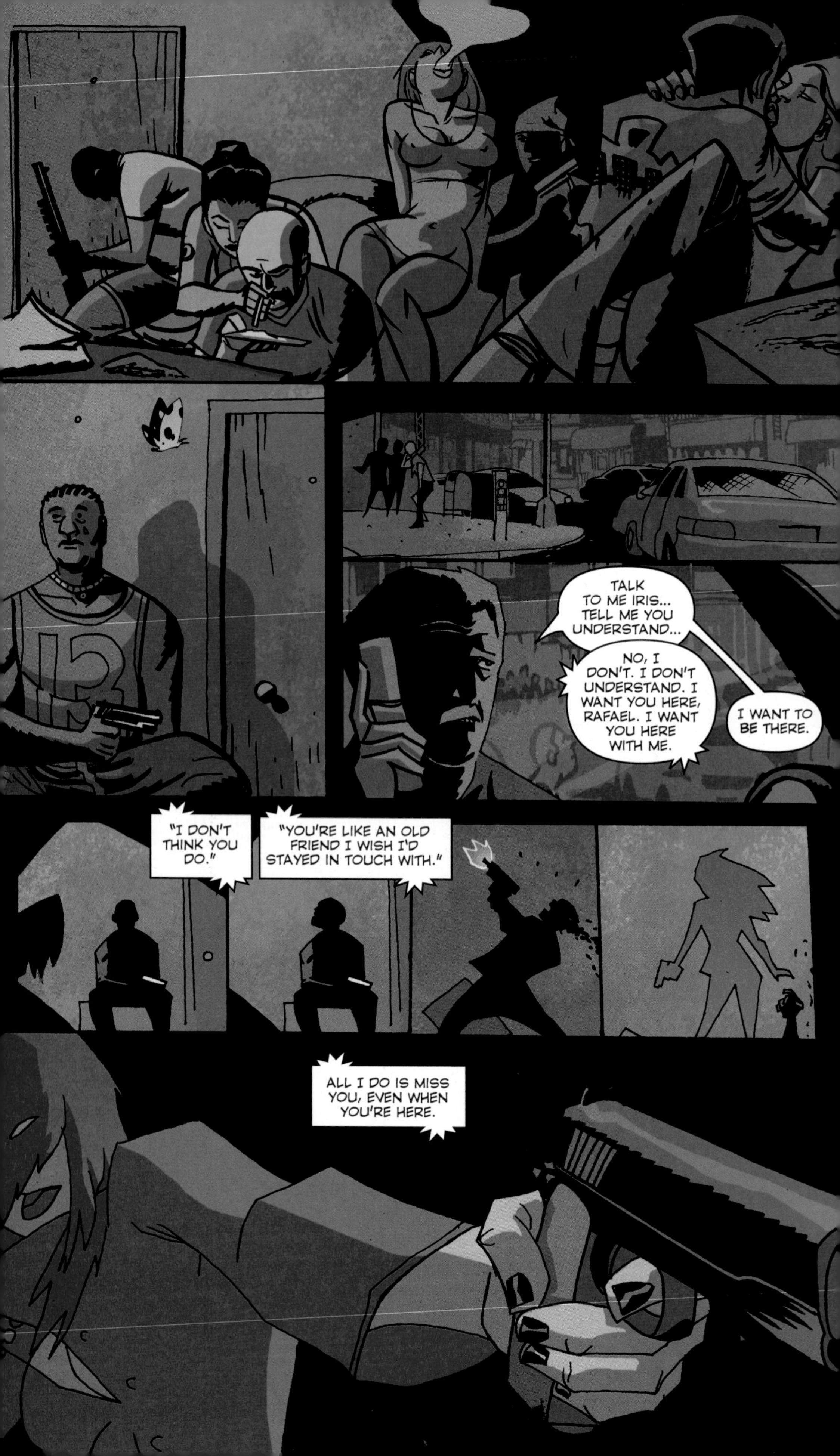
TALK TO ME IRIS... TELL ME YOU UNDERSTAND...
NO, I DON'T. I DON'T UNDERSTAND. I WANT YOU HERE, RAFAEL. I WANT YOU HERE WITH ME.
I WANT TO BE THERE.
"I DON'T THINK YOU DO."
"YOU'RE LIKE AN OLD FRIEND I WISH I'D STAYED IN TOUCH WITH."
ALL I DO IS MISS YOU, EVEN WHEN YOU'RE HERE.

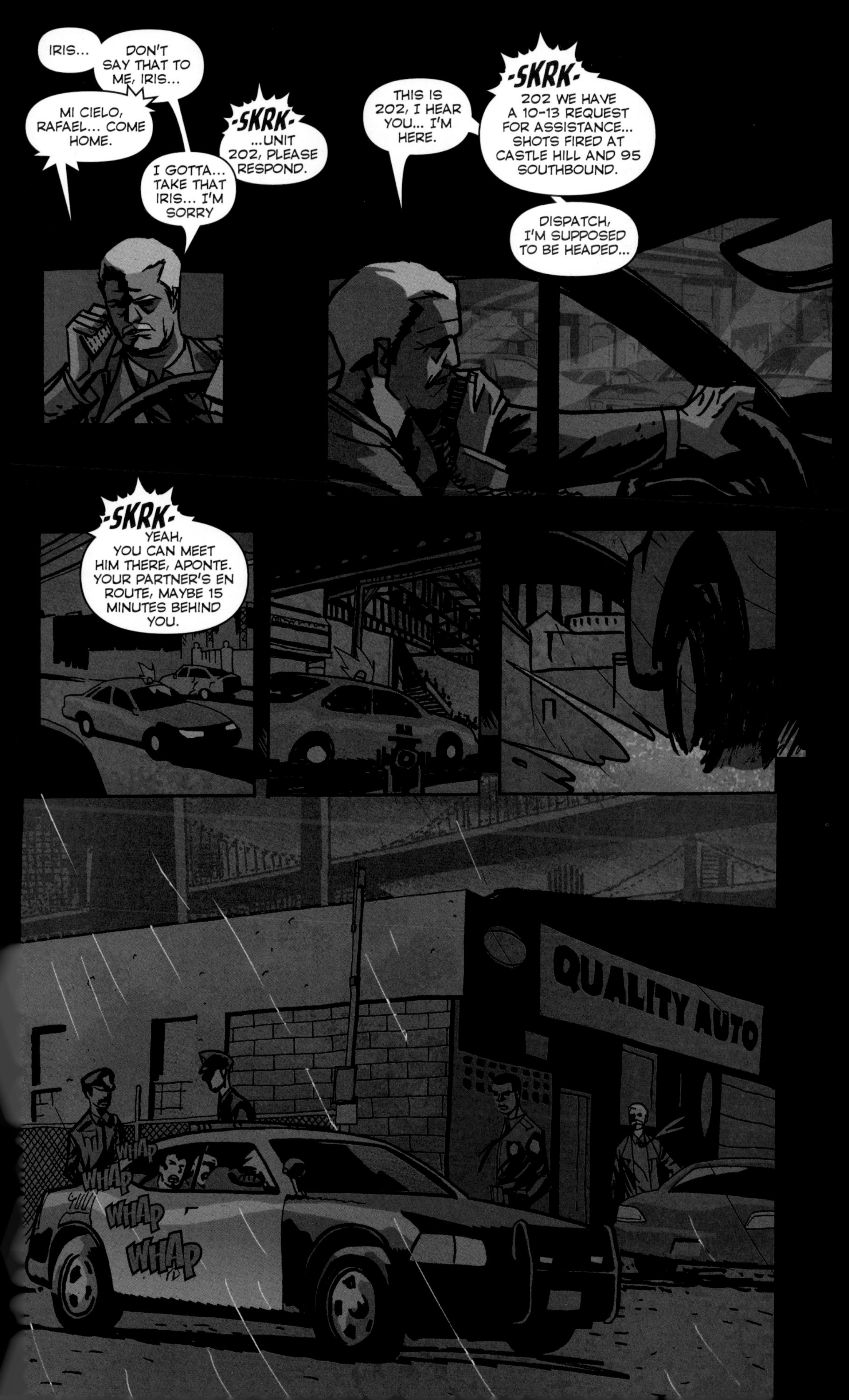
IRIS...
DON'T SAY THAT TO ME, IRIS...
MI CIELO, RAFAEL... COME HOME.
I GOTTA... TAKE THAT IRIS... I'M SORRY
-SKRK-
...UNIT 202, PLEASE RESPOND.
THIS IS 202, I HEAR YOU... I'M HERE.
-SKRK-
202 WE HAVE A 10-13 REQUEST FOR ASSISTANCE... SHOTS FIRED AT CASTLE HILL AND 95 SOUTHBOUND.
DISPATCH, I'M SUPPOSED TO BE HEADED...
-SKRK-
YEAH, YOU CAN MEET HIM THERE, APONTE. YOUR PARTNER'S EN ROUTE, MAYBE 15 MINUTES BEHIND YOU.
QUALITY AUTO
WHAP
WHAP
WHAP
WHAP

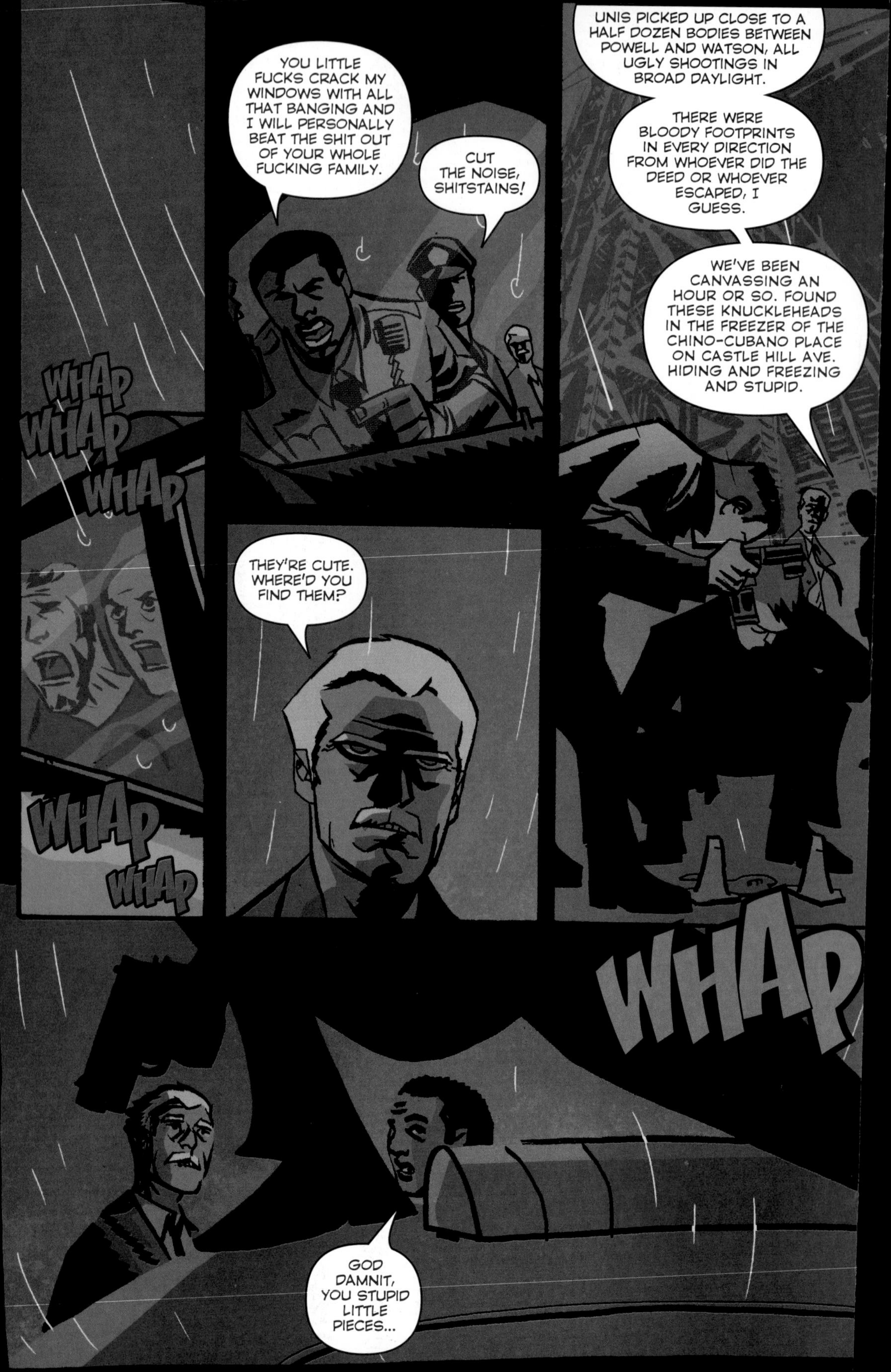
WHAP
WHAP
WHAP
YOU LITTLE FUCKS CRACK MY WINDOWS WITH ALL THAT BANGING AND I WILL PERSONALLY BEAT THE SHIT OUT OF YOUR WHOLE FUCKING FAMILY.
CUT THE NOISE, SHITSTAINS!
UNIS PICKED UP CLOSE TO A HALF DOZEN BODIES BETWEEN POWELL AND WATSON, ALL UGLY SHOOTINGS IN BROAD DAYLIGHT.
THERE WERE BLOODY FOOTPRINTS IN EVERY DIRECTION FROM WHOEVER DID THE DEED OR WHOEVER ESCAPED, I GUESS.
WE'VE BEEN CANVASSING AN HOUR OR SO. FOUND THESE KNUCKLEHEADS IN THE FREEZER OF THE CHINO-CUBANO PLACE ON CASTLE HILL AVE. HIDING AND FREEZING AND STUPID.
WHAP
WHAP
THEY'RE CUTE. WHERE'D YOU FIND THEM?
WHAP
GOD DAMNIT, YOU STUPID LITTLE PIECES...

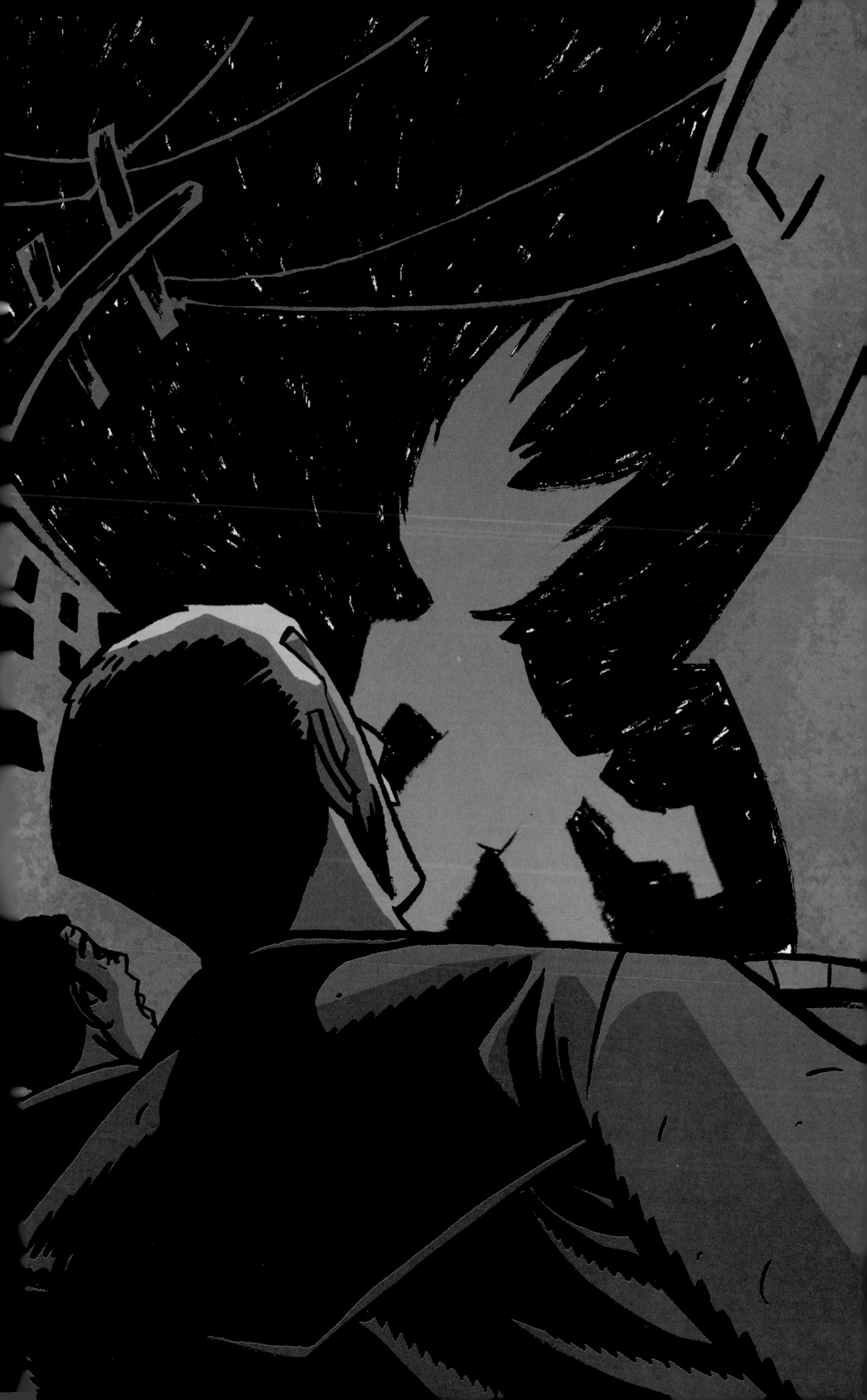

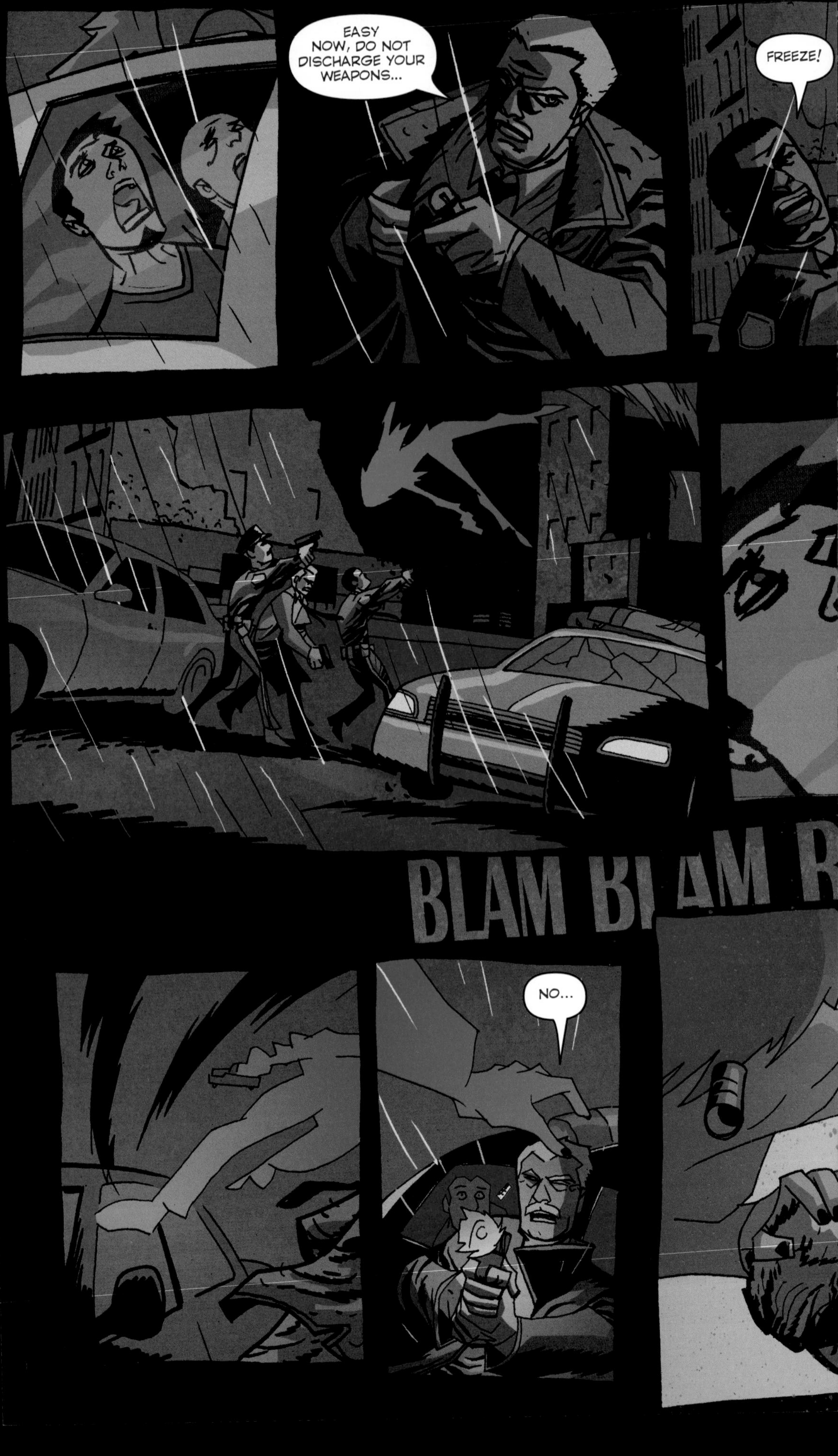
EASY NOW, DO NOT DISCHARGE YOUR WEAPONS...
FREEZE!
BLAM BLAM
NO...

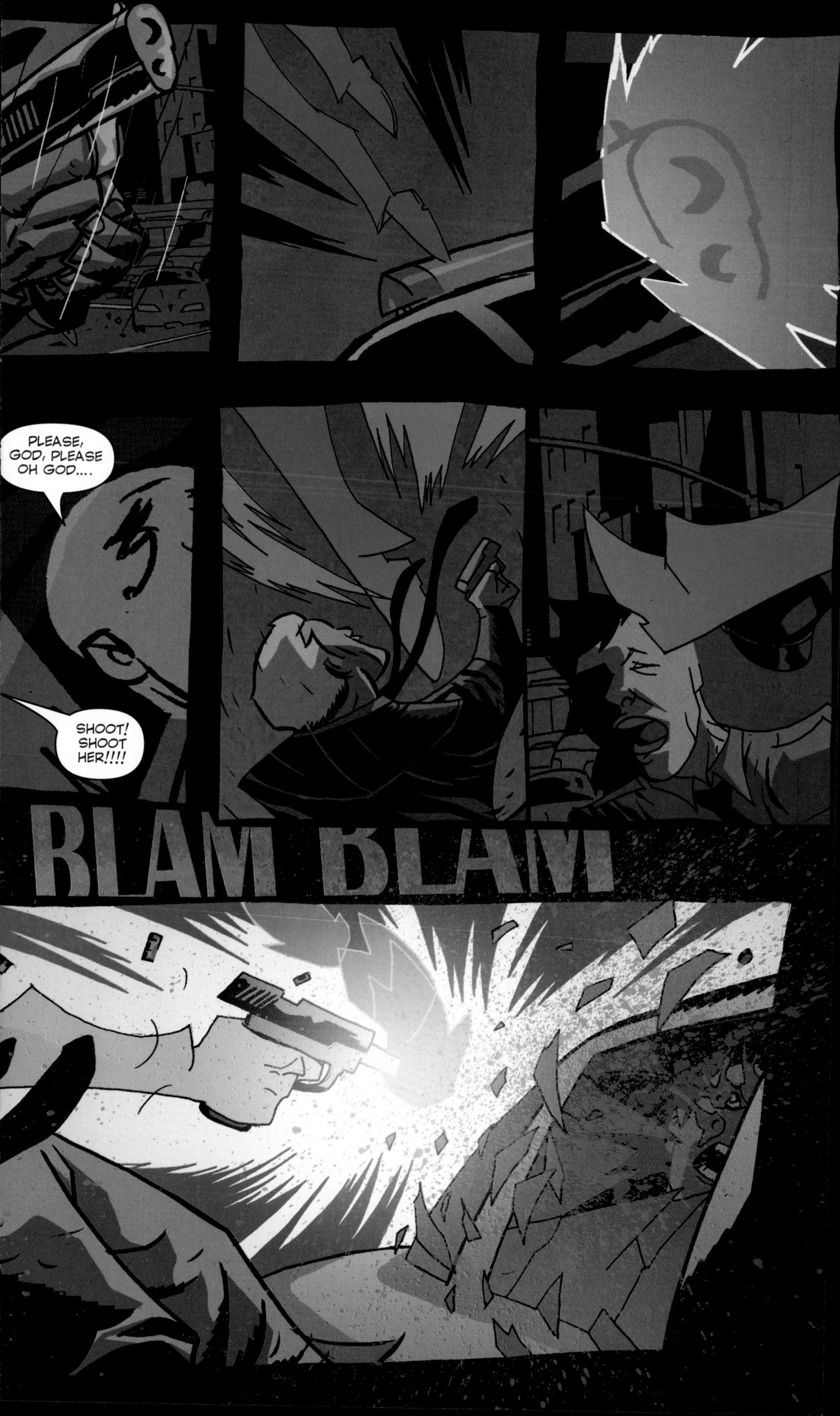
PLEASE, GOD, PLEASE OH GOD....
SHOOT! SHOOT HER!!!!
BLAM BLAM

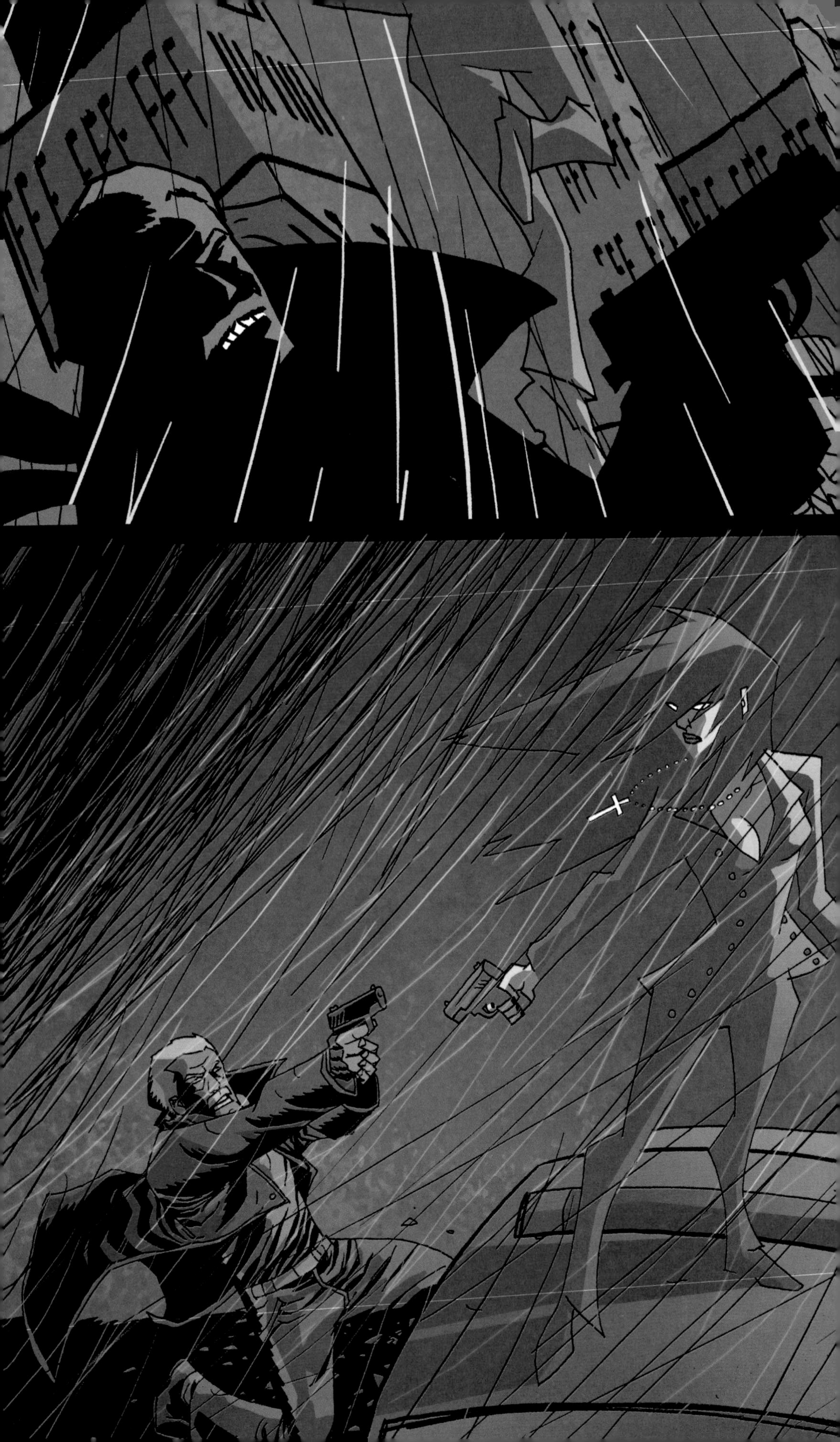

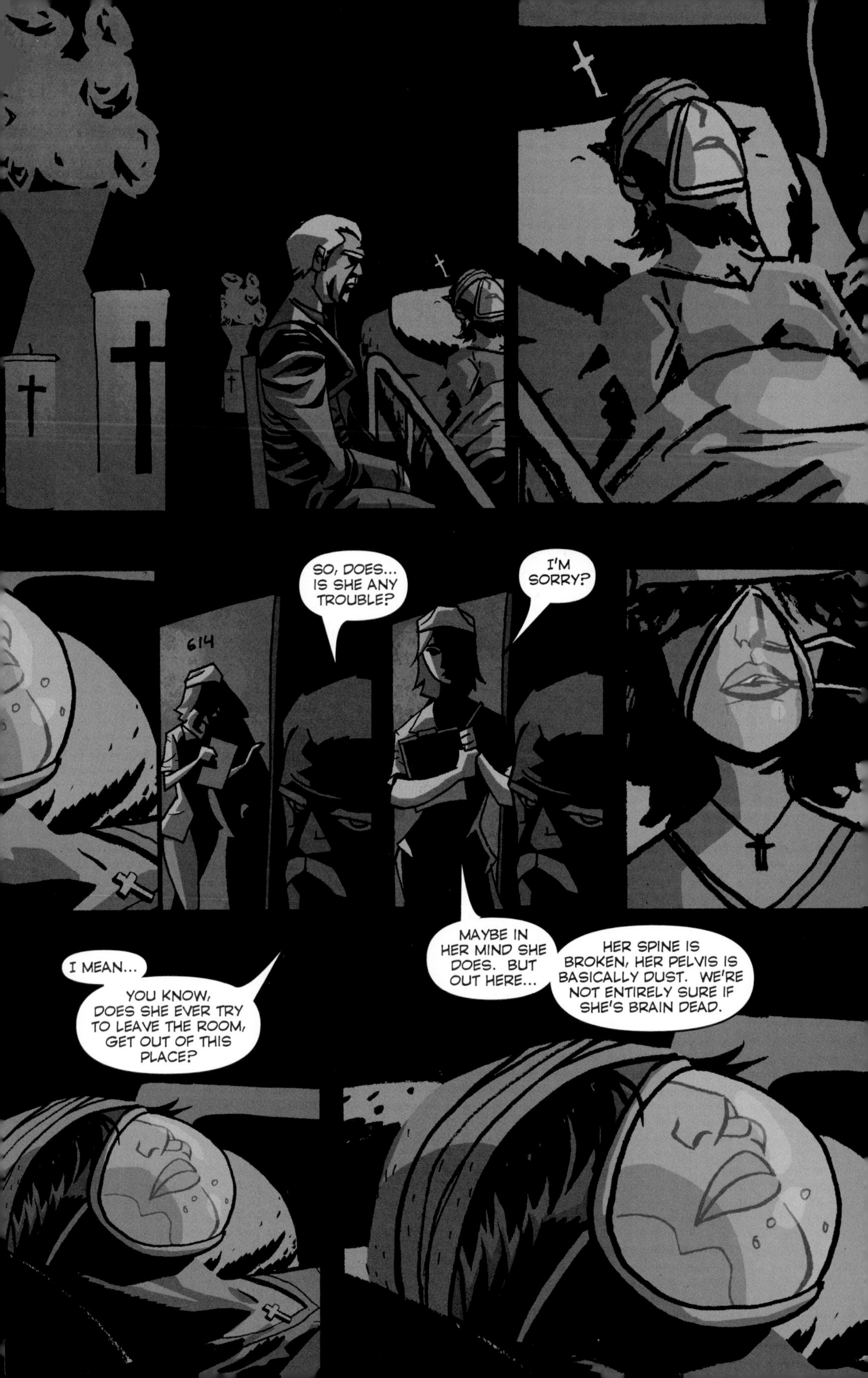
614
SO, DOES... IS SHE ANY TROUBLE?
I'M SORRY?
I MEAN...
YOU KNOW, DOES SHE EVER TRY TO LEAVE THE ROOM, GET OUT OF THIS PLACE?
MAYBE IN HER MIND SHE DOES. BUT OUT HERE...
HER SPINE IS BROKEN, HER PELVIS IS BASICALLY DUST. WE'RE NOT ENTIRELY SURE IF SHE'S BRAIN DEAD.

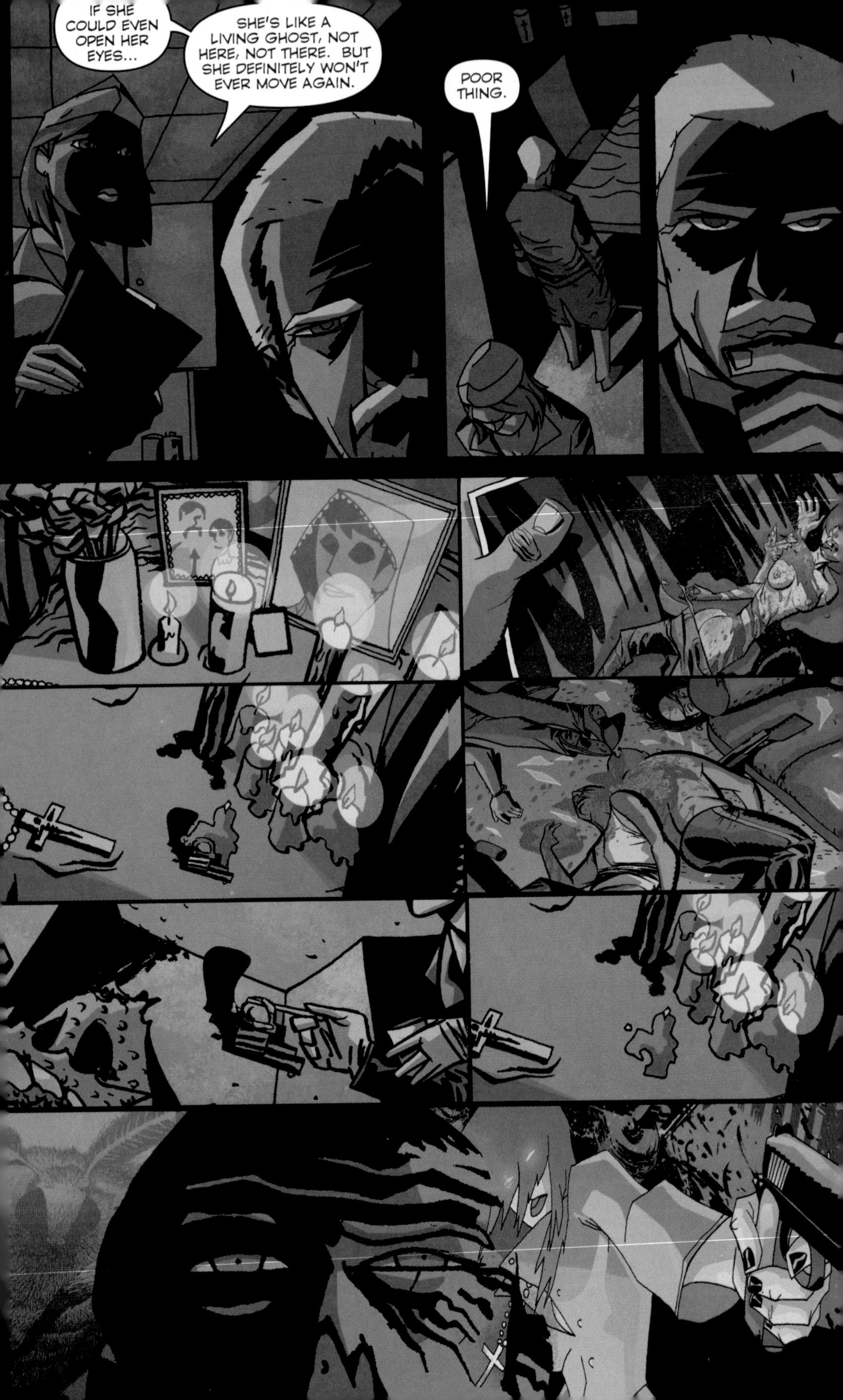
IF SHE COULD EVEN OPEN HER EYES...
SHE'S LIKE A LIVING GHOST, NOT HERE, NOT THERE. BUT SHE DEFINITELY WON'T EVER MOVE AGAIN.
POOR THING.

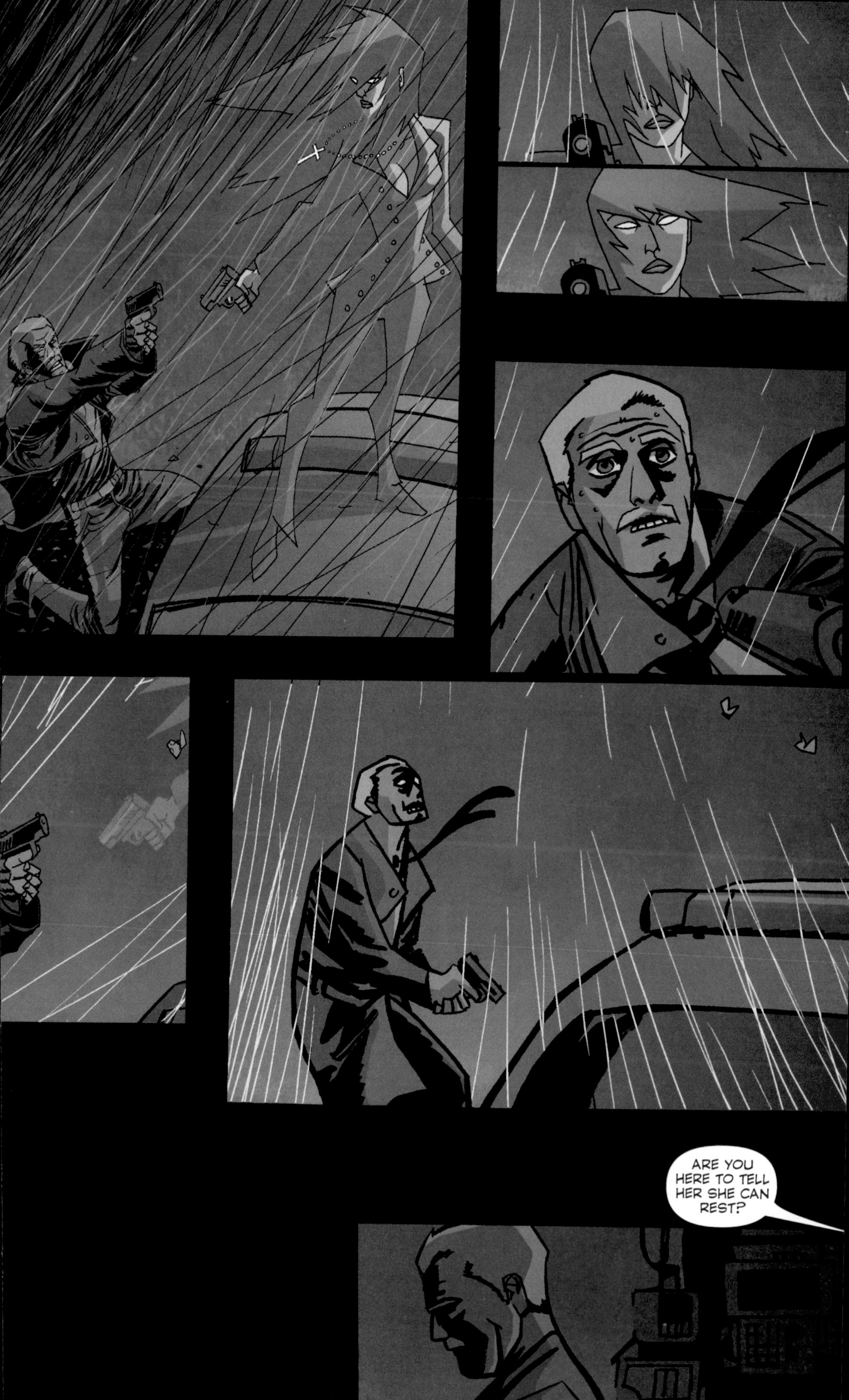
ARE YOU HERE TO TELL HER SHE CAN REST?

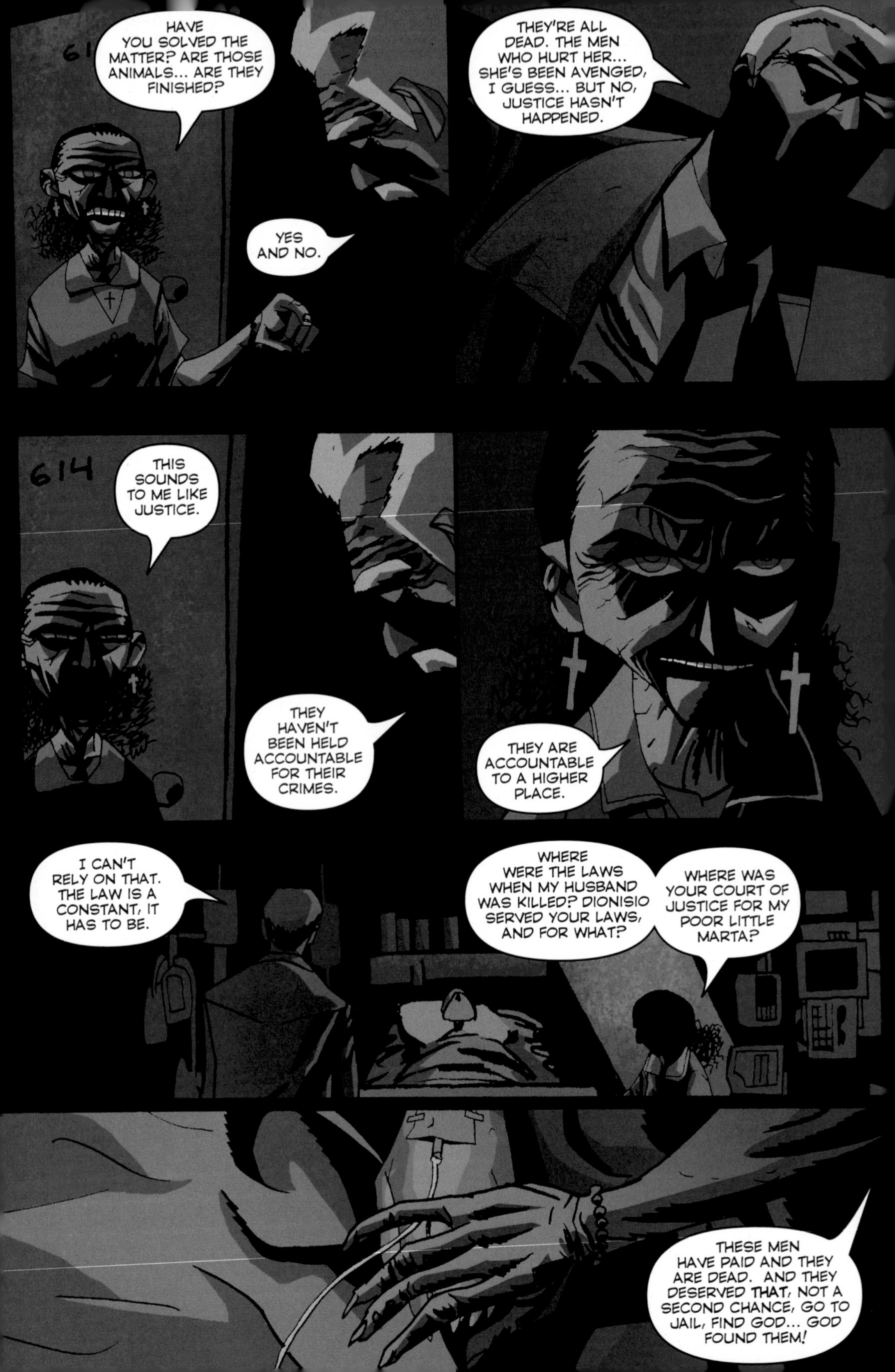
61
HAVE YOU SOLVED THE MATTER? ARE THOSE ANIMALS... ARE THEY FINISHED?
YES AND NO.
THEY'RE ALL DEAD. THE MEN WHO HURT HER... SHE'S BEEN AVENGED, I GUESS... BUT NO, JUSTICE HASN'T HAPPENED.
614
THIS SOUNDS TO ME LIKE JUSTICE.
THEY HAVEN'T BEEN HELD ACCOUNTABLE FOR THEIR CRIMES.
THEY ARE ACCOUNTABLE TO A HIGHER PLACE.
I CAN'T RELY ON THAT. THE LAW IS A CONSTANT, IT HAS TO BE.
WHERE WERE THE LAWS WHEN MY HUSBAND WAS KILLED? DIONISIO SERVED YOUR LAWS, AND FOR WHAT?
WHERE WAS YOUR COURT OF JUSTICE FOR MY POOR LITTLE MARTA?
THESE MEN HAVE PAID AND THEY ARE DEAD. AND THEY DESERVED THAT, NOT A SECOND CHANCE, GO TO JAIL, FIND GOD... GOD FOUND THEM!

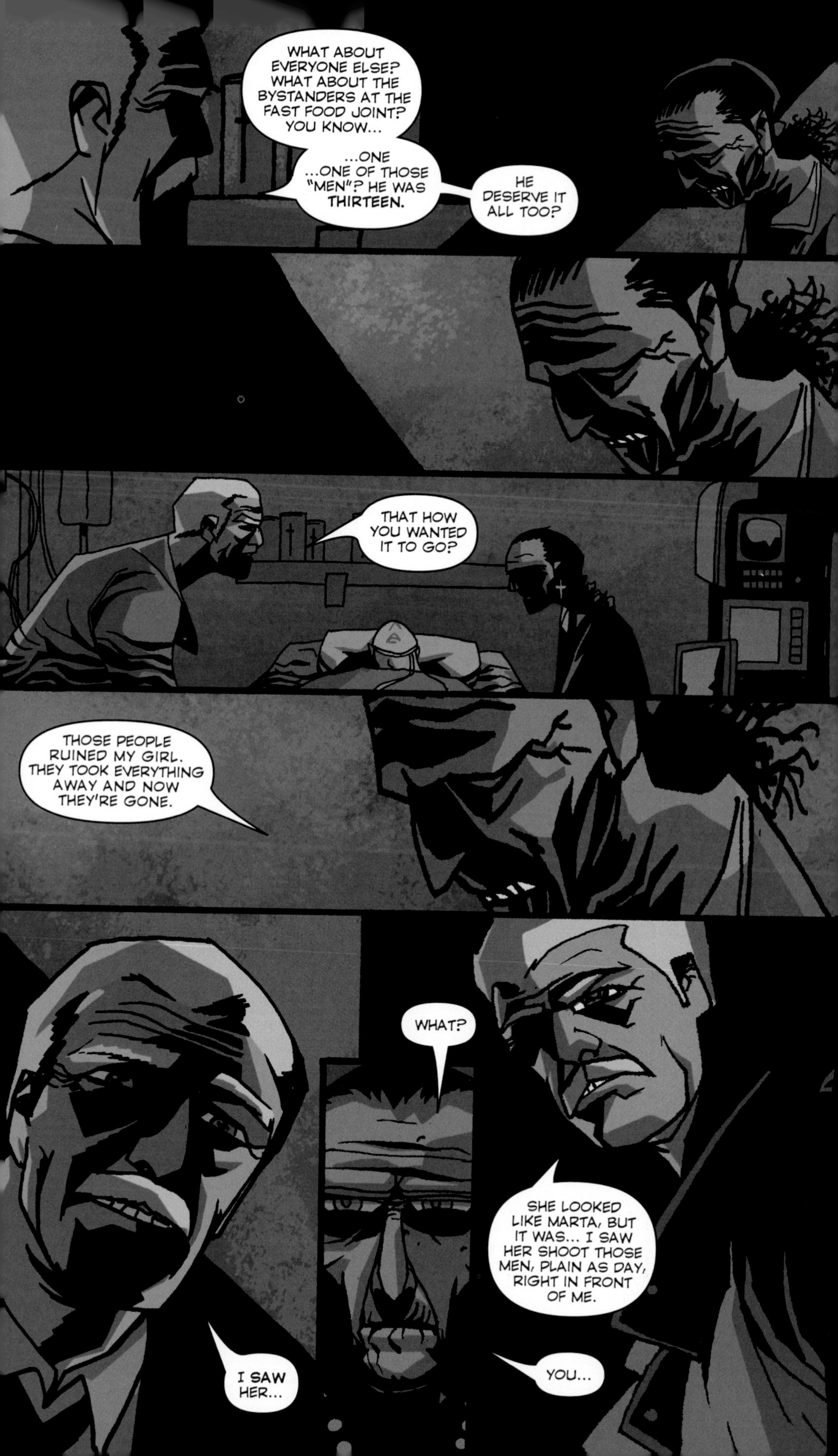
WHAT ABOUT EVERYONE ELSE? WHAT ABOUT THE BYSTANDERS AT THE FAST FOOD JOINT? YOU KNOW...
...ONE ...ONE OF THOSE "MEN"? HE WAS THIRTEEN.
HE DESERVE IT ALL TOO?
THAT HOW YOU WANTED IT TO GO?
THOSE PEOPLE RUINED MY GIRL. THEY TOOK EVERYTHING AWAY AND NOW THEY'RE GONE.
WHAT?
SHE LOOKED LIKE MARTA, BUT IT WAS... I SAW HER SHOOT THOSE MEN, PLAIN AS DAY, RIGHT IN FRONT OF ME.
I SAW HER...
YOU...

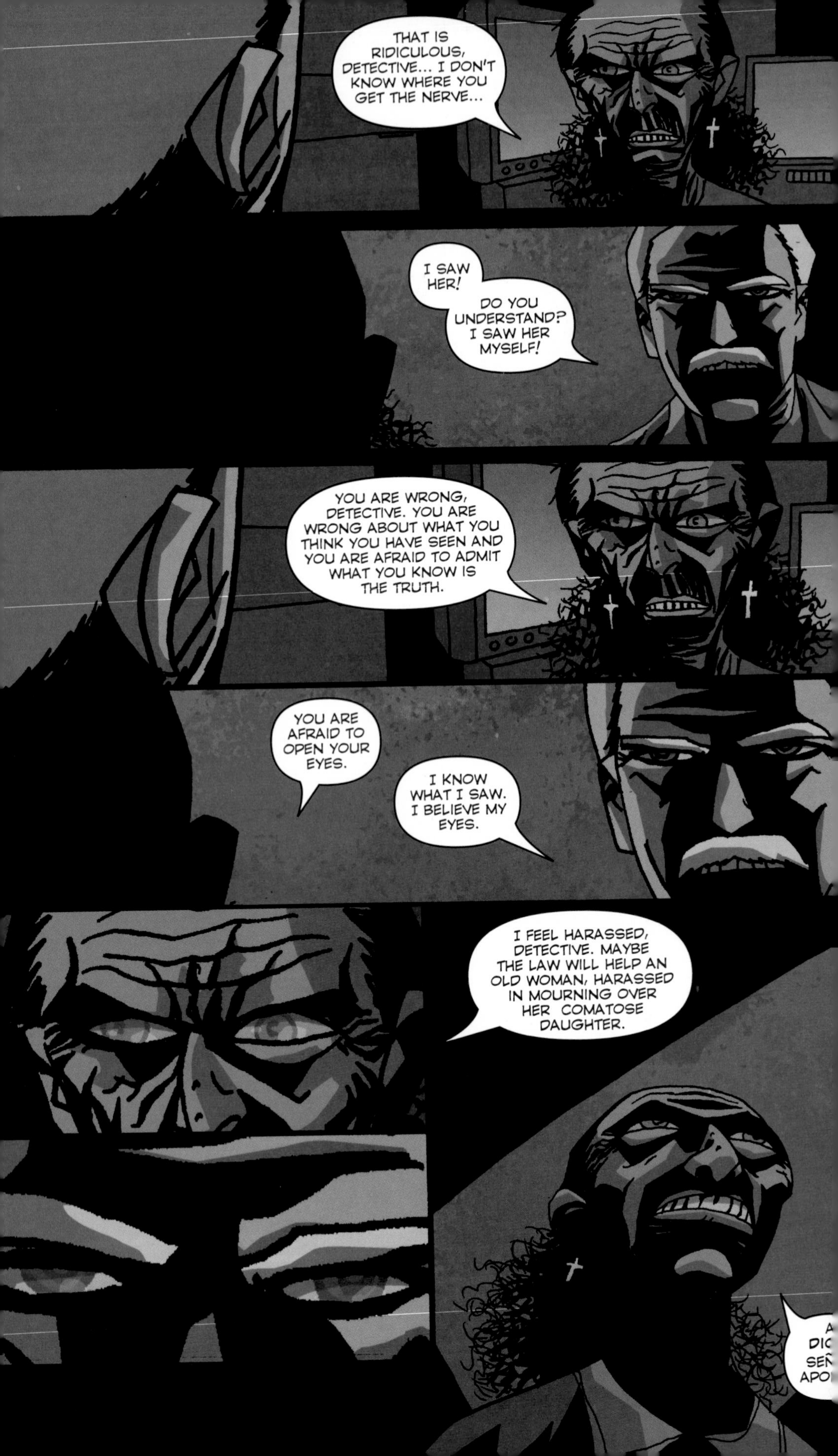
THAT IS RIDICULOUS, DETECTIVE... I DON'T KNOW WHERE YOU GET THE NERVE...
I SAW HER!
DO YOU UNDERSTAND? I SAW HER MYSELF!
YOU ARE WRONG, DETECTIVE. YOU ARE WRONG ABOUT WHAT YOU THINK YOU HAVE SEEN AND YOU ARE AFRAID TO ADMIT WHAT YOU KNOW IS THE TRUTH.
YOU ARE AFRAID TO OPEN YOUR EYES.
I KNOW WHAT I SAW. I BELIEVE MY EYES.
I FEEL HARASSED, DETECTIVE. MAYBE THE LAW WILL HELP AN OLD WOMAN, HARASSED IN MOURNING OVER HER COMATOSE DAUGHTER.

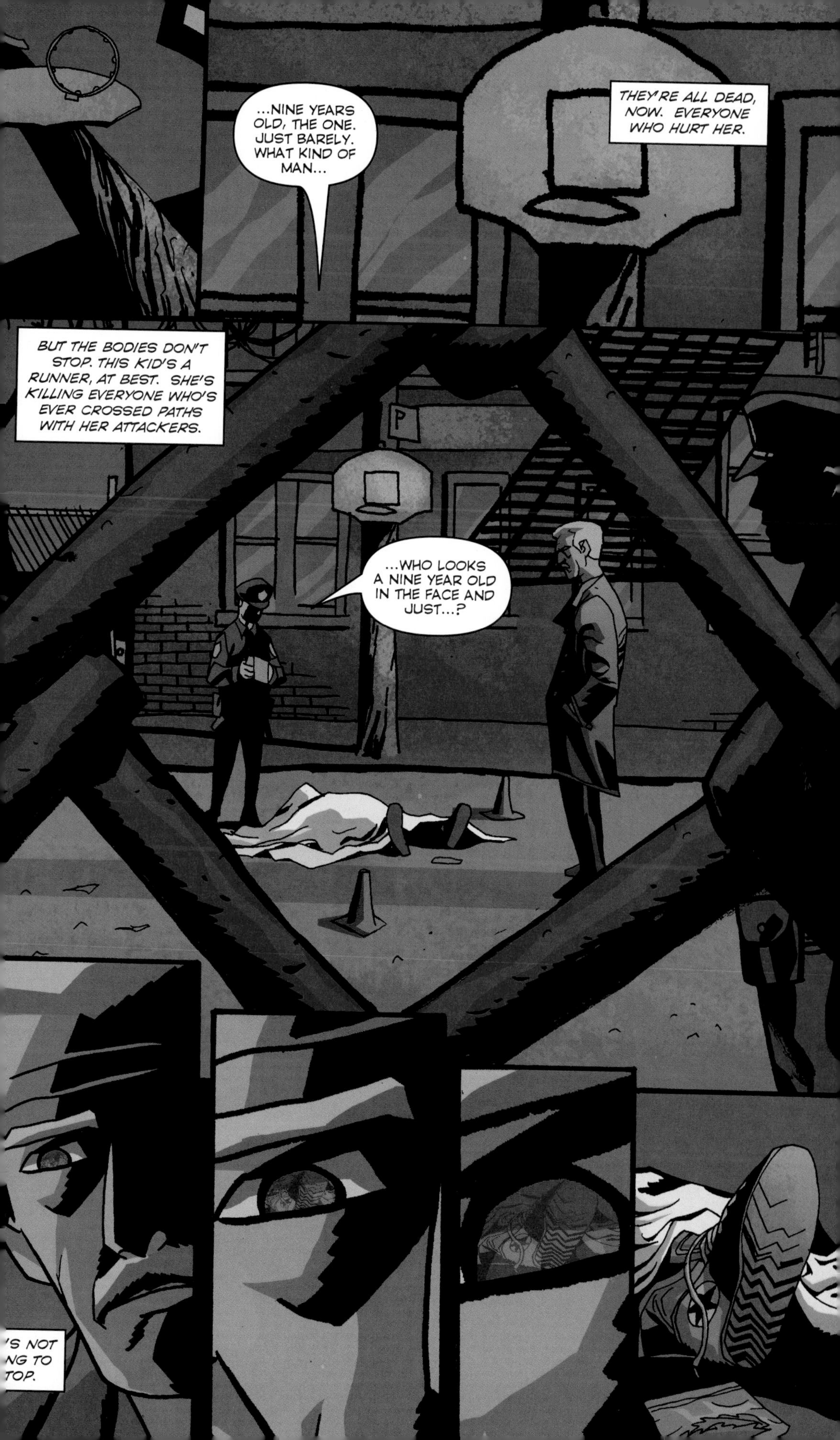
...NINE YEARS OLD, THE ONE. JUST BARELY. WHAT KIND OF MAN...
THEY'RE ALL DEAD, NOW. EVERYONE WHO HURT HER.
BUT THE BODIES DON'T STOP. THIS KID'S A RUNNER, AT BEST. SHE'S KILLING EVERYONE WHO'S EVER CROSSED PATHS WITH HER ATTACKERS.
P
...WHO LOOKS A NINE YEAR OLD IN THE FACE AND JUST...?
'S NOT NG TO TOP.

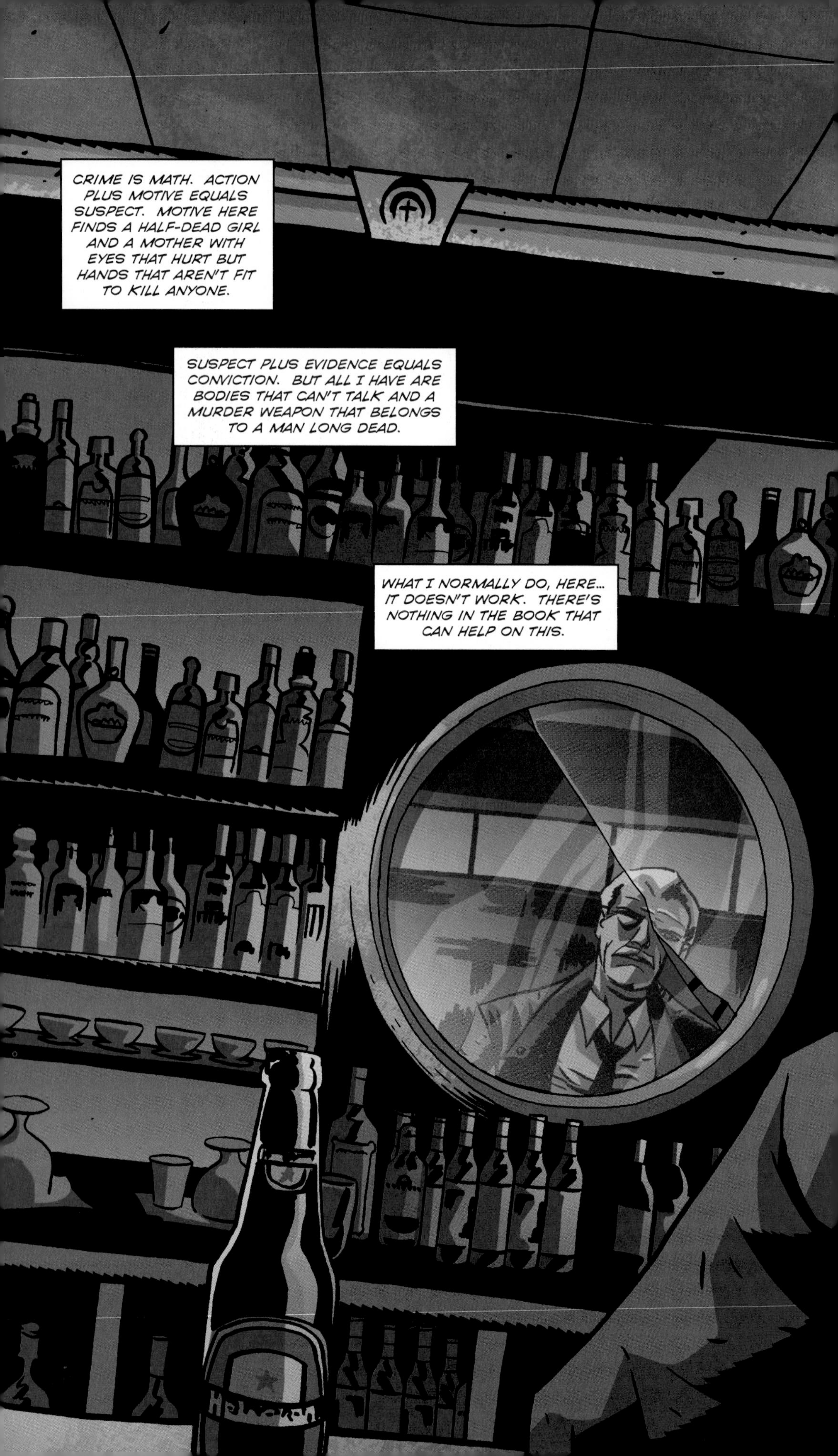
CRIME IS MATH. ACTION PLUS MOTIVE EQUALS SUSPECT. MOTIVE HERE FINDS A HALF-DEAD GIRL AND A MOTHER WITH EYES THAT HURT BUT HANDS THAT AREN'T FIT TO KILL ANYONE.
SUSPECT PLUS EVIDENCE EQUALS CONVICTION. BUT ALL I HAVE ARE BODIES THAT CAN'T TALK AND A MURDER WEAPON THAT BELONGS TO A MAN LONG DEAD.
WHAT I NORMALLY DO, HERE... IT DOESN'T WORK. THERE'S NOTHING IN THE BOOK THAT CAN HELP ON THIS.

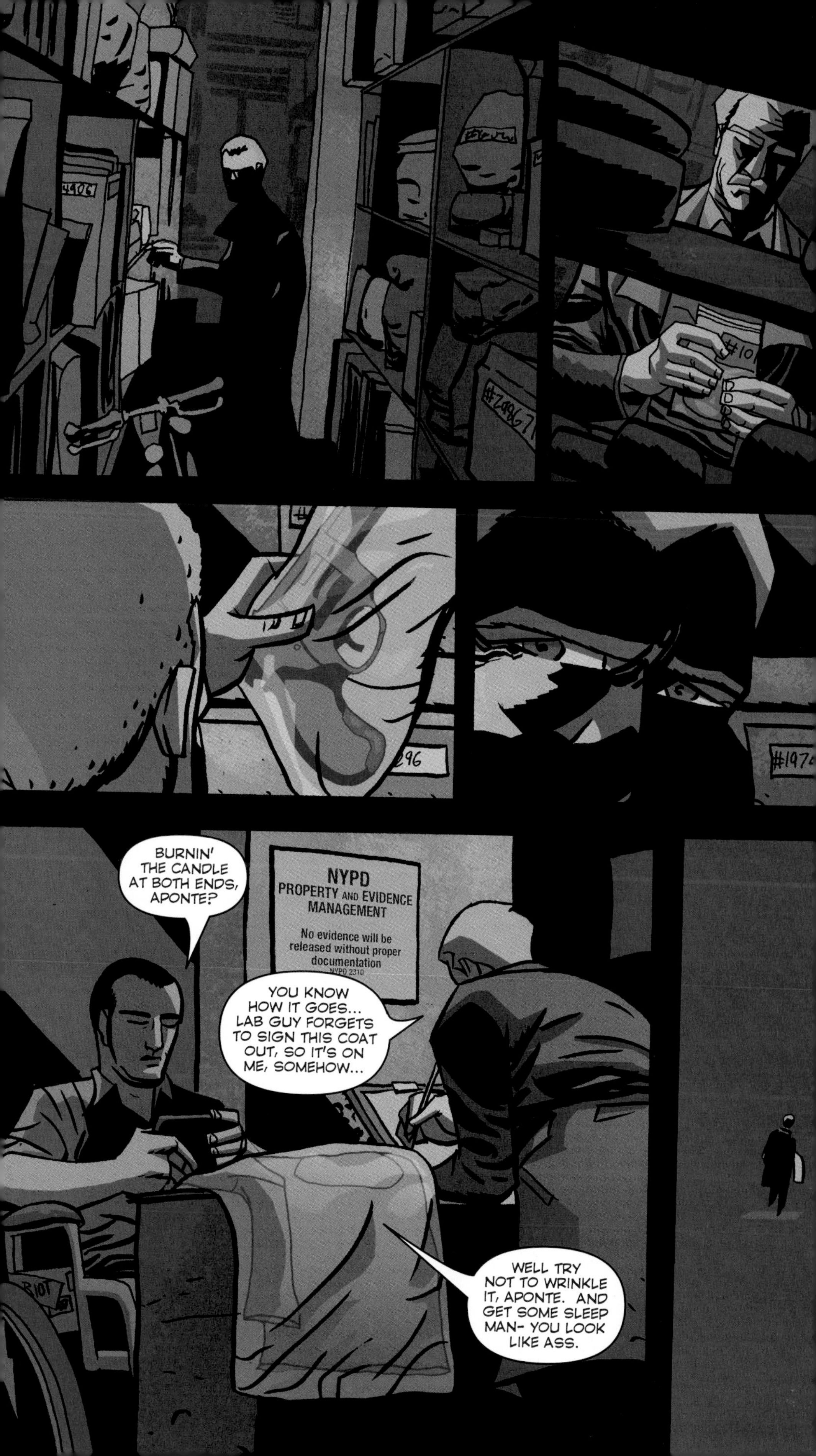
BURNIN' THE CANDLE AT BOTH ENDS, APONTE?
NYPD
PROPERTY AND EVIDENCE MANAGEMENT
No evidence will be released without proper documentation
NYPD 2310
YOU KNOW HOW IT GOES... LAB GUY FORGETS TO SIGN THIS COAT OUT, SO IT'S ON ME, SOMEHOW...
WELL TRY NOT TO WRINKLE IT, APONTE. AND GET SOME SLEEP MAN- YOU LOOK LIKE ASS.

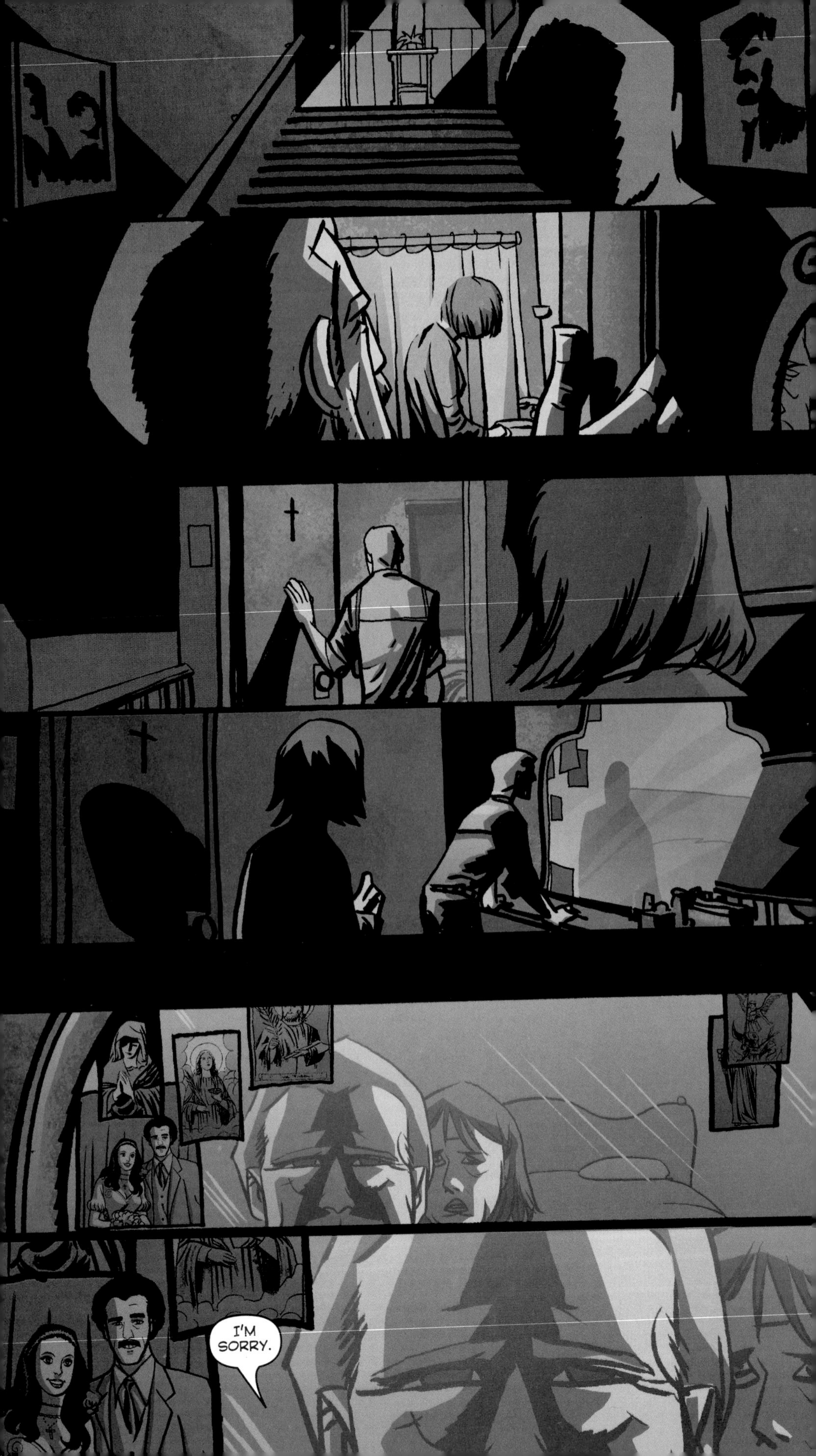
I'M SORRY.

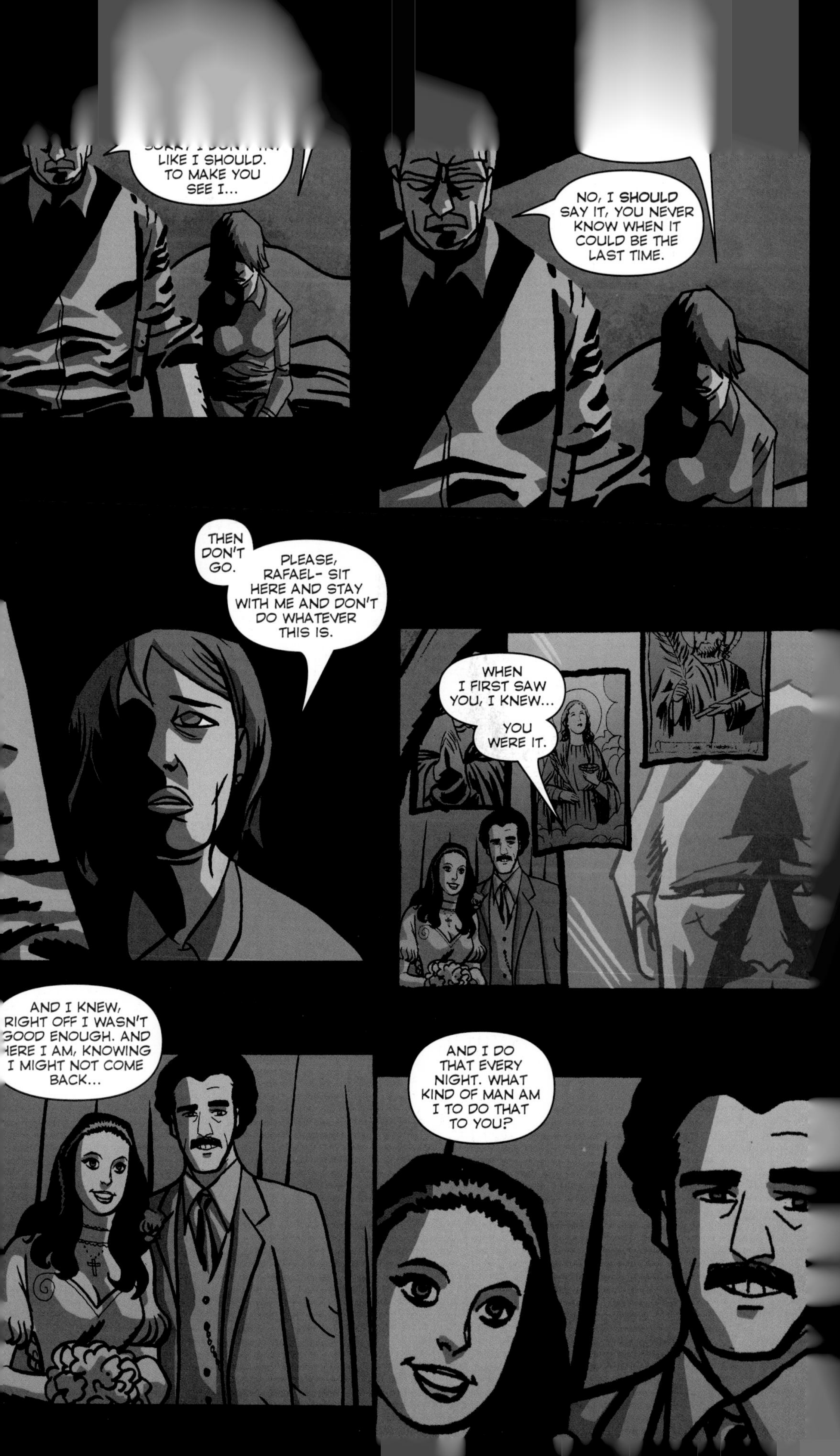

LIKE I SHOULD. TO MAKE YOU SEE I...
NO, I SHOULD SAY IT, YOU NEVER KNOW WHEN IT COULD BE THE LAST TIME.
THEN DON'T GO.
PLEASE, RAFAEL- SIT HERE AND STAY WITH ME AND DON'T DO WHATEVER THIS IS.
WHEN I FIRST SAW YOU, I KNEW...
YOU WERE IT.
AND I KNEW, RIGHT OFF I WASN'T GOOD ENOUGH. AND HERE I AM, KNOWING I MIGHT NOT COME BACK...
AND I DO THAT EVERY NIGHT. WHAT KIND OF MAN AM I TO DO THAT TO YOU?

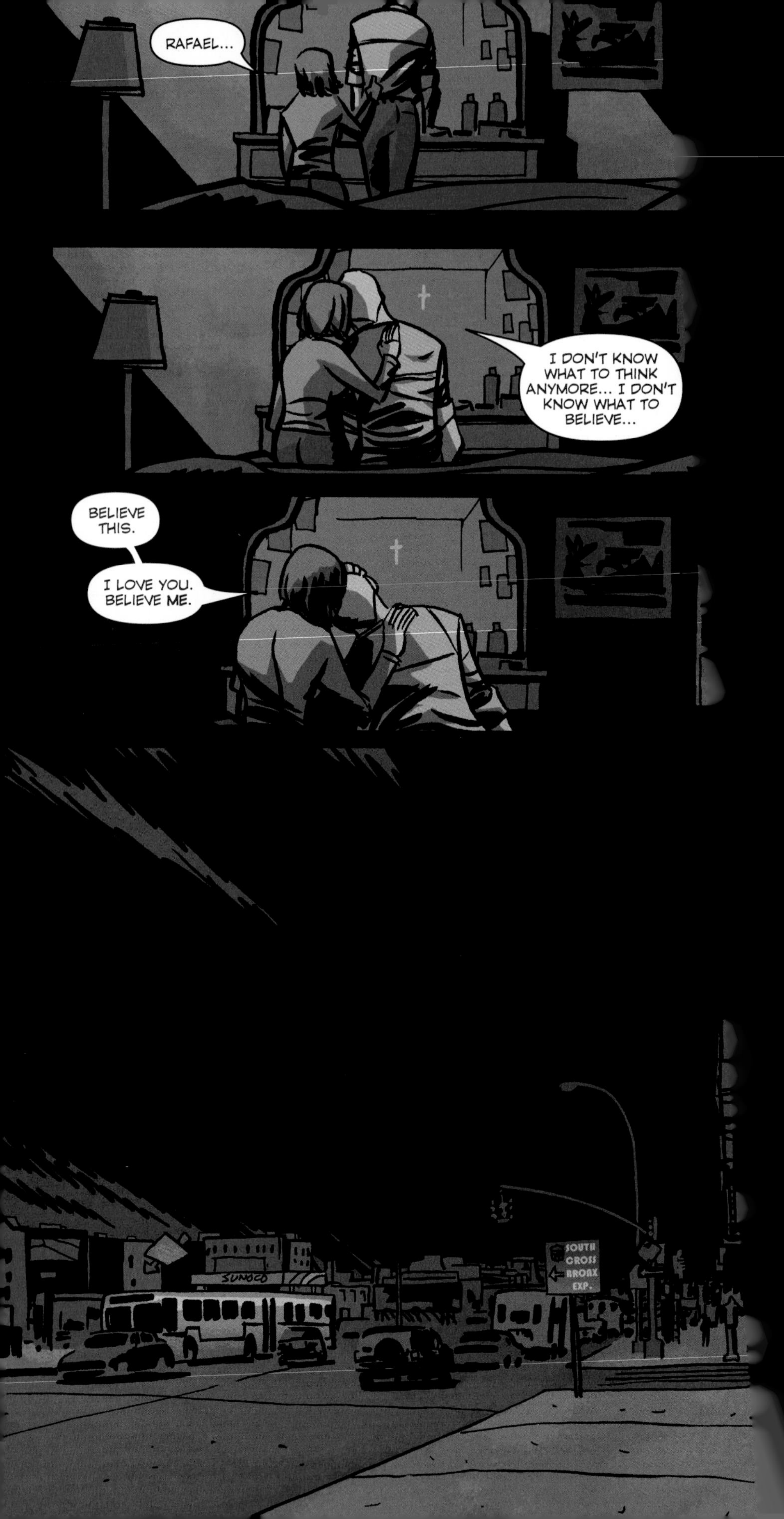
RAFAEL...
I DON'T KNOW WHAT TO THINK ANYMORE... I DON'T KNOW WHAT TO BELIEVE...
BELIEVE THIS.
I LOVE YOU. BELIEVE ME.
SUNOCO
SOUTH CROSS BRONX EXP.

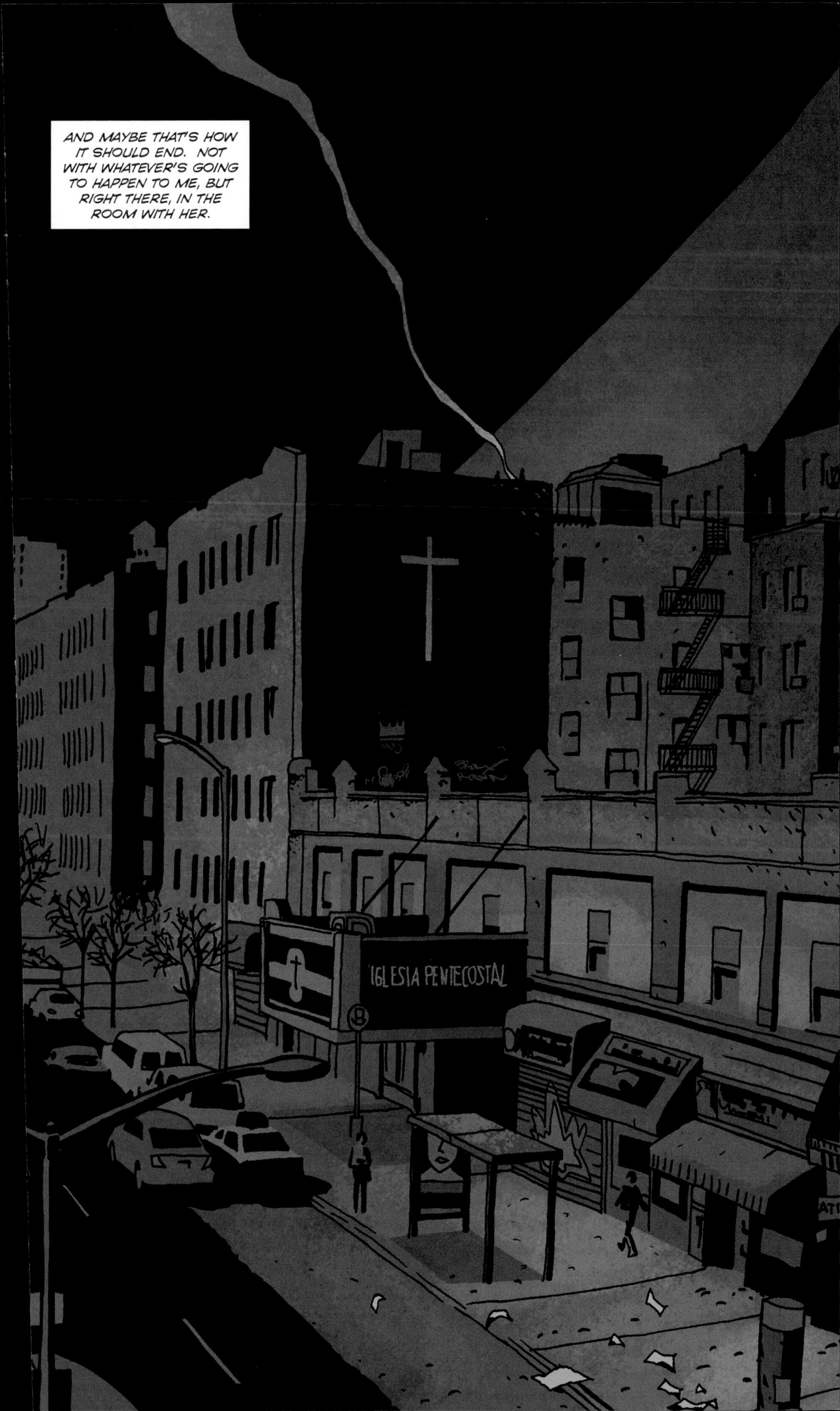
AND MAYBE THAT'S HOW IT SHOULD END. NOT WITH WHATEVER'S GOING TO HAPPEN TO ME, BUT RIGHT THERE, IN THE ROOM WITH HER.
IGLESIA PENTECOSTAL

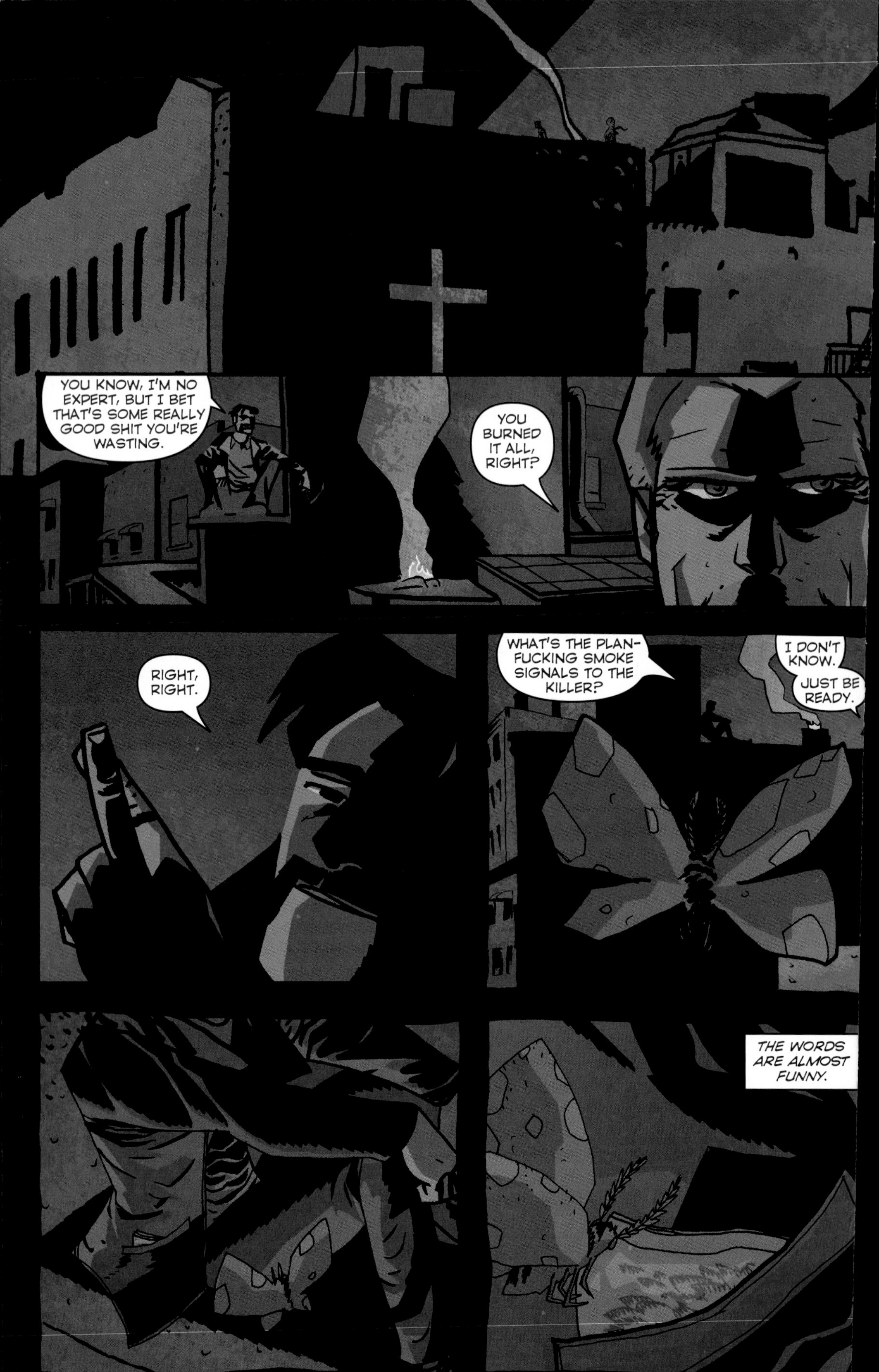
YOU KNOW, I'M NO EXPERT, BUT I BET THAT'S SOME REALLY GOOD SHIT YOU'RE WASTING.
YOU BURNED IT ALL, RIGHT?
RIGHT, RIGHT.
WHAT'S THE PLAN-FUCKING SMOKE SIGNALS TO THE KILLER?
I DON'T KNOW.
JUST BE READY.
THE WORDS ARE ALMOST FUNNY.

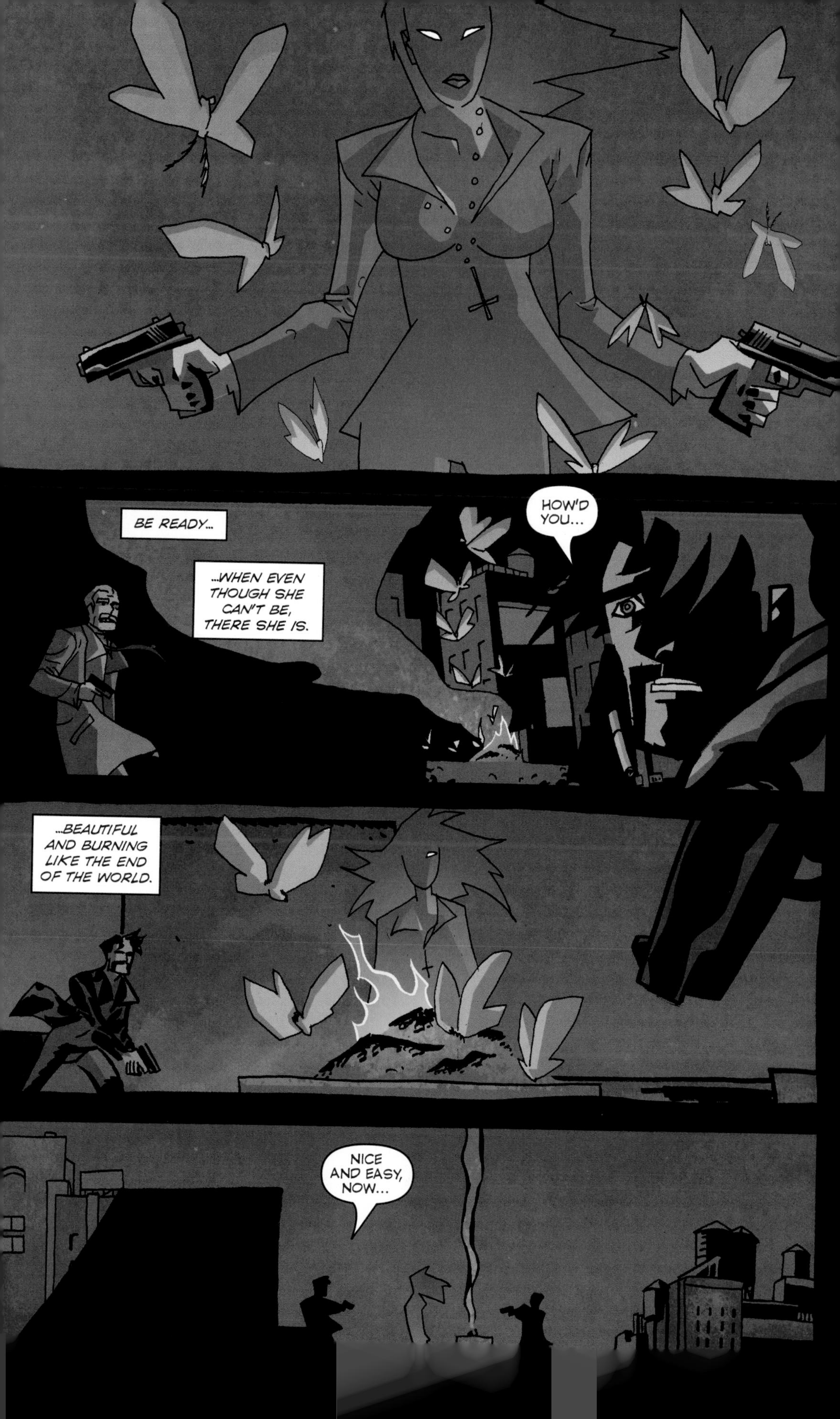
BE READY...
...WHEN EVEN THOUGH SHE CAN'T BE, THERE SHE IS.
HOW'D YOU...
...BEAUTIFUL AND BURNING LIKE THE END OF THE WORLD.
NICE AND EASY, NOW...

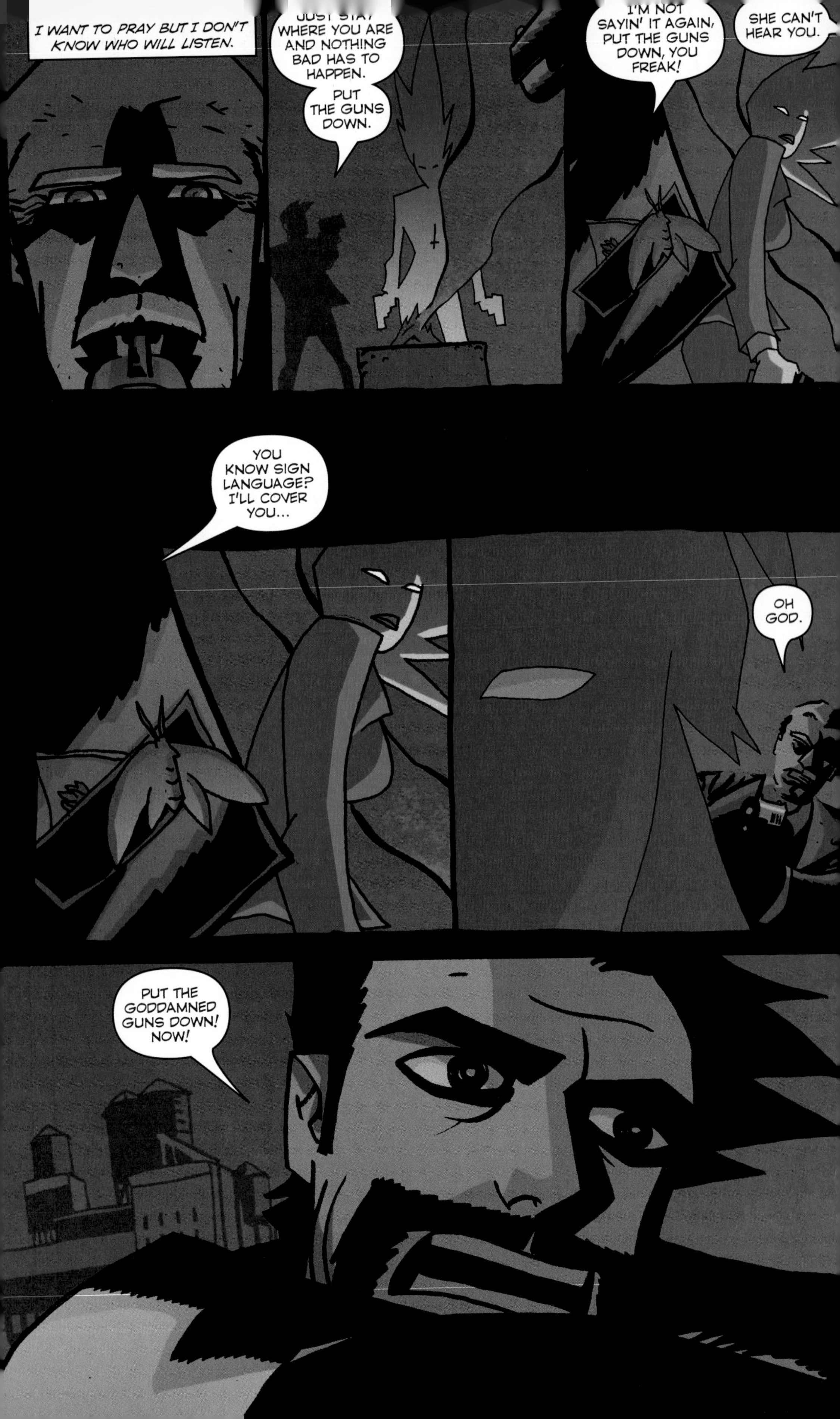
I WANT TO PRAY BUT I DON'T KNOW WHO WILL LISTEN.
WHERE YOU ARE AND NOTHING BAD HAS TO HAPPEN.
PUT THE GUNS DOWN.
I'M NOT SAYIN' IT AGAIN, PUT THE GUNS DOWN, YOU FREAK!
SHE CAN'T HEAR YOU.
YOU KNOW SIGN LANGUAGE? I'LL COVER YOU...
OH GOD.
PUT THE GODDAMNED GUNS DOWN! NOW!

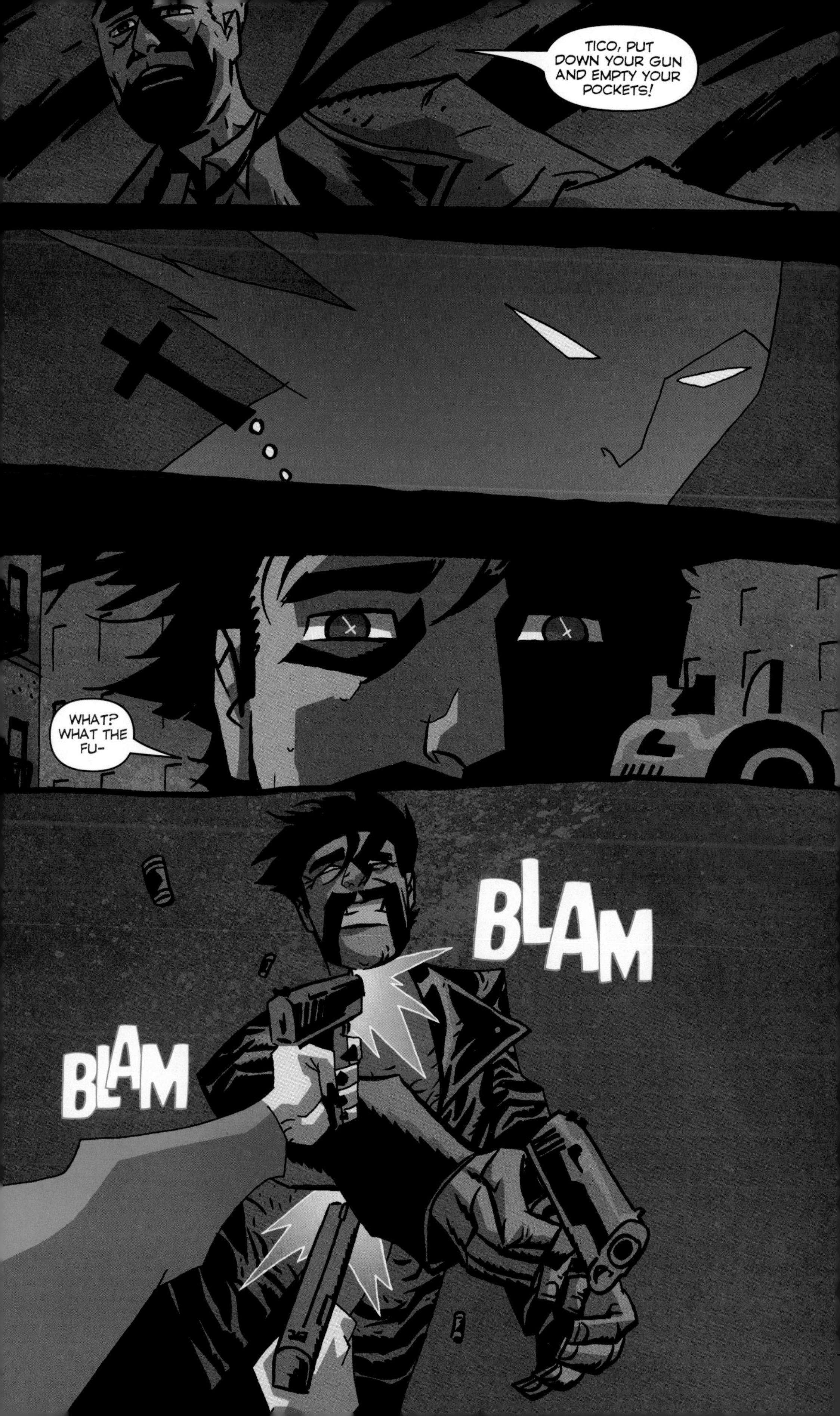
TICO, PUT DOWN YOUR GUN AND EMPTY YOUR POCKETS!
WHAT? WHAT THE FU-
BLAM
BLAM

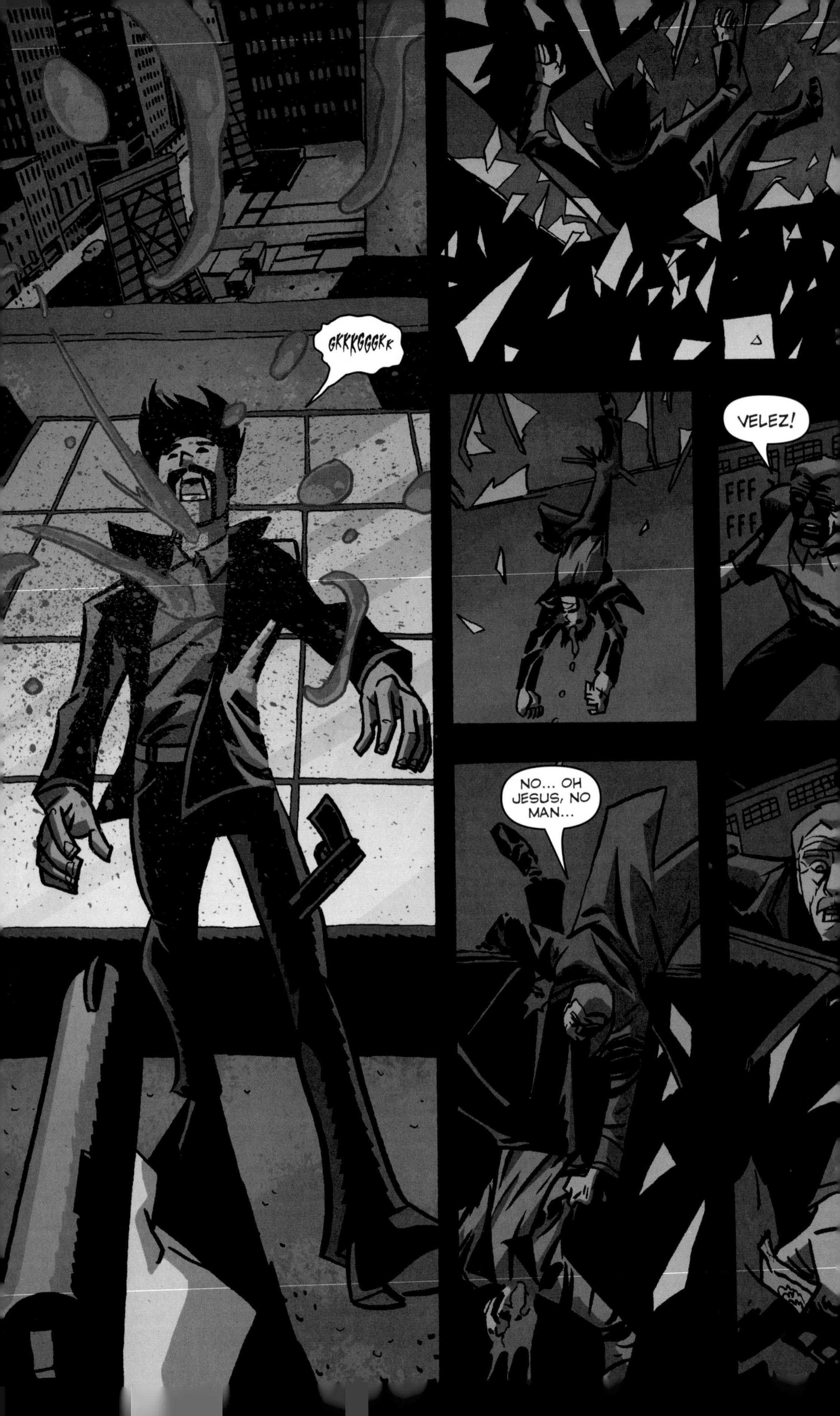
GKKKGGGKK
VELEZ!
NO... OH JESUS, NO MAN...

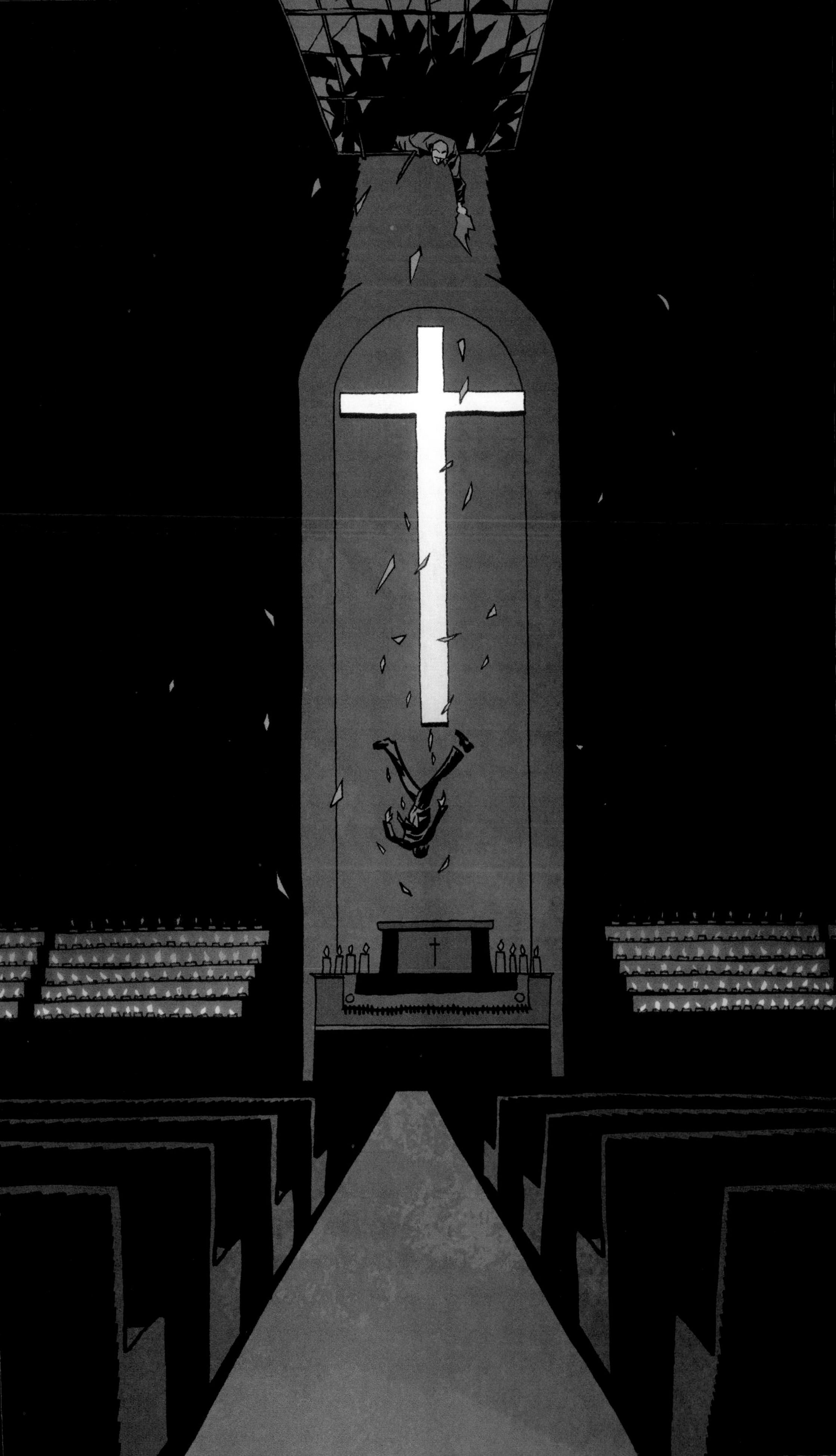

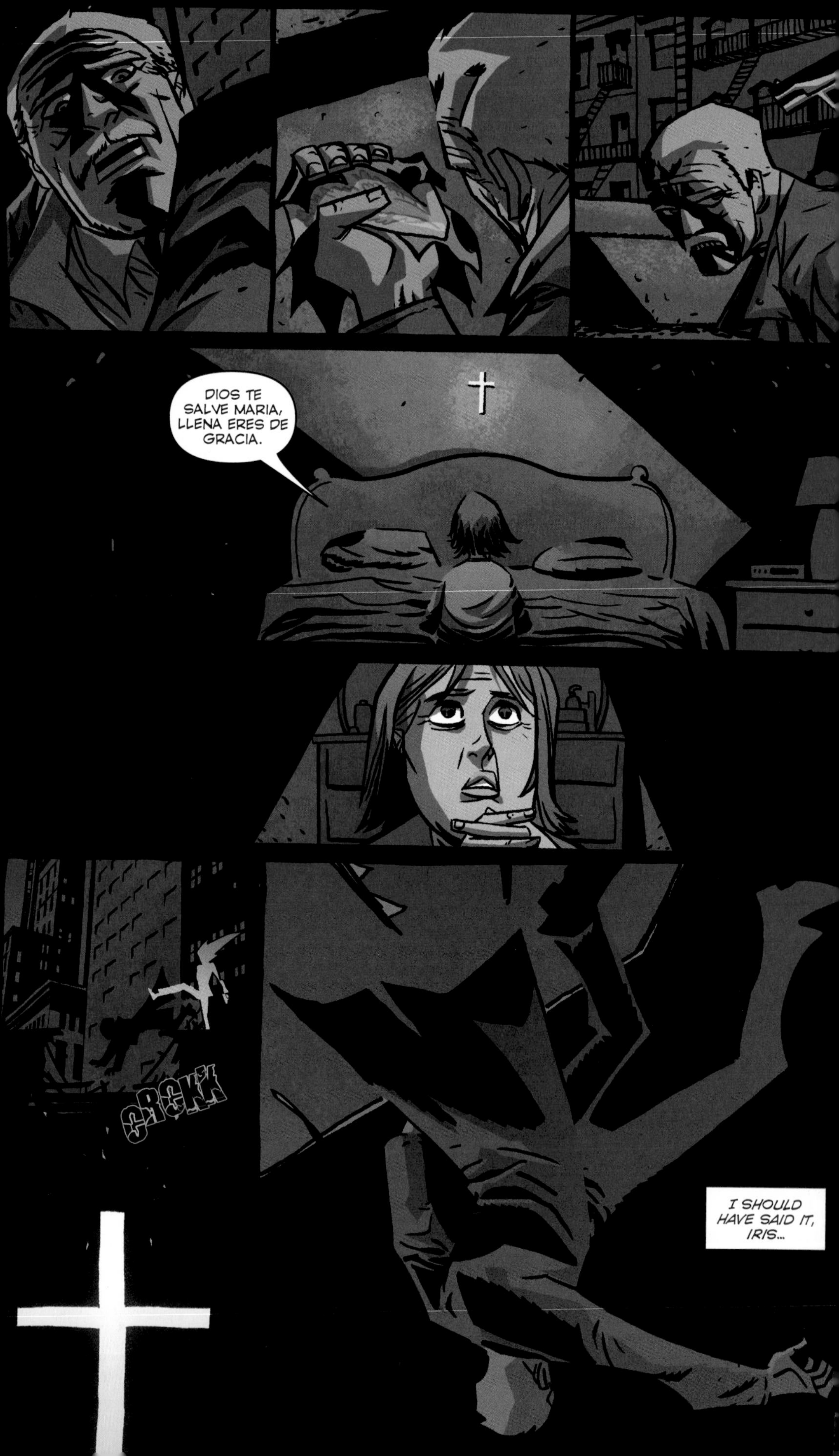
DIOS TE SALVE MARIA, LLENA ERES DE GRACIA.
CRCKK
I SHOULD HAVE SAID IT, IRIS...

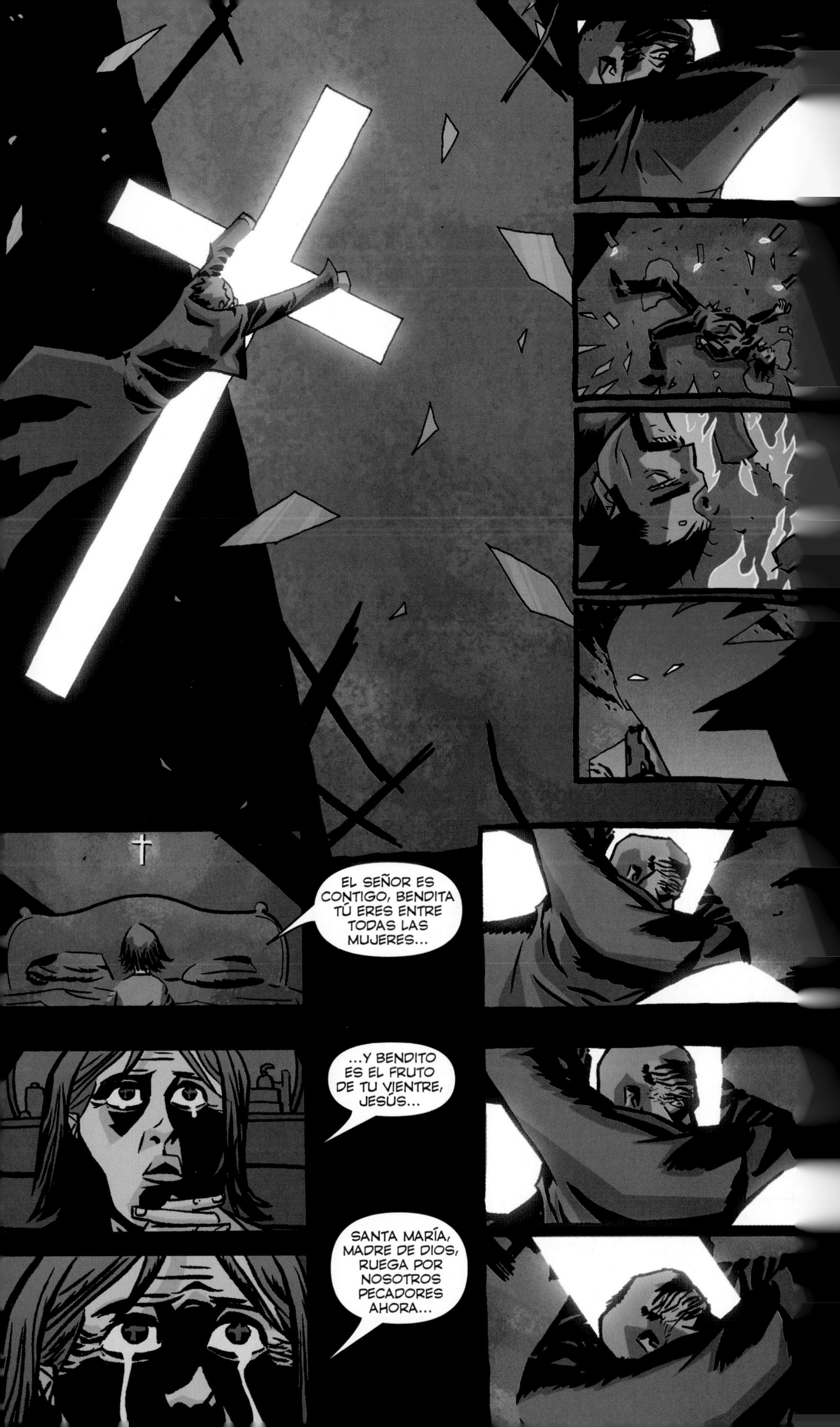
EL SEÑOR ES CONTIGO, BENDITA TÚ ERES ENTRE TODAS LAS MUJERES...
...Y BENDITO ES EL FRUTO DE TU VIENTRE, JESÚS...
SANTA MARÍA, MADRE DE DIOS, RUEGA POR NOSOTROS PECADORES AHORA...

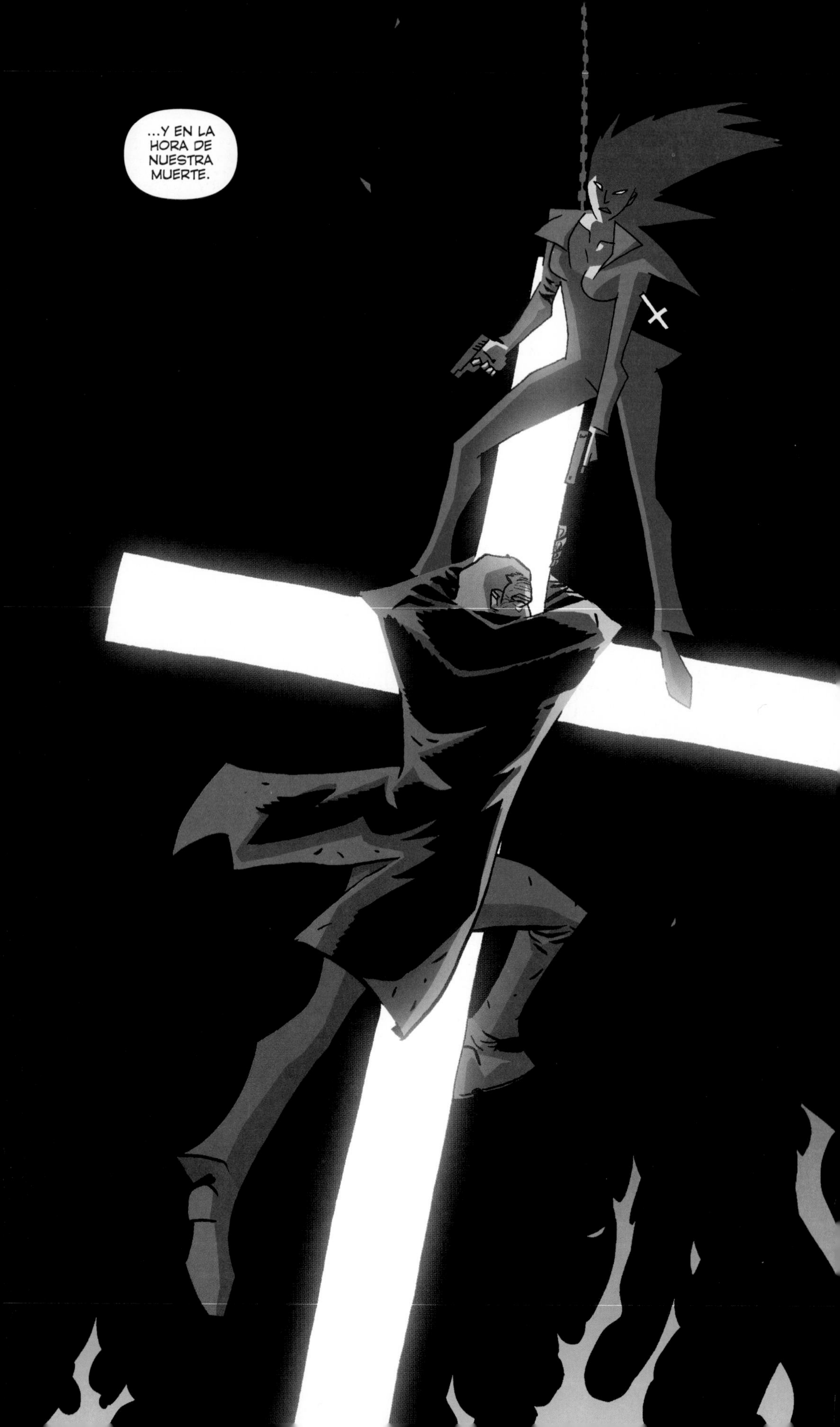
...Y EN LA HORA DE NUESTRA MUERTE.

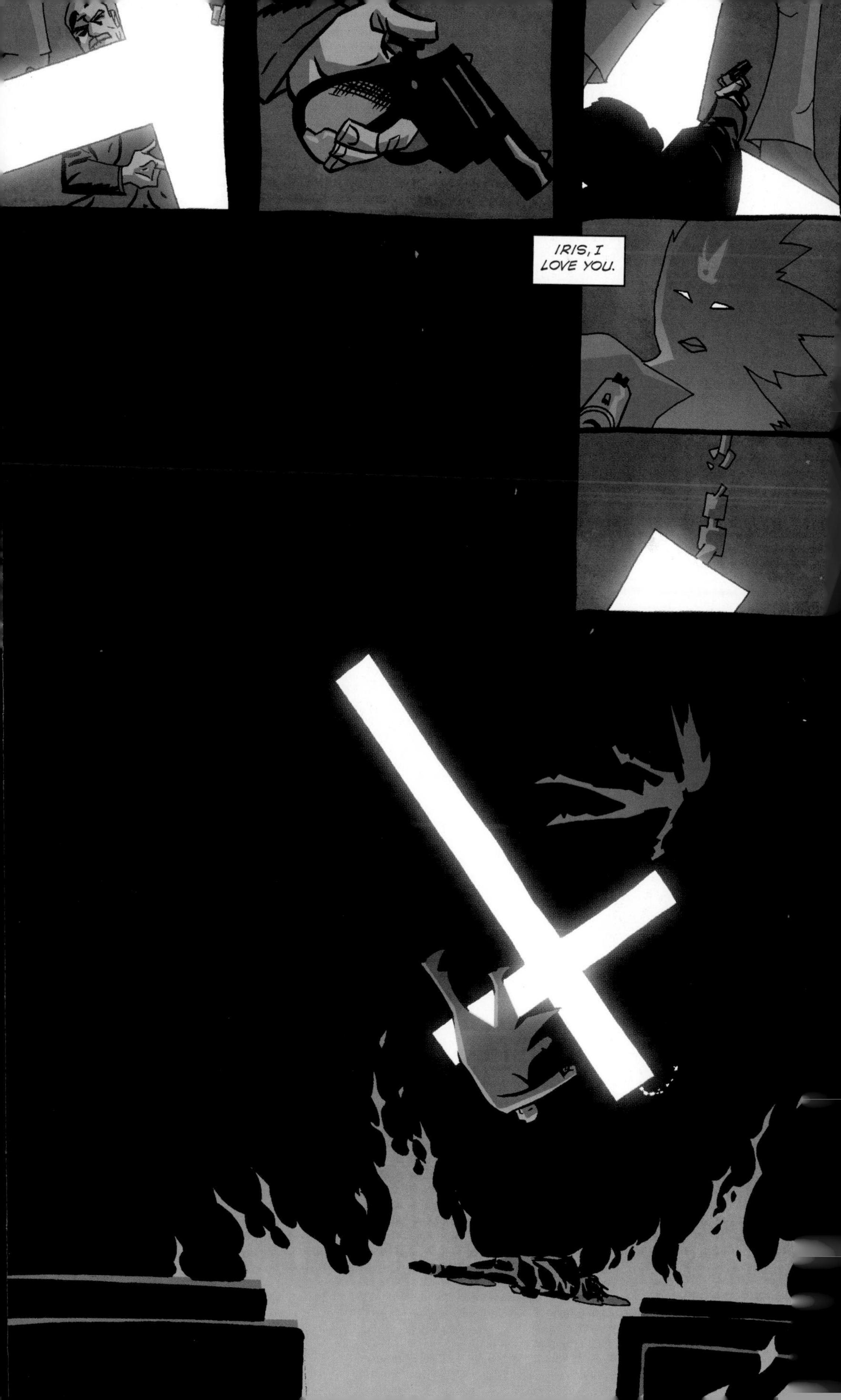
IRIS, I LOVE YOU.

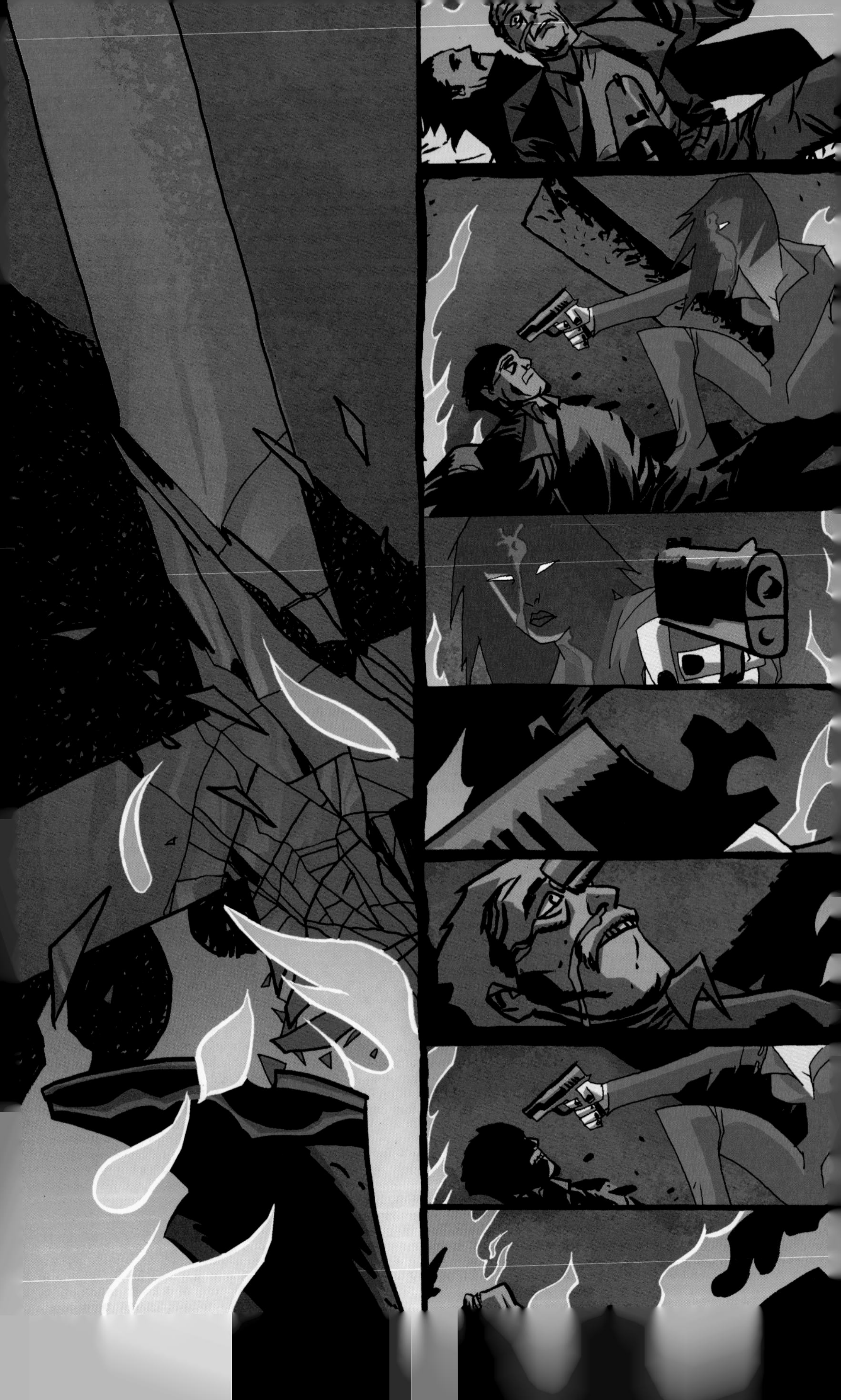

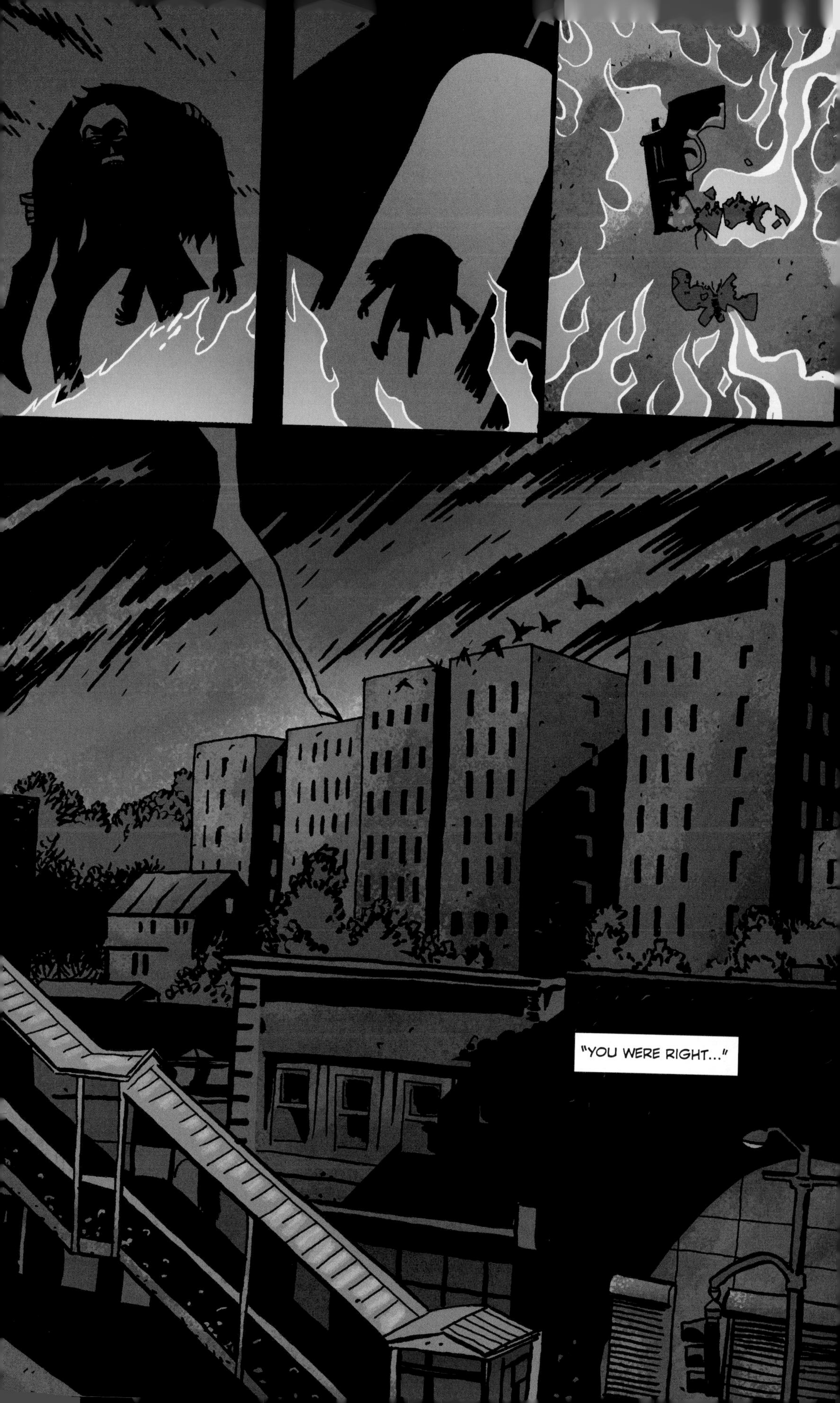
"YOU WERE RIGHT..."

"...I DON'T BELIEVE EVEN MY EYES, ANYMORE... I DON'T KNOW WHAT I BELIEVE."

"TELL ME WHAT HAPPENED TO ME."

"WHEN SHE APPEARED BEFORE ME, LIKE AN ANGEL... I KNEW HER SPIRIT WAS GONE FROM HER BODY..."

"SHE DID WHAT YOUR PEO[...] COULD NOT, SHE ENDED TH[...] THAT HURT HER."

ONE LAST ACT OF EARTHLY JUSTICE, ROSA; AND THEN WE'RE DONE.

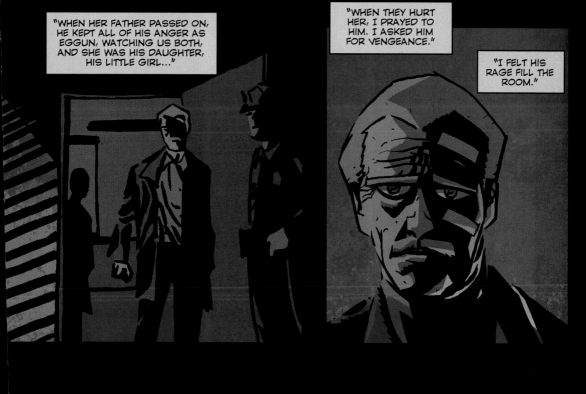

"WHEN HER FATHER PASSED ON, HE KEPT ALL OF HIS ANGER AS EGGUN, WATCHING US BOTH, AND SHE WAS HIS DAUGHTER, HIS LITTLE GIRL..."

"WHEN THEY HURT HER, I PRAYED TO HIM. I ASKED HIM FOR VENGEANCE."

"I FELT HIS RAGE FILL THE ROOM."

"BUT THEN SHE WOULDN'T STOP. THOSE CHILDREN... SHE JUST WOULDN'T STOP..."

"I HAD TO STOP IT. I HAD TO LET HER GO."

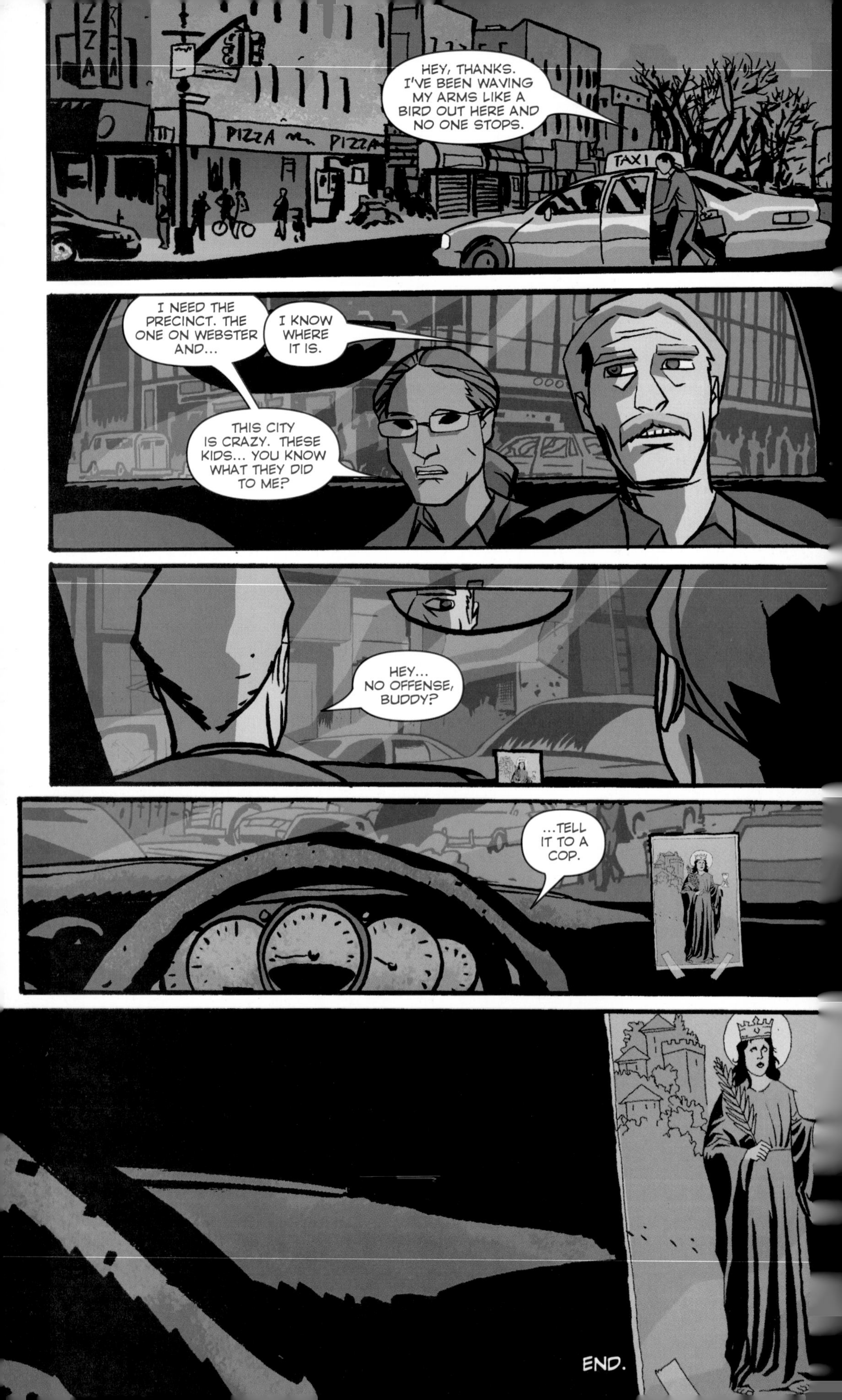
PIZZA
PIZZA
PIZZA
HEY, THANKS. I'VE BEEN WAVING MY ARMS LIKE A BIRD OUT HERE AND NO ONE STOPS.
TAXI
I NEED THE PRECINCT. THE ONE ON WEBSTER AND...
I KNOW WHERE IT IS.
THIS CITY IS CRAZY. THESE KIDS... YOU KNOW WHAT THEY DID TO ME?
HEY... NO OFFENSE, BUDDY?
...TELL IT TO A COP.
END.

COVERS
ORIGINAL SERIES
MICHAEL AVON OEMING

CROSS BRONX
TAXI

1

CROSS BRONX

2

CROSS BRONX

3

CROSS BRONX

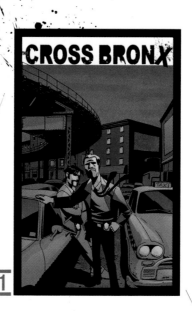

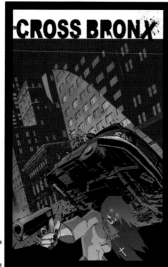

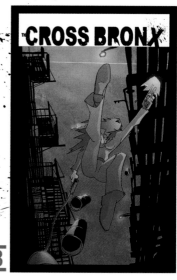

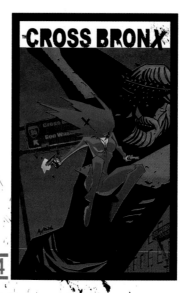

4

COVERS
VARIANTS

1
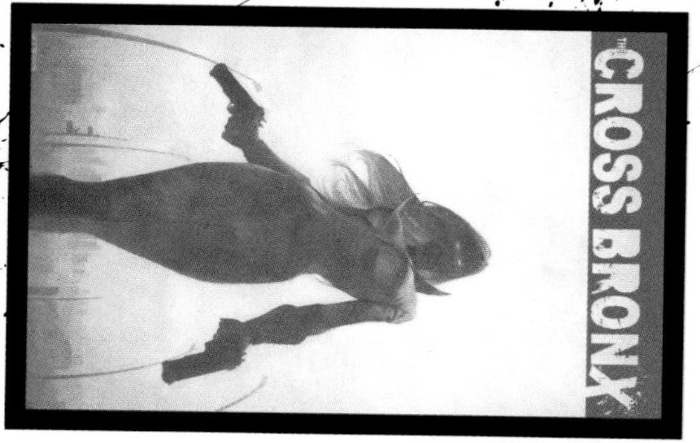
THE CROSS BRONX
ESAD RIBIC

2
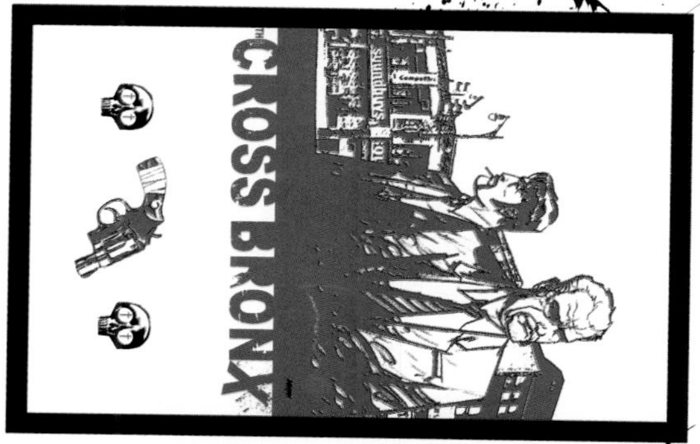
THE CROSS BRONX
DAVE JOHNSON

3
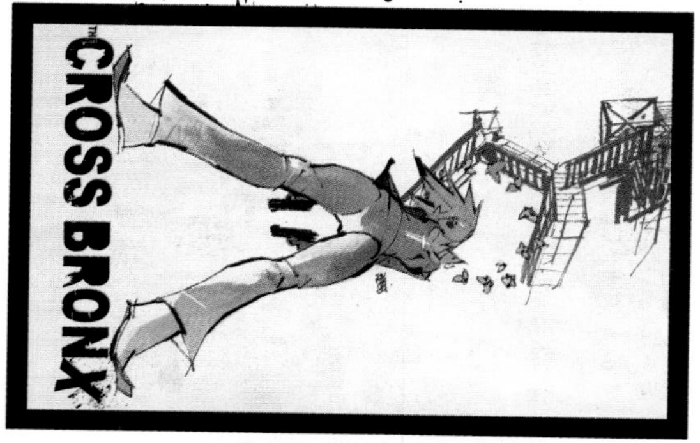
THE CROSS BRONX
ASHLEY WOOD

4
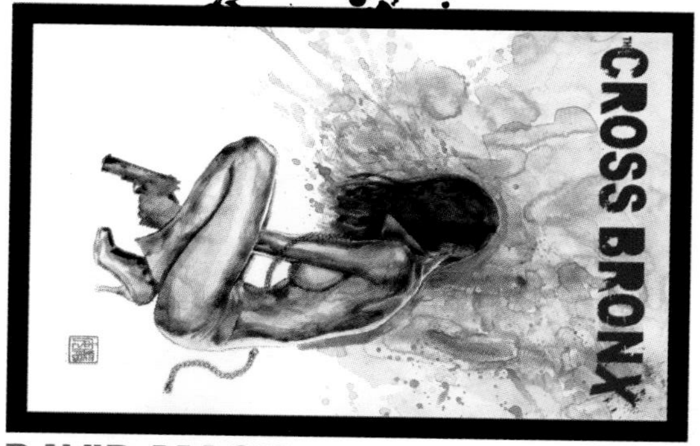
THE CROSS BRONX
DAVID MACK

HE CROSS BRONX

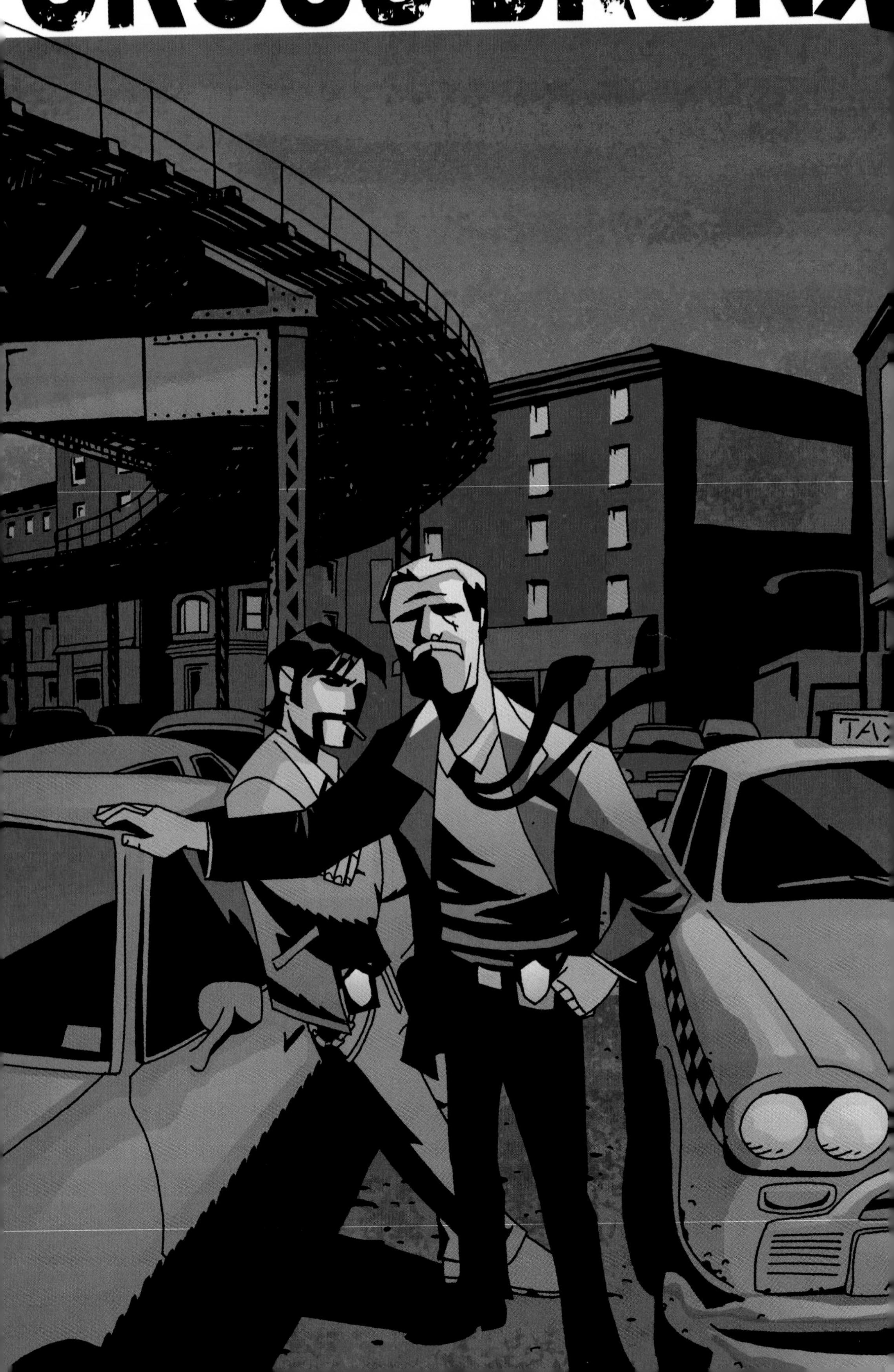

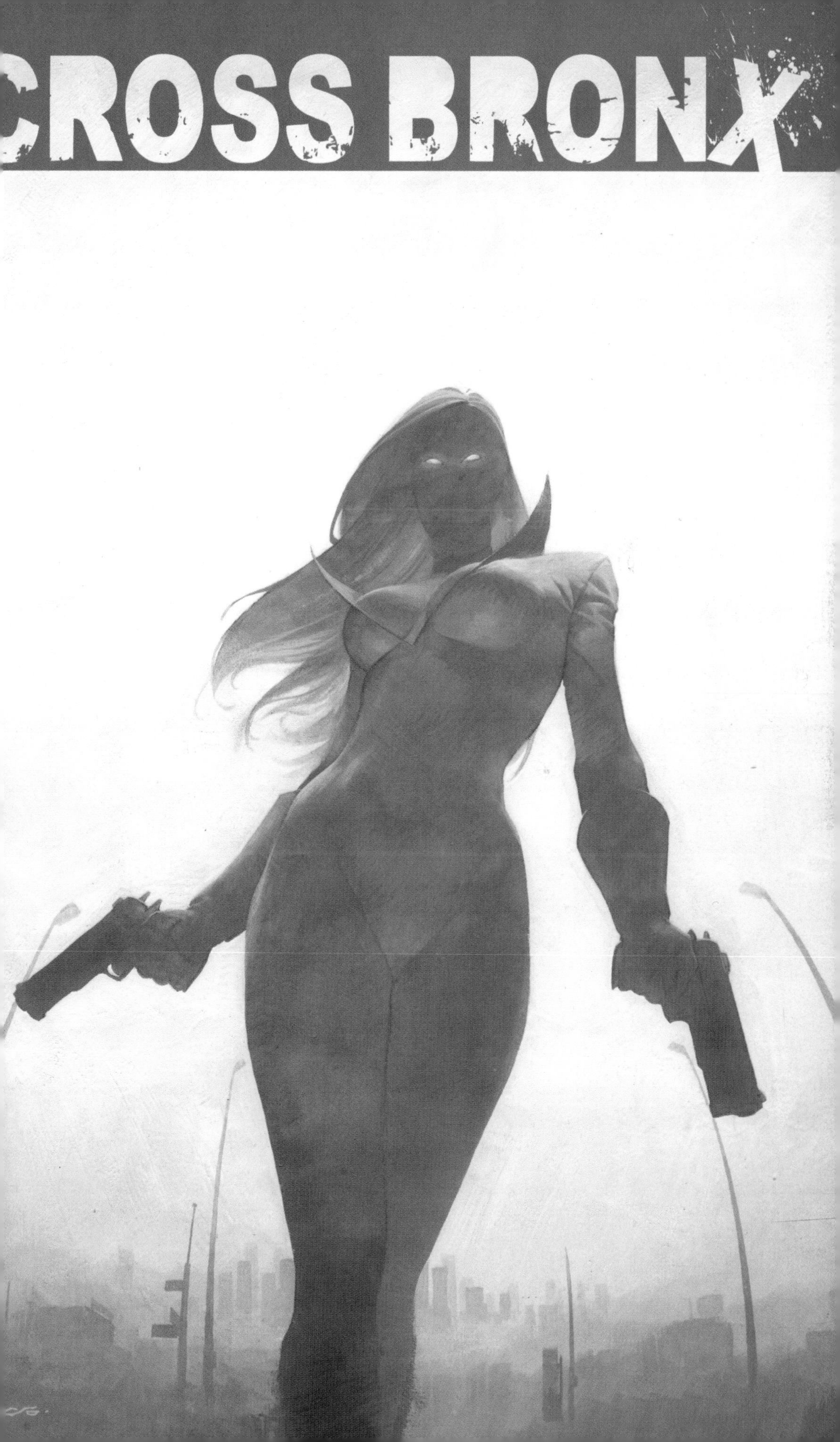
CROSS BRONX

THE CROSS BRONX

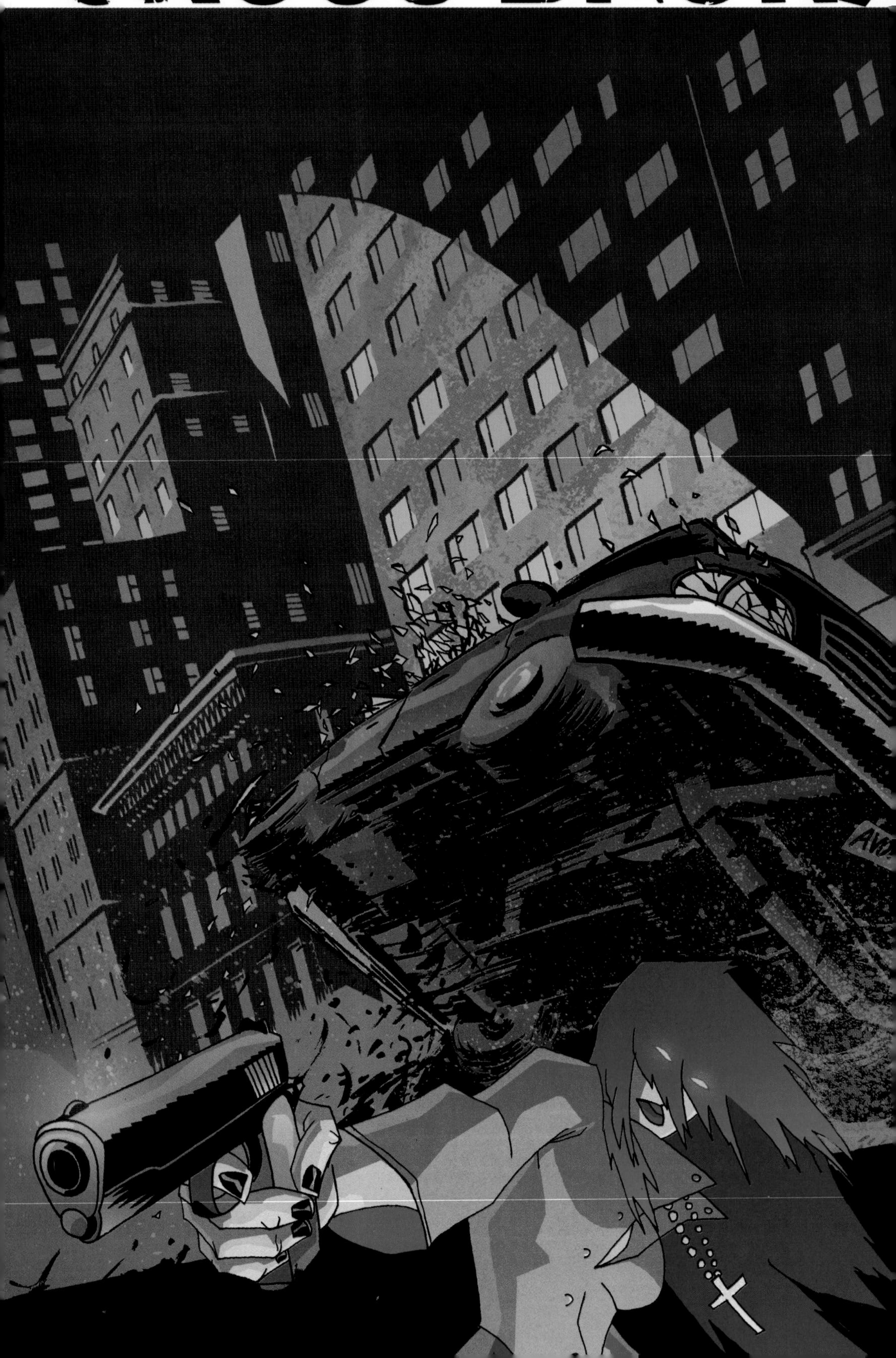

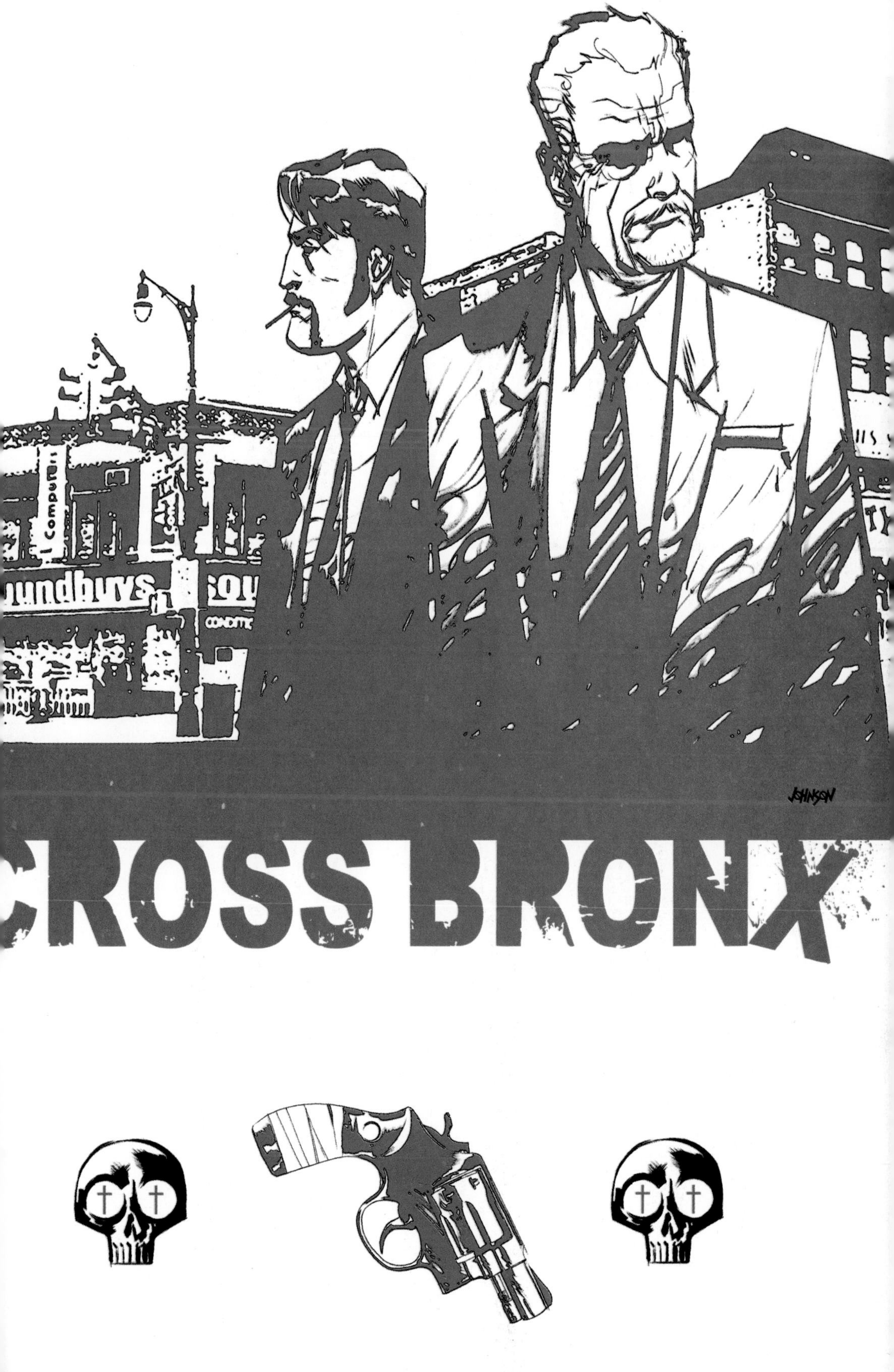
JOHNSON
CROSS BRONX

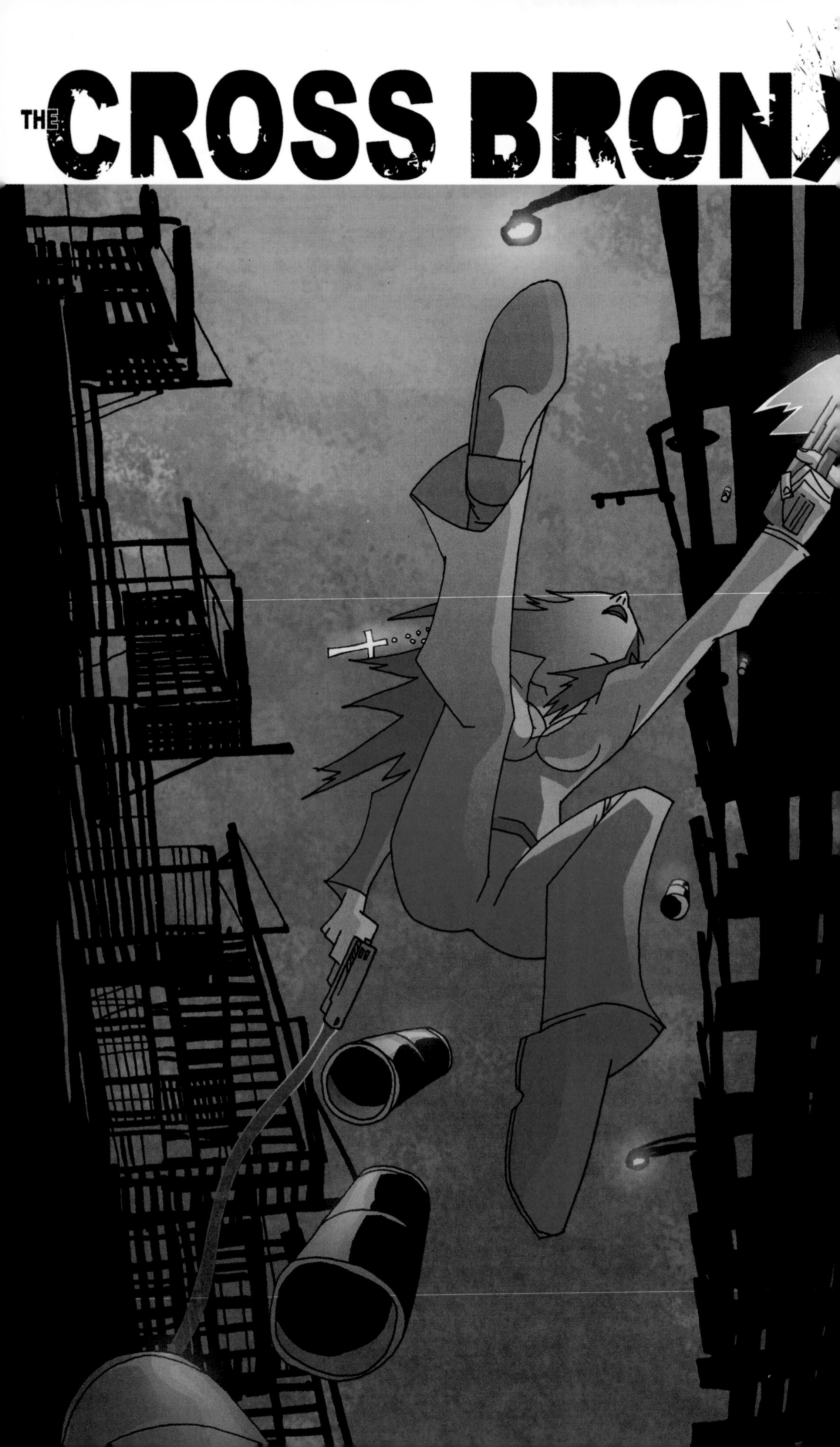
THE CROSS BRONX

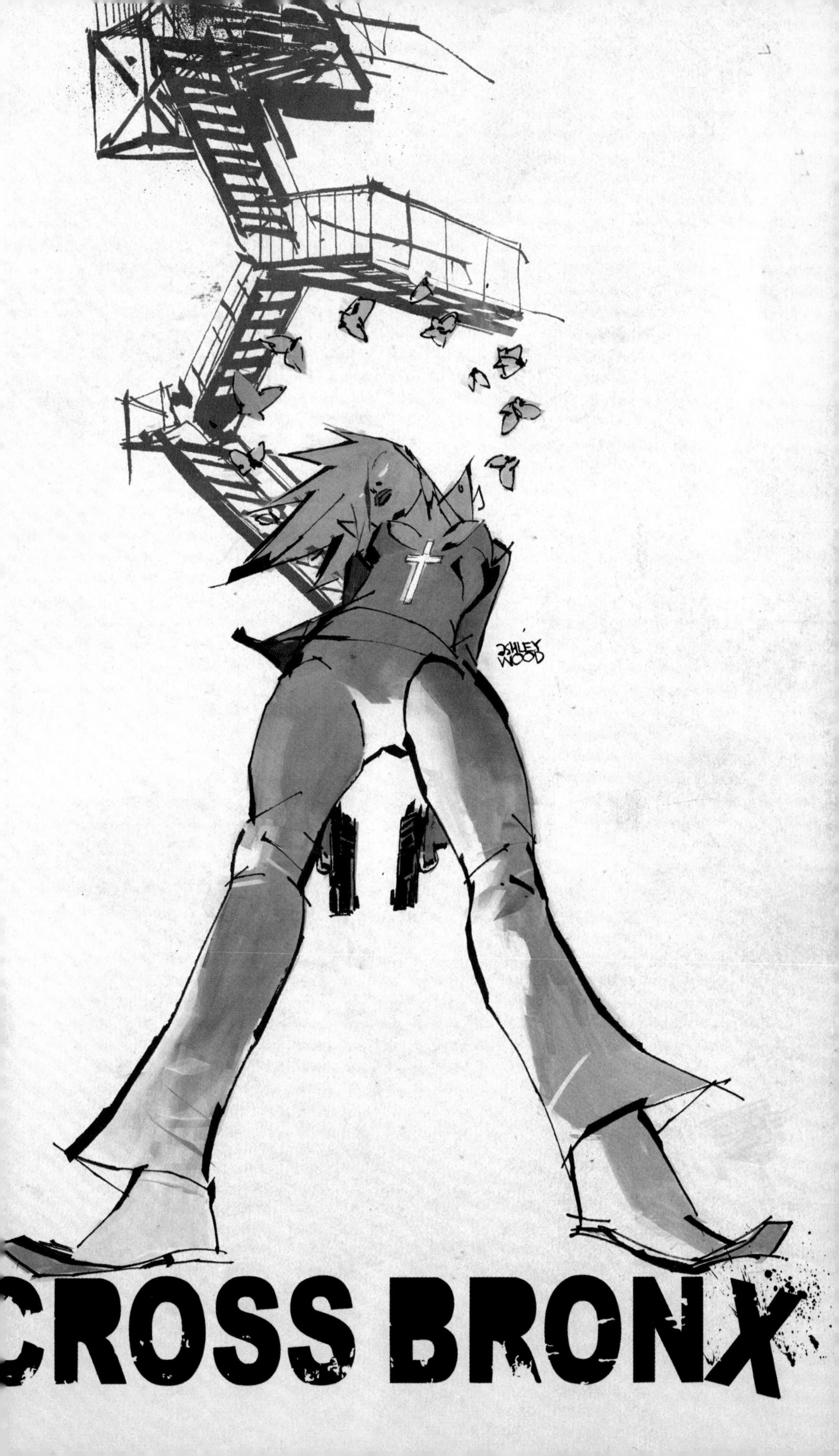
ASHLEY WOOD
CROSS BRONX

THE CROSS BRONX

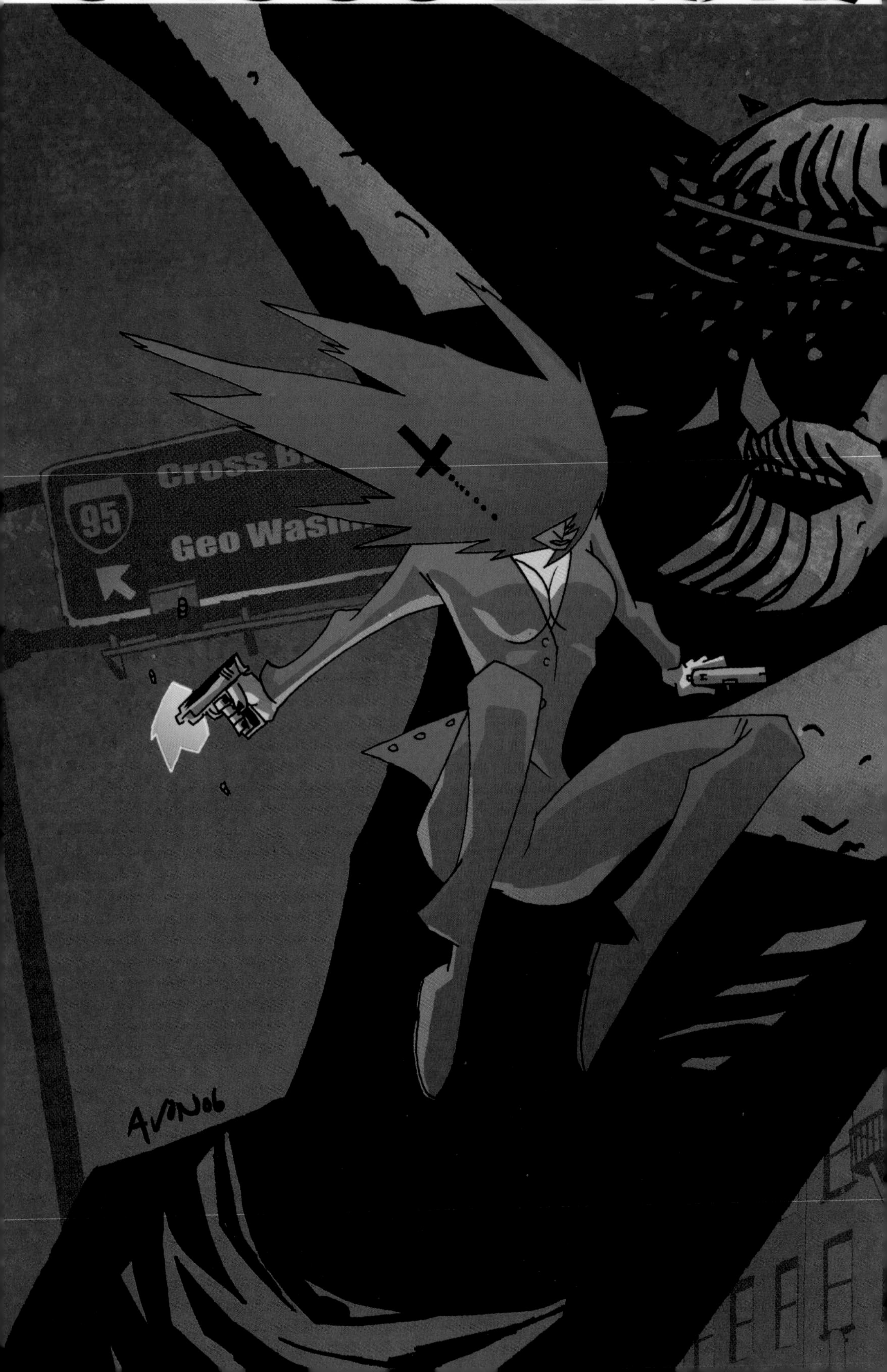
Cross B
95
Geo Wash

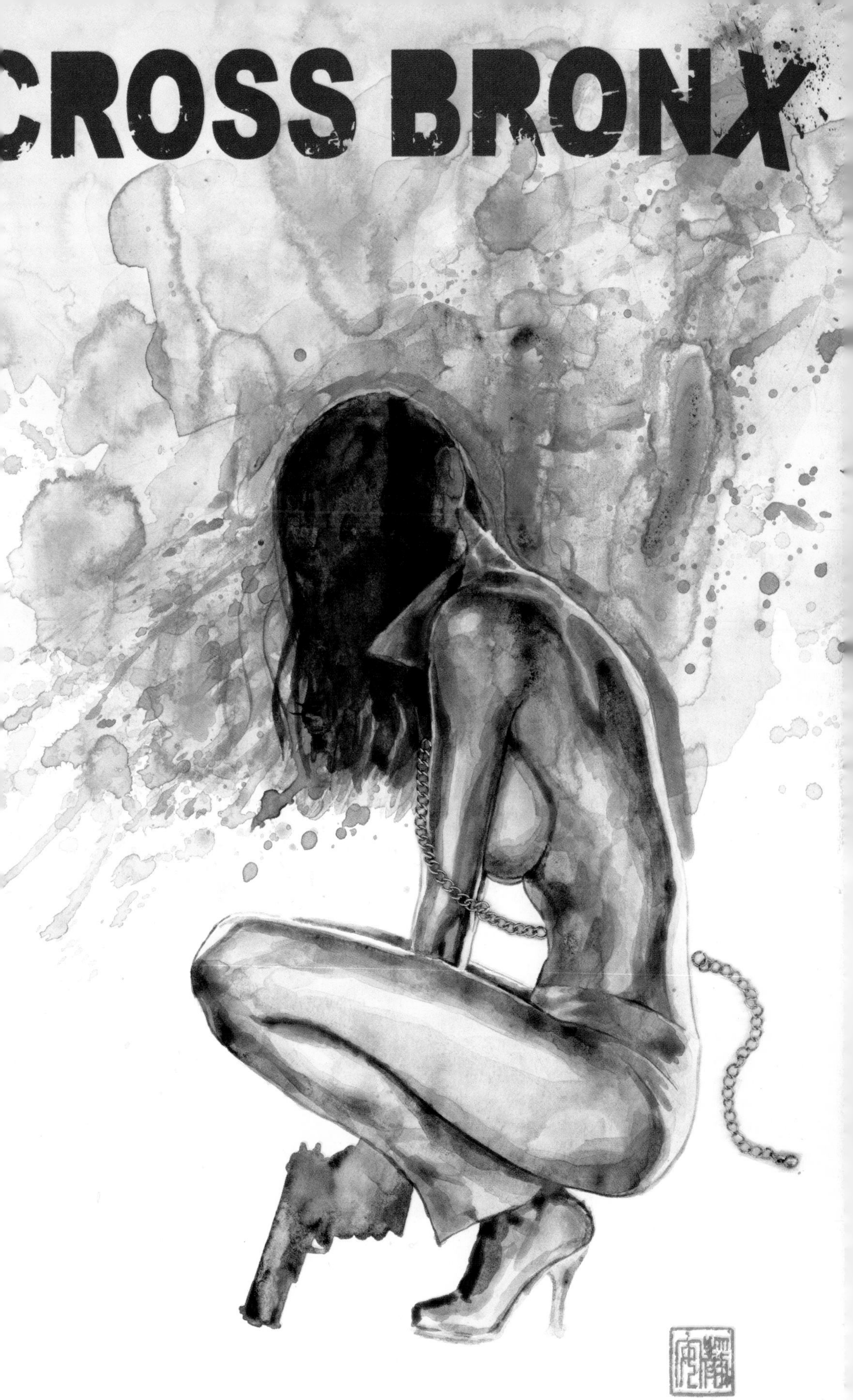
CROSS BRONX
MACK

|PINUPS|

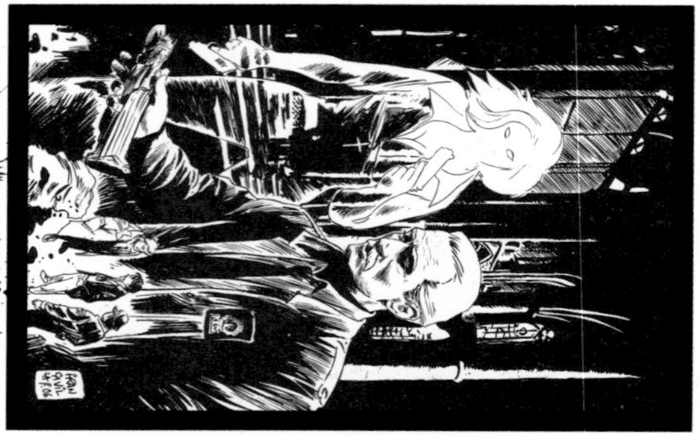

FRANCESCO FRANCAVILLA

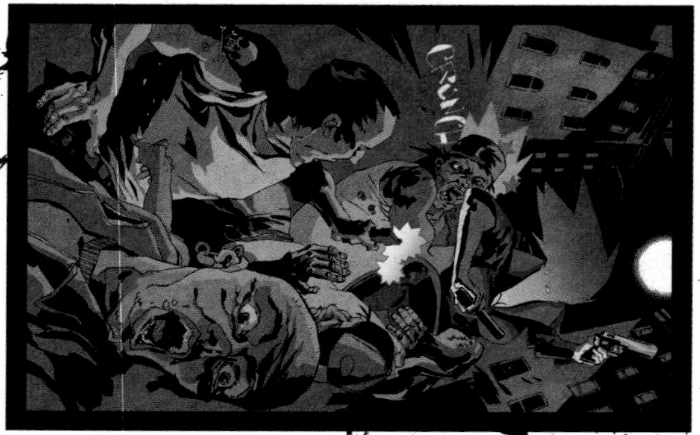

NICK STAKAL

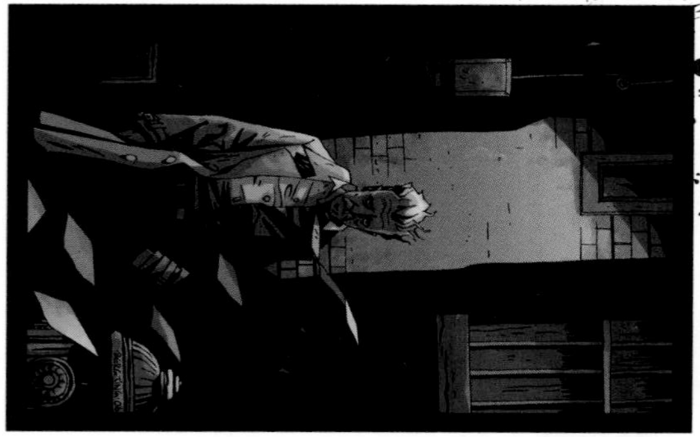

PETER BERGTING

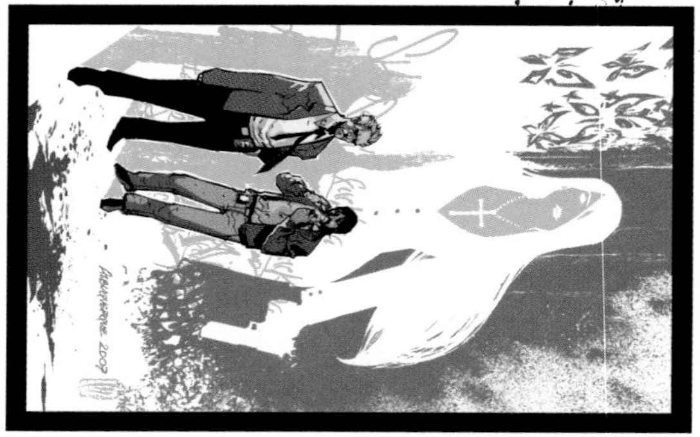

RAFAEL ALBUQUERQUE

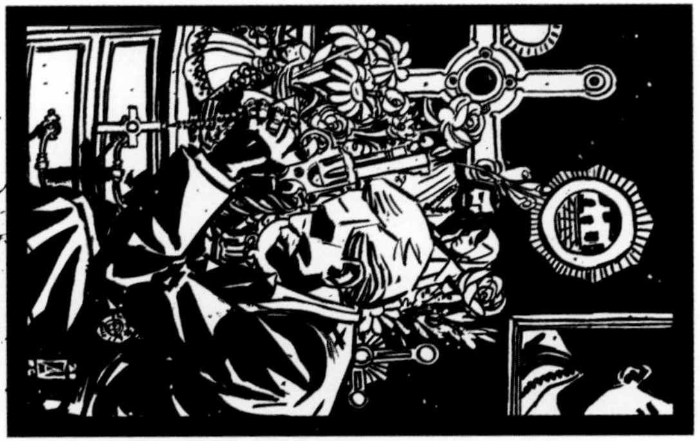

PAUL AZACETA

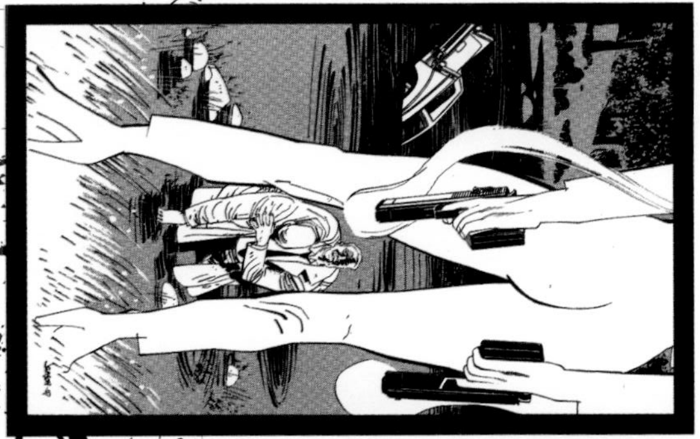

KLAUS JANSON

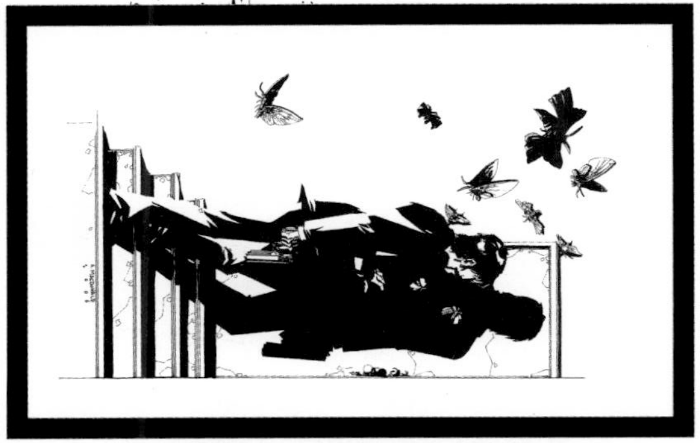

ANDY MACDONALD

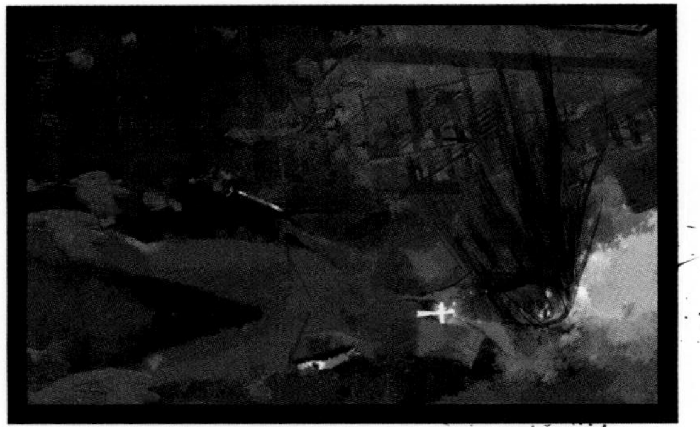

ERIC NGUYEN

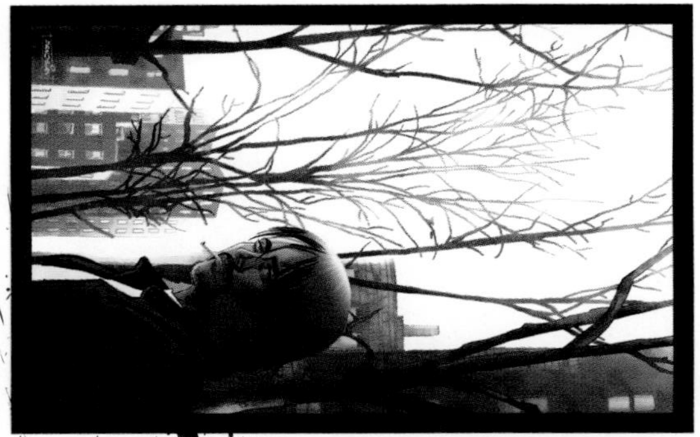

DAN PANOSIAN

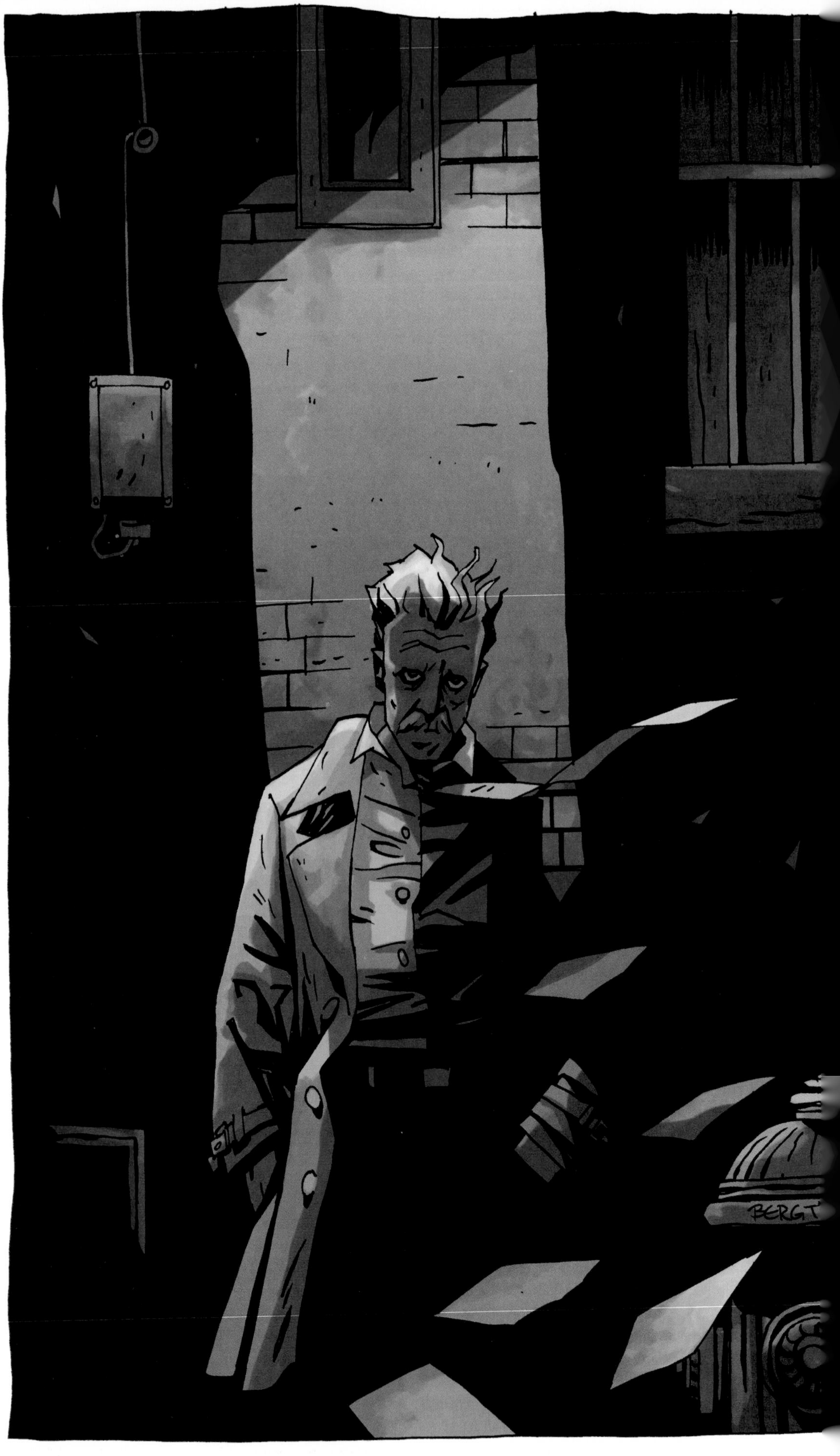
BERGT

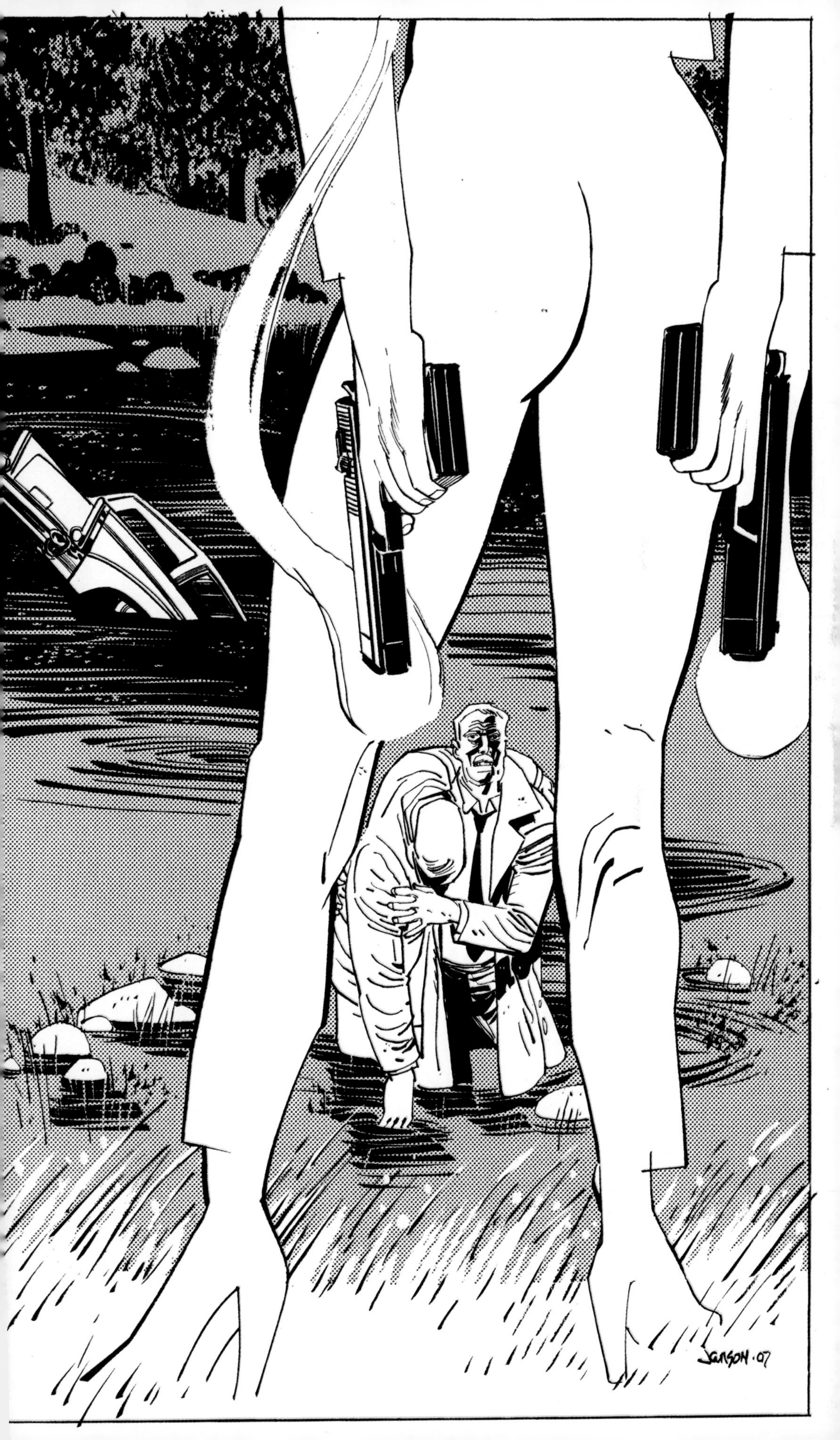
JASON ·07

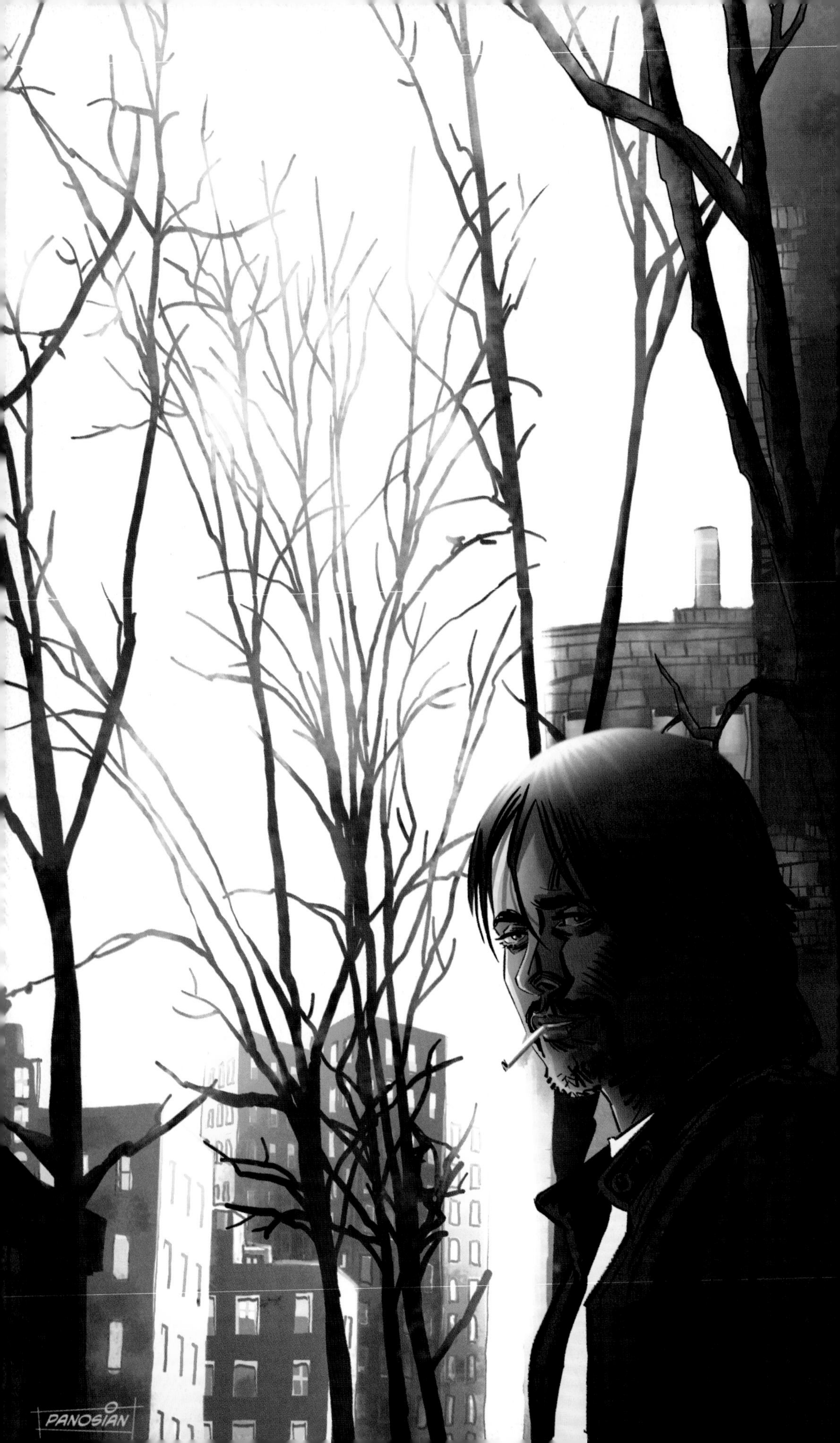
PANOSIAN

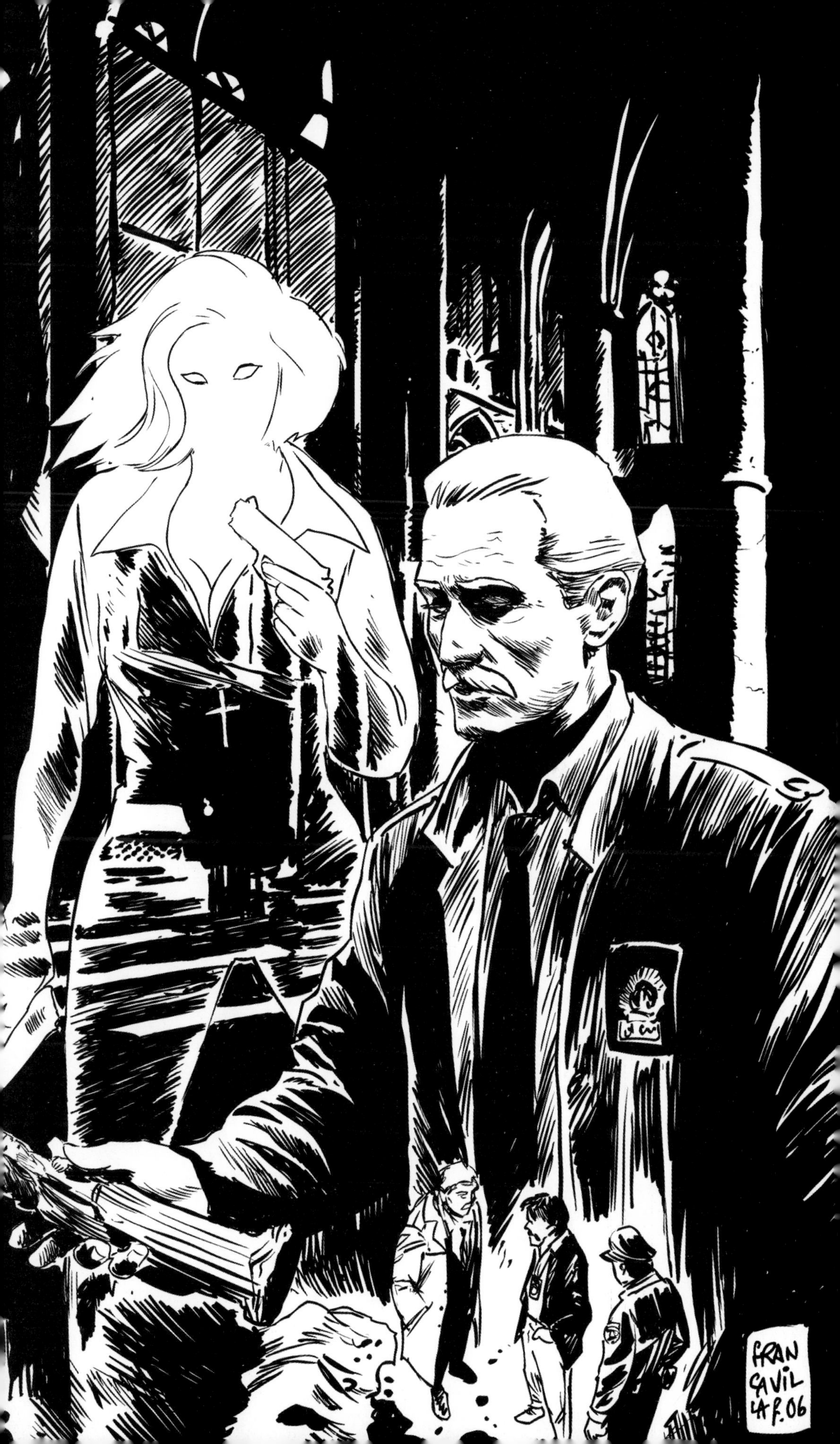
FRAN
CAVIL
LA F.06

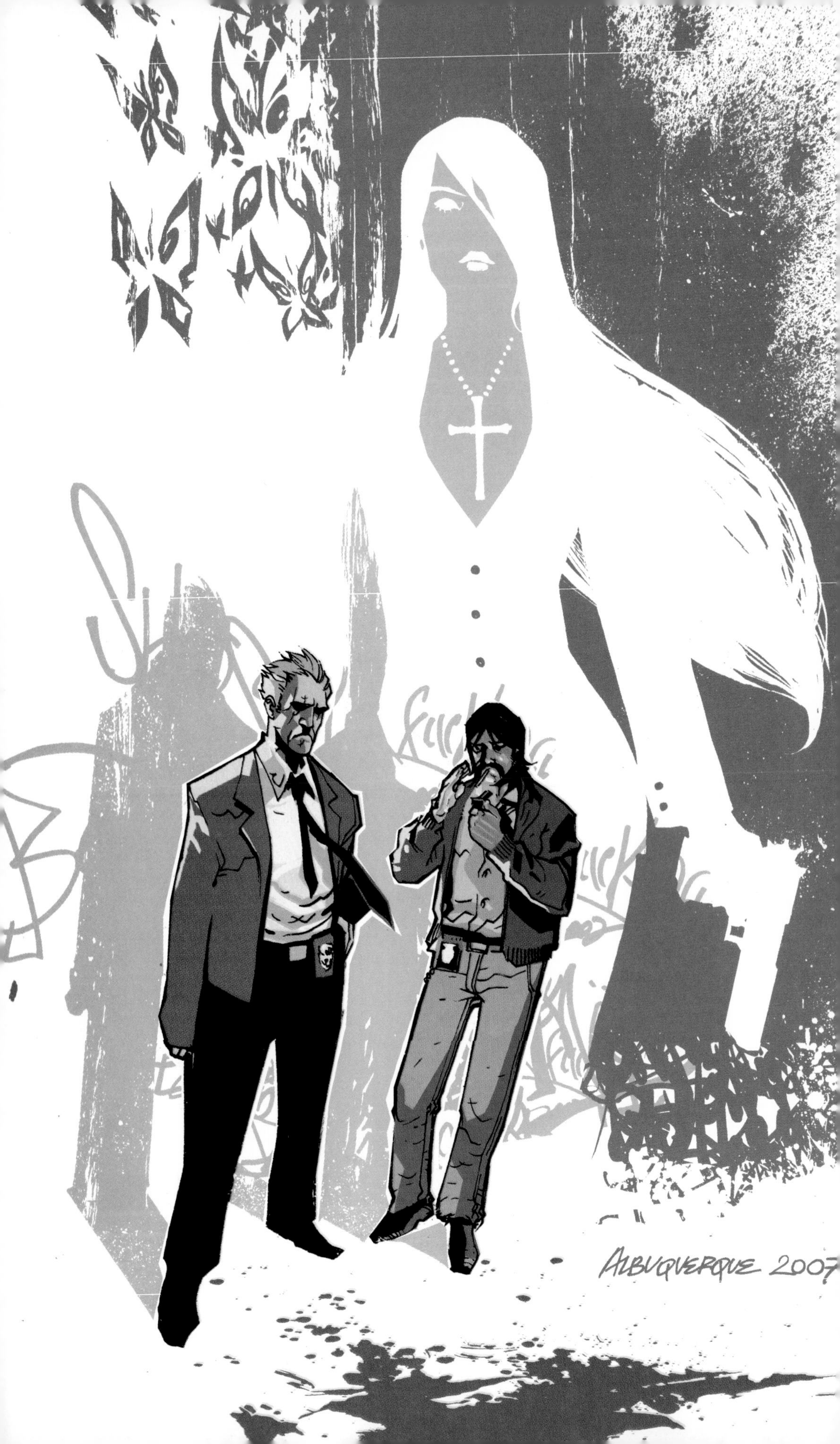
ALBUQUERQUE 2007

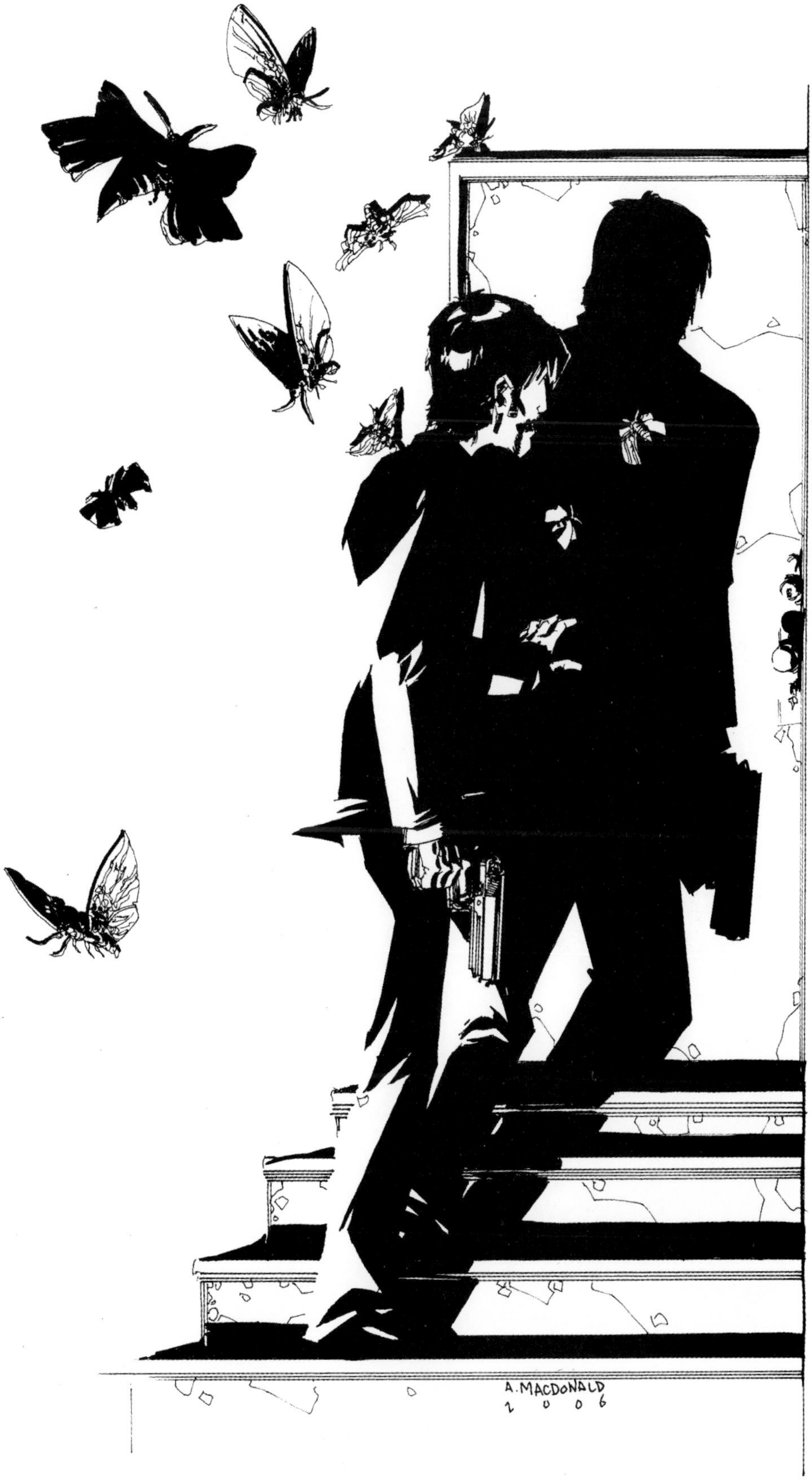
A. MACDONALD
2006

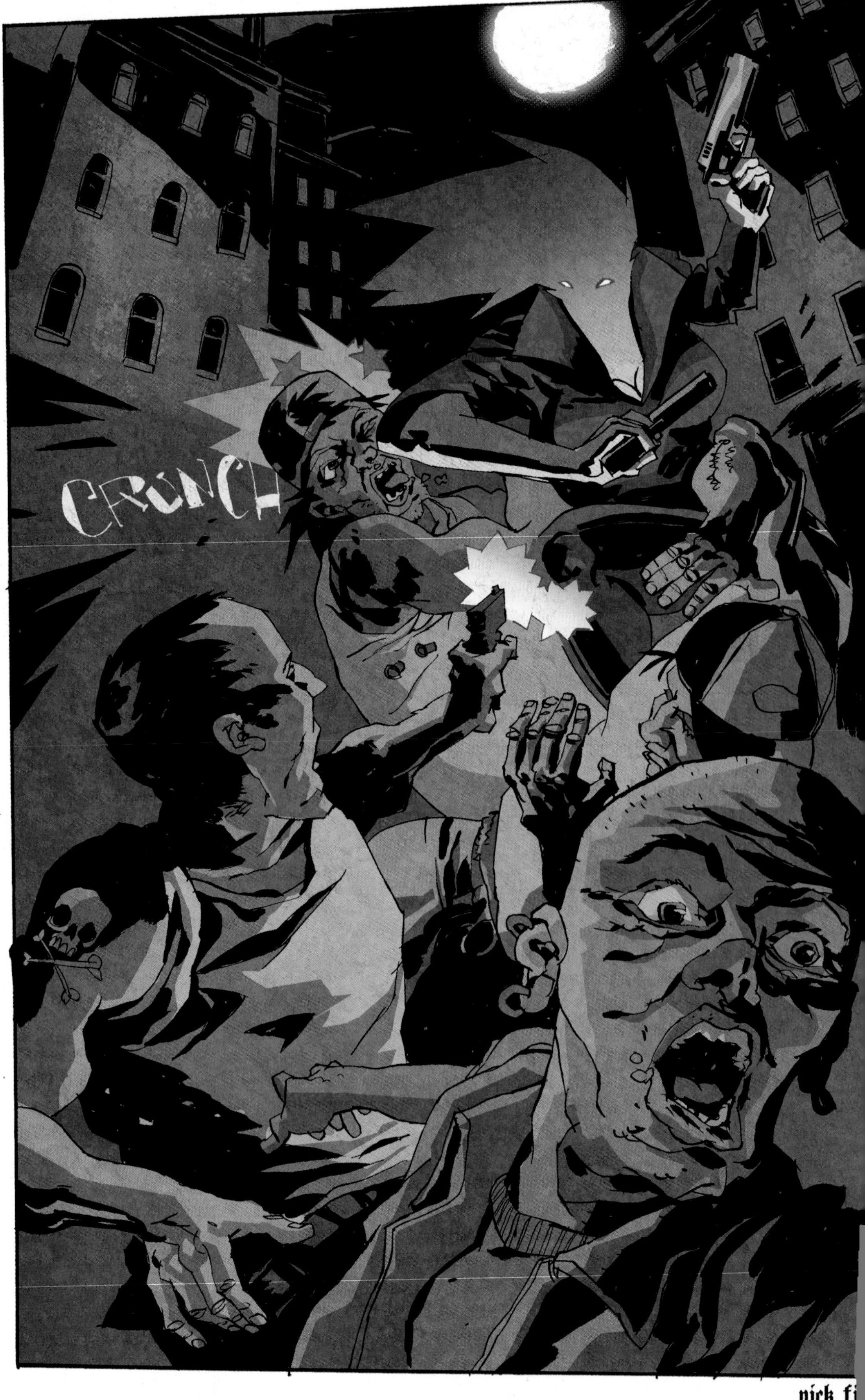
CRUNCH

nick fi

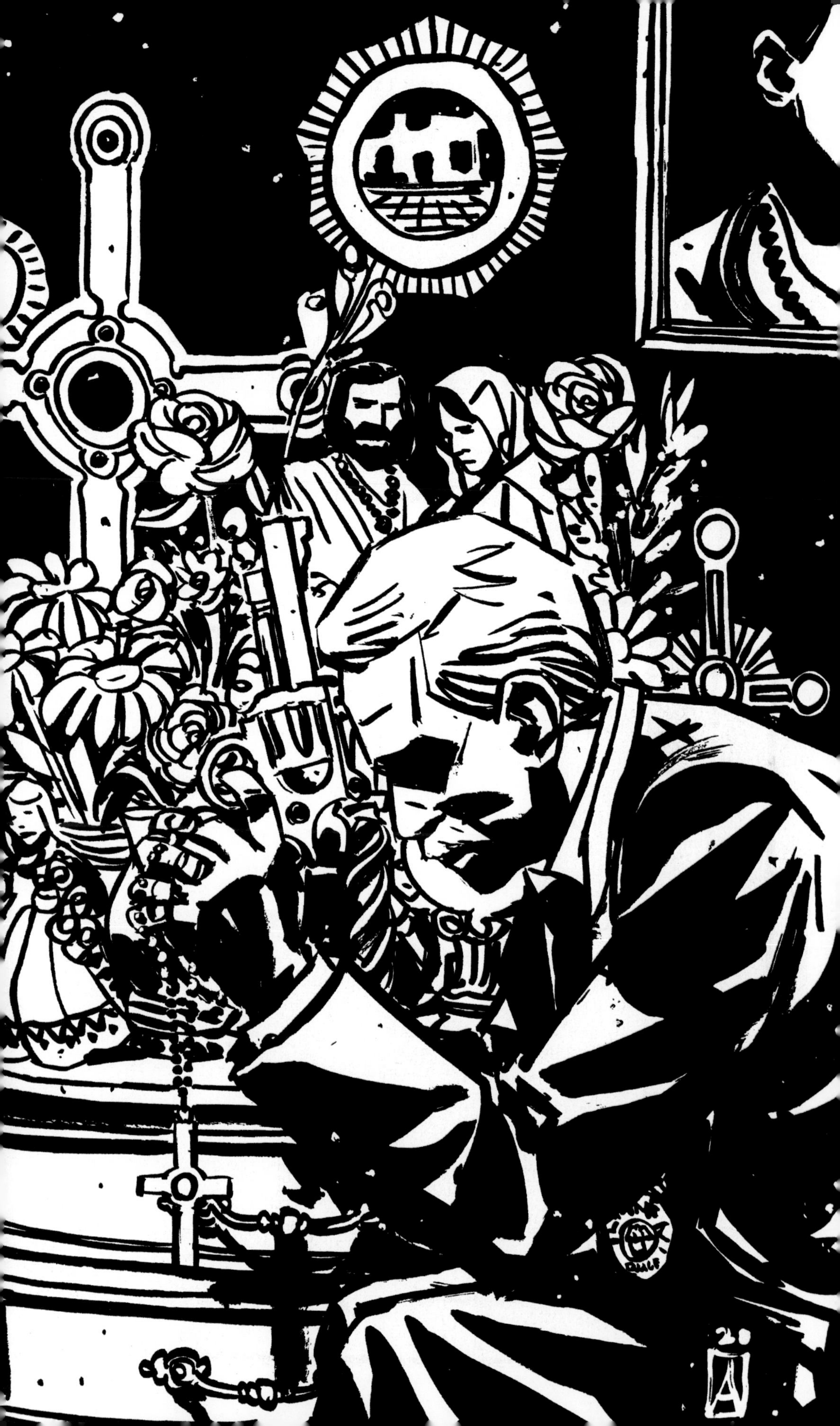

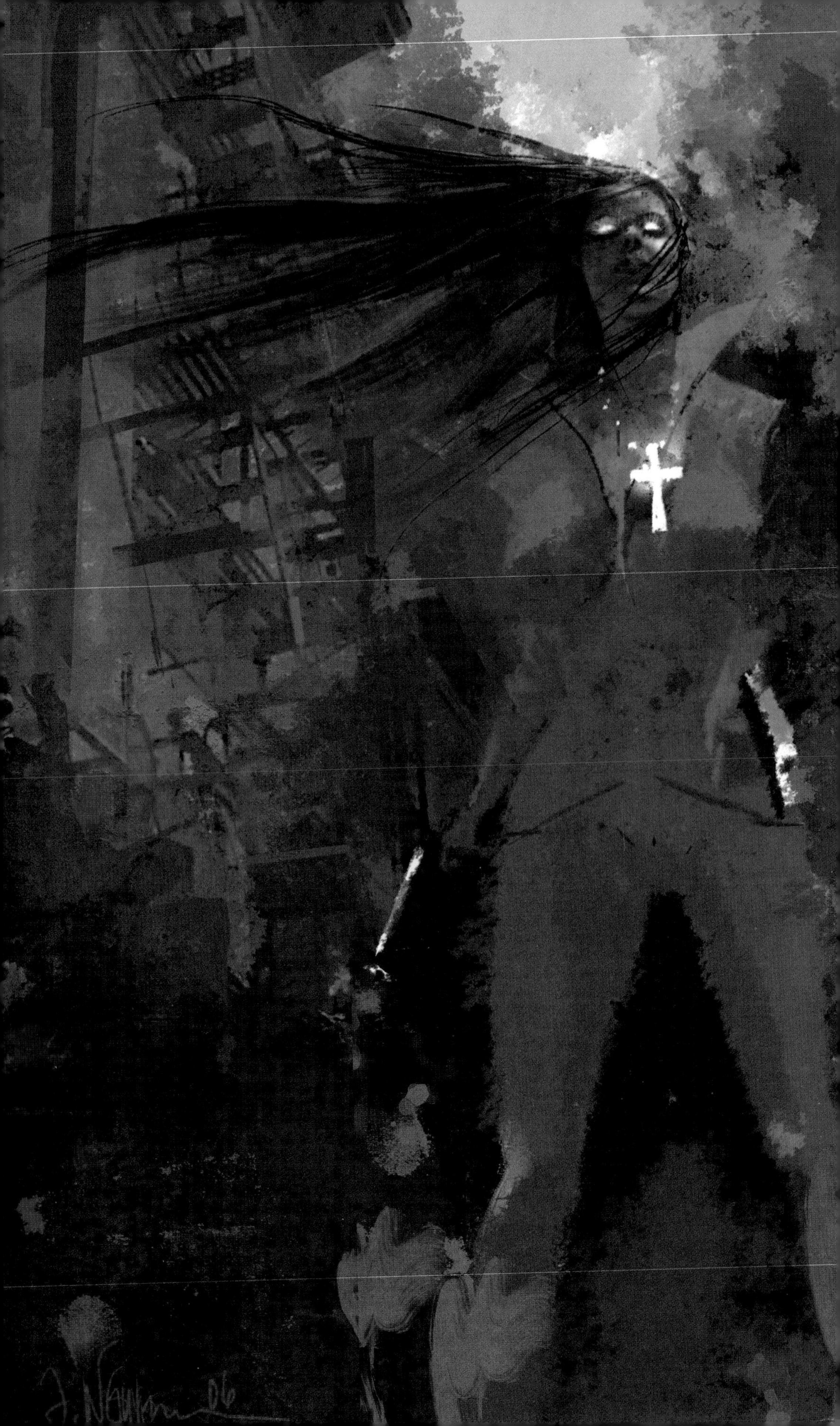